INTERMEDIATE
CHINESE
WITH AUDIO CD
SECOND EDITION

INTERMEDIATE
CHINESE
WITH AUDIO CD
SECOND EDITION

Yong Ho
Illustrations by Youli Hu

Hippocrene Books, Inc.
New York

For information, address:
HIPPOCRENE BOOKS, INC.
171 Madison Avenue
New York, NY 10016
www.hippocrenebooks.com

MIX
Paper from
responsible sources
FSC
www.fsc.org
FSC® C011935

Illustrations by Youli Hu.

Library of Congress Cataloging-in-Publication Data

Ho, Yong.
  Intermediate Chinese with audio cd / Yong Ho. -- Second Edition.
    pages cm
  ISBN-13: 978-0-7818-1311-2 (pbk.)
  ISBN-10: 0-7818-1311-5 (pbk.)
  1. Chinese language--Textbooks for foreign speakers--English. 2. Chinese
language--Spoken Chinese. 3. Chinese language--Sound recordings for
English speakers. I. Title.
  PL1129.E5H64 2013
  495.1'82421--dc23
                                                2013010173

Printed in the United States of America

CONTENTS

TRACK LIST FOR AUDIO CD

LESSONS FOR INTERMEDIATE CHINESE

1. Lesson One
2. Lesson Two
3. Lesson Three
4. Lesson Four
5. Lesson Five
6. Lesson Six
7. Lesson Seven
8. Lesson Eight
9. Lesson Nine
10. Lesson Ten

INTRODUCTION

Intermediate Chinese is a continuation of my *Beginner's Chinese* first published in 1997 and republished in 2010 by Hippocrene Books. After I wrote *Beginner's Chinese*, I didn't plan to write a follow-up book, although I did publish a number of other books on Chinese and Chinese history in the meantime. Since its publication, *Beginner's Chinese* has been very well received by students of Chinese. Since 1997, the book has undergone quite a few printings, becoming a bestseller for Hippocrene. Both the publisher and I have received many encouraging letters from people, some of whom wrote from as far as China. Many of them asked for a second book.

Part of the success of *Beginner's Chinese* lies in its organizational principles and manner of presentation, but I attribute a larger part to the upsurge in the interest in learning Chinese in the United States and elsewhere. The interest stems from a number of fronts. The following is a dramatic chart showing the top ten languages spoken in the world (speakers are in millions):

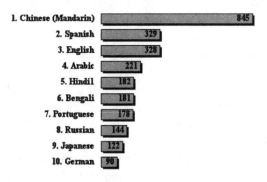

1. Chinese (Mandarin)	845
2. Spanish	329
3. English	328
4. Arabic	221
5. Hindil	182
6. Bengali	181
7. Portuguese	178
8. Russian	144
9. Japanese	122
10. German	90

Source: *Ethnologue*, 16th Edition

What was listed for Chinese are Mandarin speakers, but since Mandarin is the *lingua franca* in China, the actual number of people speaking and understanding Mandarin is much higher. The need to communicate with a quarter of the world's population and learn about its culture and society is certainly a stimulating factor. Another reason for the enhanced interest in Chinese is the strong growth of the Chinese population in the U.S. In 2010, the U.S. Census Bureau published national statistics highlighting the prevalence of foreign languages spoken in U.S. households by persons age five years and over. While Spanish remains the most prevalent foreign language spoken in the U.S. with 34,547,077 speakers, Chinese is now ranked #2 in the nation with 2,464,572 speakers, an increase of almost 300% as compared with the number of Chinese speakers in 1980. Over 80% of Chinese-Americans now report that they speak Chinese at home. In our neighboring country Canada, Chinese dominates the immigrant language list with more than one million speakers.

Aside from these, there are two additional notable sources that are spurring the interest in learning Chinese: the economic vitality of the Chinese-speaking world and the well-publicized need by the U.S. government for personnel with Chinese language skills. Chinese has been designated by the U.S. government as a "critical language" (Critical Languages are the ones for which there is large demand for language professionals but little supply). Realizing the value and importance of learning Chinese, more and more schools in the U.S., particularly those at the pre-collegiate level, are now offering Chinese programs.

As teachers of Chinese, we are both excited and challenged. One of the challenges we face is to select and create good and effective textbooks for learners of Chinese, particularly for elementary and intermediary students because they rely more on the textbook than advanced students. *Intermediate Chinese*, together with *Beginner's Chinese*, is an effort in this direction. This book, like *Beginner's Chinese*, is based on the premise that less is more and is communication-oriented. It tries to present basic sentence patterns and vocabulary necessary for dealing with particular communicative topics. While the focus is still very much on conversation, attention is also paid to reading and writing.

This book is written with the adult learners in mind, college students included. The communicative scenes and vocabulary selected thus reflect the adult scenes: work, study, travel, recreation and survival needs.

Nine years have lapsed since the book was first published in 2004. Although that is a relatively short span, in this fast-changing information age many phenomena have become outdated and many have come into being. This edition has updated the texts to reflect what is in common use in today's China. The resource section of the book has been overhauled. The suggested resources now given in the back are those that have been observed to be useful and reliable. A number of mobile apps, which were non-extant when the earlier version was published, have been included.

This edition has regulated the number of new words and expressions for each lesson at 30-35 and supplementary words and expressions at 15.

Thus we have a total vocabulary stock of about 350 new words and expressions and 150 supplementary words and expressions. Between *Beginners Chinese* and this edition of *Intermediate Chinese*, we have a total vocabulary of about 800 new words and expressions, which constitutes the core vocabulary of Chinese. Counting the supplementary words and expressions, the total exceeds 1,000—adequate for expressing everyday needs and the essential needs for travel, work and school.

One of the stumbling blocks for students of Chinese is writing the characters. With the advancement of computer and mobile technology, students can now avail themselves of a multitude of software programs and apps to produce Chinese characters on the computer and smart phones (see the section at the back of the book for Internet resources and apps). A set of downloadable worksheets of all the new characters that appear in the book, complete with stroke order and pinyin, can be found at:

http://hippocrenebooks.com/intermediatechineseworksheets.zip

To assist learners with making a smooth transition, this book also provides a vocabulary list of words that appeared in *Beginner's Chinese* (see pages 247-267).

Happy learning!

Yong Ho

GRAMMATICAL TERMS EXPLAINED

Adverbial
A word, phrase or clause that functions to modify a verb, an adjective or another adverb, providing such information as time, place, manner, reason, condition and so on.

Aspect
Manner in which an action takes place. English distinguishes four aspects: indefinite, continuous, perfect and perfect continuous, whereas Chinese distinguishes indefinite, continuous and perfect. The indefinite aspect indicates the habitual or repeated action. The continuous aspect indicates the continuation or progression of the action. The perfect aspect indicates the completion of an action.

Classifier
A word used between a numeral and a noun to show a sub-class to which the noun belongs. See an extensive discussion of the subject in *Beginner's Chinese*.

Complement
That part of the sentence that follows the verb and provide additional information about the verb. As such, they are also called verb complements. The most common complements in Chinese are those of direction, result and degree. Directional complements indicate the direction of the action in relation to the speaker and are not separated from the verb by any particle. Result and degree complements indicate the result and the degree of the action expressed by the verb and they are separated from the verb by the particle 得 de.

Existential sentence
This refers to a type of sentence that is similar to the "there is/are" structure in English. The pattern for existential sentences in Chinese is (在 zài) Adverbial of Place + 有 (yǒu, *there is/are*) + Subject. The adverbial of place precedes, instead of following the verb 有 (yǒu). *There is a Bank of China in Chinatown* is thus expressed in Chinese as 中国城有中国银行 (Zhōngguóchéng yǒu Zhōngguó yínháng). In an existential sentence, the initial (在 zài) is always dropped.

Object
A noun, pronoun, phrase or clause that is used after, and affected in some way by, a transitive verb. If it is affected in a direct way, it is called the direct object. If it is affected in an indirect way, it is called the indirect object. In the sentence *he gave me a book*, *a book* is the direct object and *me* is the indirect object.

Particle
A word that has only grammatical meaning, but no lexical meaning, such as 吗 ma, 呢 ne, and 吧 ba in Chinese.

Predicate
That part of a sentence that states or asserts something about the subject. This role is only assumed by the verb in English, but can also be assumed by the adjective in Chinese.

Subject
Something about which a statement or assertion is made in the rest of the sentence.

Transitive and intransitive verb
A transitive verb is one that needs to take an object such as *we study Chinese*. An intransitive verb is one that does not take an object such as *walk, run*, and *go*.

ABBREVIATIONS

adjective.................................*adj.*

adverb....................................*adv.*

noun...*n.*

somebody ....*sb.*

something...............................*sth.*

verb...*v.*

LESSON 1
PAST & FUTURE

CONVERSATIONS

(English translation, pages 24-25)

A：玛莉，你 最近 怎么样？
Mǎlì,   nǐ zuìjìn zěnmeyàng?

B：坐 下，我 要 告诉 你 一件 事。
Zuò xià, wǒ yào gàosù nǐ yí jiàn shì.

A：什么 事？
Shénme shì?

B：我 快 结婚 了。
Wǒ kuài jiéhūn le.

A：你 要 当 新娘 了？ 太好 了。祝贺 你！
Nǐ yào dāng xīnniáng le?   Tài hǎo le.   Zhùhè nǐ!
新郎 是 谁？
Xīnláng shì shuí?

B：是 大卫。
Shì Dàwèi.

A：你 是 什么 时候 认识 他 的？
Nǐ shì shénme shíhou rènshi tā de?

B：我 是 去年 认识 他 的。
Wǒ shì qùnián rènshi tā de.

A：你 是 在 哪儿 认识 他 的？
Nǐ shì zài nǎr   rènshi tā de?

B：我 是 在 北京 认识 他 的。 当时   我们 都 在 北京
Wǒ shì zài Běijīng rènshi tā de.   Dāngshí wǒmen dōu zài Běijīng
学 中文。
xué Zhōngwén.

A：你们 是在 什么 学校 学 的中文？
Nǐmen shì zài shénme xuéxiào xué de Zhōngwén?

B：我们 是在 北京 大学 学 的中文。
Wǒmen shì zaì Běijīng Dàxué xué de Zhōngwén.

A：你们 打算 什么 时候 结婚？
Nǐmen dǎsuan shénme shíhou jiéhūn?

B：下个月 三 号。你很 快 就会 收到 我们的 请帖。
Xià ge yuè sān hào.　Nǐ hěn kuài jiù huì shōudào wǒmende qǐngtiě.
到时 你 一定 要 来 参加 我们的 婚礼。
Dàoshí nǐ yídìng yào lái cānjiā wǒmende hūnlǐ.

A：我 一定 来。婚礼 以后，你们 要 去 哪儿度蜜月？
Wǒ yídìng lái.　Hūnlǐ yǐhòu, nǐmen yào qù nǎr　dù mìyuè?

B：我们 要 去 香港。
Wǒmen yào qù Xiānggǎng.

A：你们 以前 去过 香港 吗？
Nǐmen yǐqián qù guo Xiānggǎng ma?

B：没有，这 是第一次。听说 香港 是个 很 有意思
Méiyou, zhè shì dì yī cì.　Tīngshuō Xiānggǎng shì ge hěn yǒuyìsi
的 地方。
de dìfang.

A：你回来 以后 告诉 我 是 不 是 这样。
Nǐ huí lái　yǐhòu gàosù wǒ shì bu shì zhèyàng.

B：一 定。
Yídìng.

*　　*　　*　　*　　*

A：玛莉，你们 是 什么 时候 从 香港 回 来 的？
Mǎlì, nǐmen shì shénme shíhou cóng Xiānggǎng huí lai de?

B：我们 是 上 星期 回 来 的。
Wǒmen shì shàng xīngqī huí lai de.

A：你们 在 香港 玩儿了几 天？
Nǐmen zài Xiānggǎng wánr le jǐ tiān?

B：我们 在 香港 玩儿 了一 个 星期。
Wǒmen zài Xiānggǎng wánr le yí ge xīngqī.

A：香港 怎么样？
Xiānggǎng zěnmeyàng?

B：香港 很 好玩儿，风景 也 很 美。
Xiānggǎng hěn hǎowánr, fēngjǐng yě hěn měi.

A：除了 香港， 你们 还 去 了哪儿？
Chúle Xiānggǎng, Nǐmen hái qù le nǎr?

B：我们 还 去了澳门。
Wǒmen hái qù le Àomén.

A：是 吗？你们 是 怎么 去 澳门 的？是 不 是 坐 飞机去
Shì mǎ? Nǐmen shì zěnme qù Àomén de? Shì bu shì zuò fēijī qù
的？
de?

B：我们 不是坐飞机去 的，我们 是 坐 船 去 的。
Wǒmen bú shì zuò fēijī qù de, wǒmen shì zuò chuán qù de.

A：从 香港 坐 船 到 澳门 要 多 长 时间？
Cóng Xiānggǎng zuò chuán dào Àomén yào duō cháng shíjiān?

B：澳门 离 香港 很 近，坐 船 只要 一 个 小时。
Aòmén lí Xiānggǎng hěn jìn, zuò chuán zhǐ yào yí ge xiǎoshí.

* * * * *

A：王 先生， 我 想 问 你一件 私事。不 知道 你
Wáng Xiānsheng, wǒ xiǎng wèn nǐ yí jiàn sī shì. Bù zhīdào nǐ
会不 会 介意？
huì bu huì jièyì?

B：你 问 吧。
Nǐ wèn ba.

A：你 有 没有 结婚？
Nǐ yǒu méiyou jiéhūn?

B：我 结 了。
Wǒ jié le.

A：你是什么 时候 结的 婚？
Nǐ shì shénme shíhou jié de hūn?

B：我 是三年 前 结 的。你呢，李 先生？
Wǒ shì sān nián qián jié de. Nǐ ne, Lǐ Xiānsheng?
你 有 没有 结婚？
Nǐ yǒu méiyou jiéhūn?

A：还 没有。
Hái méiyou.

B：有 女朋友 吗？
Yǒu nǚpéngyou ma?

A：有。她 和 我 在 一 个 单位。
Yǒu. Tā hé wǒ zài yí ge dānwèi.

B：你们 准备 什么 时候 结婚？
Nǐmén zhǔnbèi shénme shíhou jiéhūn?

A：现在 还 不 知道。可能 两 年 以后 吧。
Xiànzài hái bù zhīdào. Kěnéng liǎng nián yǐhòu bā.

READING PASSAGE

我的朋友大卫快结婚了。我下星期要参加他的婚礼。大
卫的新娘是玛莉。大卫和玛莉都是美国人。他们是去年
在北京大学学中文的时候认识的。来北京以前，大卫在
银行工作，玛莉是小学老师。他们要在中国结婚。他们
的爸爸妈妈都要来北京参加他们的婚礼。大卫和玛莉结
婚后要去南京大学教英语。他们一年以后回美国。

Wǒde péngyou Dàwèi kuài jiéhūn le. Wǒ xià xīngqī yào cānjiā tāde hūnlǐ.
Dàwèi de xīnniáng shì Mǎlì. Dàwèi hé Mǎlì dōu shì Měiguórén. Tāmen
shì qùnián zài Běijīng Dàxué xué Zhōngwén de shíhou rènshi de. Lái
Běijīng yǐqián, Dàwèi zài yínháng gōngzuò. Mǎlì shì xiǎoxué lǎoshī.
Tāmen yào zài Zhōngguó jiéhūn. Tāmen de bàba māma dōu yào lái
Běijīng cānjiā tāmende hūnlǐ. Dàwèi hé Mǎlì jiéhūn hòu yào qù Nánjīng
Dàxué jiāo Yīngyǔ. Tāmen yì nián yǐhòu huí Měiguó.

(English translation, page 25)

NEW WORDS AND EXPRESSIONS

最近	zuìjìn	recently; shortly; these days
事	shì	matter; thing (to do)
快 ... 了	kuài ... le	about to
当	dāng	become; act as
新娘	xīnniáng	bride
祝贺	zhùhè	congratulate; congratulations
新郎	xīnláng	bridegroom
当时	dāngshí	at that time
打算	dǎsuan	plan (v./n.)
结婚	jiéhūn	get married
就	jiù	right away
会	huì	will (modal verb)
收到	shōudào	receive
请帖	qǐngtiě	invitation card/letter
到时	dàoshí	at that (future) time
参加	cānjiā	participate (in); join; take part (in)
婚礼	hūnlǐ	wedding
以后	yǐhòu	after; later; in the future
以前	yǐqián	before; previously; in the past; ago
蜜月	mìyuè	honeymoon
有意思	yǒuyìsi	interesting
这样	zhèyàng	so; like this
回	huí	return (to a place); reply
风景	fēngjǐng	scenery
美	měi	pretty; beautiful
除了	chúle	besides; in addition to
还	hái	also; additionally
澳门	Àomén	Macao

SUPPLEMENTARY WORDS AND EXPRESSIONS

私	sī	private
介意	jièyì	mind (*v.*)
吧	ba	*sentence-final particle*
举行	jǔxíng	hold (an event)
教	jiāo	teach
将来	jiānglái	future; in the future
订婚	dìnghūn	be engaged (to)
离婚	líhūn	divorce (*v.*)
再婚	zàihūn	remarry
未婚夫	wèihūnfū	fiancé
未婚妻	wèihūnqī	fiancée
爱	ài	love (*v./n.*)
谈恋爱	tán liàn'ài	date (*v.*)
送	sòng	give as a present
礼物	lǐwù	gift; present
夫妇	fūfù	husband and wife; couple
主人	zhǔrén	host; hostess
宴会	yànhuì	banquet
亲戚	qīnqī	relatives
贵宾	guìbīn	distinguished guests; VIP

LANGUAGE POINTS

你最近怎么样 nǐ zuìjìn zěnmeyàng?

Unlike *"recently"* in English, 最近 zuìjìn can refer to future as well as past. Basically it refers to a point, past or future, that is closest to the present. So we can say both of the following:

我 最近 去了中国。
Wǒ zuìjìn qù le Zhōngguó.
I went to China recently.

我 最近要 去 中国。
Wǒ zuìjìn yào qù Zhōngguó.
I'm going to China soon.

Indication of the future

Chinese does not have a tense system. The following words and expressions are often used in conjunction with a verb to indicate future:

1. 要 yào:

下 个星期我 要 去 非洲。
Xià ge xīngqī wǒ yào qù Fēizhōu.
I'm going to Africa next week.

你长 大以后要 做 什么?
Nǐ zhǎng dà yǐhòu yào zuò shénme?
What are you going to do when you grow up?

2. 打算 dǎsuan (*plan*), both as a noun and a verb:

A: 你 毕业以后 有 什么 打算?
Nǐ bìyè yǐhòu yǒu shénme dǎsuan?
What's your plan after you graduate?

B: 我 打算 工作。
Wǒ dǎsuan gōngzuò.
I plan to work.

3. 准备 zhǔnbèi (*plan*):

你 今年 准备　在 哪儿 过 年?

Nǐ jīnnián zhǔnbèi zài nǎr　guò nián?

Where are you planning to spend your New Year this year?

Note: While 打算 dǎsuan is more often used in spoken language,
准备 zhǔnbèi occurs more in written language.

4. 会 huì (*will*) is a modal verb expressing a future possibility:

老师　明天　会 来 吗?

Lǎoshī míngtiān huì lái ma?

Will the teacher come tomorrow?

今天 不 会 下雨。

Jīntiān bú huì xiàyǔ.

It won't rain today.

To indicate imminence, Chinese basically uses the expression:

要 ... 了

yào ... le

be going to; be about to

我　妈妈 要 来 美国　了。

Wǒ māma yào lái Měiguó le.

My mother is coming to America soon.

要 yào in this sense is often preceded by 就 jiù or 快 kuài for additional
emphasis on imminence. Once 就 jiù or 快 kuài is used, 要 yào can be
left out.

快　下课 了。

Kuài xiàkè le.

The class will be over soon.

火车　就 来 了。

Huǒchē jiù lái le.

The train is about to arrive.

就 jiù conveys a sense of more imminence than 快 kuài.

Indication of the past

Since Chinese does not have a tense system, there is no specific verbal form that indicates a past occurance. Past events are usually indicated by time words such as 现在 xiànzài (*now*), 过去 guòqù (*in the past*), 三年前 sān nián qián (*three years ago*) or the context. Please disassociate the particle 了 le from the English suffix -ed, which is used to indicate the past. In one of its many uses, 了 le serves as an aspect marker indicating the completion of an action. Although most completed actions took place in the past, they can also take place in the future such as when we say in English, *I will have finished reading the book by the end of this week*. Additionally, 了 le is not to be used when the verb is cognitive in nature or when the verb indicates a past habitual action (see *Beginner's Chinese*, Lesson 10).

When asking questions about the time, place and manner of a past event, Chinese uses the 是 shì . . . 的 de construction, where the item following 是 shì is highlighted. Additionally, 是 shì can be omitted, but not 的 de:

他 (是) 什么 时候 去 中国   的？
Tā (shì) shénme shíhou qù Zhōngguó de?
When did he go to China?

你 (是) 在 哪儿 认识 你 太太 的？
Nǐ shì zài nǎr rènshi nǐ tàitai de?
Where did you meet your wife?

你今天 (是) 怎么 来 的？
Nǐ jīntiān (shì) zěnme lái de?
How did you come today?

When the verb is a transitive one, 的 de is usually placed between the verb and the object:

你今天 (是) 在 哪儿 吃 的中饭？
Nǐ jīntiān (shì) zài nǎr chī de zhōngfàn?
Where did you eat lunch today?

你 (是) 在 哪儿上   的 大学？
Nǐ (shì) zài nǎr shàng de dàxué?
Where did you go to college?

Note that the response to the questions above should take the same form. If the object is a pronoun or if it is a noun followed by a directional complement (*see below*), 的 de must be placed at the end of the sentence:

你 是 在 哪儿认识 他 的？
Nǐ shì zài nǎr   rènshi tā de?
Where did you become acquainted with him?

他 是 昨天 回 上海   的。
Tā shì zuótiān huí Shànghǎi de.
He returned to Shanghai yesterday.

If the sentence takes the negative form, 不 bù is used before 是 shì, which cannot be omitted:

我 不 是 在 北京 大学 学 的 中文。
Wǒ bú shì zài Běijīng Dàxué xué de Zhōngwén.
I didn't study Chinese at Beijing University.

以后 yǐhòu and 以前 yǐqián

Unlike *after* and *before* in English, which are prepositions and conjunctions, 以后 yǐhòu and 以前 yǐqián are nouns in Chinese used adverbially to indicate time.

When used by itself, 以后 yǐhòu means *later* or *in the future*. Since it is used to indicate time, it appears before the verb:

我 以后 要 当 老师。
Wǒ yǐhòu yào dāng lǎoshī.
I would like to become a teacher in the future.

你 还 小，我 以后 告诉 你。
Nǐ hái xiǎo, wǒ yǐhòu gàosù nǐ.
You are still young. I'll tell you later.

When modified by a noun, a phrase or a sentence, 以后 yǐhòu means (time) *after*. Additionally, the 以后 yǐhòu phrase always appears before the main clause:

2012 年 以后
2012 nián yǐhòu
after 2012

下班 以后, 他们 要 去 看 电影。
Xiàbān yǐhòu, tāmen yào qù kàn diànyǐng.
They are going to see a movie after work.

我 来 美国 以后 住 在 纽约。
Wǒ lái Měiguó yǐhòu zhù zài Niǔyuē.
I lived in New York after I came to America.

When used by itself, 以前 yǐqián means *before* or *previously*. Since it is used to indicate time, it appears before the verb:

我 以前 没有 吃 过 广东 菜。
Wǒ yǐqián méiyou chī guo Guǎngdōng cài.
I have not had Cantonese food before.

When modified by a noun, a phrase or a sentence, 以前 yǐqián means *(time) before.* Additionally, the 以前 yǐqián phrase always appears before the main sentence:

三 天 以前
sān tiān yǐqián
three days ago

吃饭 以前 要 洗 手。
Chīfàn yǐqián yào xǐ shǒu.
Wash your hands before eating.

你 来 美国 以前 会 不 会 说 英语?
Nǐ lái Měiguó yǐqián huì bu huì shuō Yīngyǔ?
Did you speak English before you came to America?

以 yǐ in 以前 yǐqián and 以后 yǐhòu can be left out when used at the end of a phrase, particularly in written Chinese:

三 天 前
sān tiān qián
three days ago

来 美国 前
lái Měiguó qián
before coming to America

一个 月 后
yí ge yuè hòu
a month later

结婚 后
jiéhūn hòu
after getting married

香港是个很有意思的地方 **Xiānggǎng shì ge hěn yǒuyìsi de dìfang.**

A monosyllabic adjective can directly modify a noun:

好 人
hǎo rén
good person

旧 车
jiù chē
old car

But 的 de is needed when the adjective is disyllabic or polysyllabic:

高兴 的 事
gāoxìng de shì
happy event

有意 思 的电影
yǒuyìsi de diànyǐng
interesting movie

A monosyllabic attributive adjective modified by an adverb also requires the use of 的 de before a noun:

很 好 的人
hěn hǎo de rén
very good person

非常 热 的夏天
fēicháng rè de xiàtiān
extremely hot summer

你们是什么时候从香港回来的 **Nǐmen shì shénme shíhou cóng Xiānggǎng huí lái de?**
When used after a verb, 来 lái indicates the direction of the action in relation to the speaker. As such, it is usually used after certain verbs of motion such as 到 dào (*go to*), 带 dài (*bring, carry*), 寄 jì (*mail*), 上 shàng (*go up*), 下 xià (*go down*), 进 jìn (*enter*), 出 chū (*exit*), 回 huí (*return*). This use of 来 lái is opposed to 去 qù. Compare: 进来 jìn lai (*come in*—in the direction of the speaker) and 进去 jìn qu (*go in*—away from the speaker); 上来 shàng lai (*come up*—the speaker is up) and 上去 shàng qu (*go up*—away from the speaker). This use of 来 lái and 去 qù is referred to in grammar as the directional complement. When used as a directional complement, 来 lái and 去 qù are pronounced in the neutral tone.

香港很好玩儿 Xiānggǎng hěn hǎowánr

好 hǎo is often used with certain verbs to form adjectives. Examples are: 好吃 hǎochī (*delicious*), 好喝 hǎohē (*good to drink*), 好听 hǎotīng (*ear-pleasing; good to listen to*), 好看 hǎokàn (*pretty, good-looking*), and 好玩儿 hǎowánr (*fun*).

的时候 de shíhou

What precedes 的时候 de shíhou is an attribute, usually in the form of a verb or a sentence. Additionally, the phrase or clause with 的时候 de shíhou always appears before the main clause:

吃饭 的 时候, 不要 说话。
Chīfàn de shíhou, búyào shuōhuà.
Don't talk while eating.

我 在 中国　 的 时候, 去过 青岛。
Wǒ zài Zhōngguó de shíhou, qù guo Qīngdǎo.
I visited Qingdao when I was in China.

你们在香港玩儿了几天 Nǐmen zài Xiānggǎng wánr le jǐ tiān?

In *Beginner's Chinese*, mention was made that adverbials of time should precede verbs in Chinese, but we should also know that this rule only applies to a point of time. If the time refers to a duration or period that the action expressed by the verb experienced, it should follow the verb in the sentence:

他 在 那 个公司 工作 了 三 年。

Tā zài nà ge gōngsi gōngzuò le sān nián.

He worked at that company for three years.

雨 下 了五 个 小时。

Yǔ xià le wǔ ge xiǎoshí.

It rained for five hours.

可能两年以后吧 kěnéng liǎng nián yǐhòu ba

吧 ba is a sentence-final particle, used to indicate:

1. A supposition or guess as in the sentence cited: *probably in two years.*

2. Suggestion, request or command:

我们   开始学习 吧。

Wǒmen kāishǐ xuéxí ba.

Let's begin our study.

3. Confirmation:

你 是 中国人   吧?

Nǐ shì Zhōngguórén ba?

You are Chinese, aren't you?

你是什么时候结的婚 Nǐ shì shénme shíhou jié de hūn?

A large number of verbs in Chinese are formed by a verb and an object such as 见面 jiànmiàn (*see face, meet*), 结婚 jiéhūn (*form a marital tie, marry*) and 帮忙 bāngmáng (*render assistance, help*). Many of these verbs would be transitive in English, but they are not to be followed by an object in Chinese, as there is already an "embedded object." The idea that would be expressed by an object in English are usually expressed in China by an adverbial before the verb or an attribute before the embedded object:

跟他见面 gēn tā jiànmiàn (*meet with him*), 跟同事结了婚 gēn tóngshì jié le hūn (*married a colleague*), 帮了我的忙 bāng le wǒde máng (*helped me*; *did me a favor*). In the cited sentence above, 的 is inserted before 婚 hūn because 婚 hūn is an embedded object.

EXERCISES

Answer key, pages 269-271

I. Answer the following questions:

1. 你是 什么 时候 开始 学 中文 的？
   Nǐ shì shénme shíhou kāishǐ xué zhōngwén de?

2. 你 在 这儿 住 了几年 了？
   Nǐ zài zhèr zhù le jǐ nián le?

3. 你 今天 吃 了中饭 吗？你 是 在 哪儿 吃 的 中饭？
   Nǐ jīntiān chī le zhōngfàn ma? Nǐ shì zài nǎr chī de zhōngfàn?

4. 你 今天 是 怎么 来 学校 的？
   Nǐ jīntiān shì zěnme lái xuéxiào de?

5. 你 今天 怎么 回 家？你 回 家 以后 要 做 什么？
   Nǐ jīntiān zěnme huí jiā? Nǐ huí jiā yǐhòu yào zuò shénme?

6. 你 今年 夏天 打算 做 什么？
   Nǐ jīnnián xiàtiān dǎsuan zuò shénme?

7. 你 现在 住 哪儿？你 以前 住 哪儿？
   Nǐ xiànzài zhù nǎr? Nǐ yǐqián zhù nǎr?

8. 你 以前 去 过 中国 吗？你 以后 会 去 中国 吗？
   Nǐ yǐqián qù guo Zhōngguó ma? Nǐ yǐhòu huì qù Zhōngguó ma?

9. 你 学习 的 时候，喜欢 听 音乐 吗？
   Nǐ xuéxí de shíhou, xǐhuan tīng yīnyuè ma?

10. 除了 今天，这 星期 你 还 有 中文 课 吗？
    Chúle jīntiān, zhè xīngqī nǐ hái yǒu Zhōngwén kè ma?

II. How do you say the following:

1. married for thirty years
2. divorced for five years
3. attend a friend's wedding
4. go to Hawaii (夏威夷 Xiàwēiyí) for honeymoon
5. let's go
6. bride and groom
7. ten years ago; in ten years
8. before going to work; after getting off work
9. when they got married
10. return from America

III. Fill in the blanks with the following words and expressions:

最近 zuìjìn	是 … 的 shì … de
要 yào	快 … 了 kuài … le
以前 yǐqián	… 的时候 … de shíhou
以后 yǐhòu	

1. 我 下班 ＿＿＿＿＿ 要 去看 一个 朋友。
   Wǒ xiàbān ＿＿＿＿＿ yào qù kàn yí ge péngyou.

2. 你 今天 ＿＿＿＿＿ 几点 起床 ＿＿＿＿＿?
   Nǐ jīntiān ＿＿＿＿＿ jǐ diǎn qǐchuáng ＿＿＿＿＿?

3. 我的 老师 ＿＿＿＿＿ 去 了香港。
   Wǒde lǎoshī ＿＿＿＿＿ qù le Xiānggǎng.

4. 他 在 北京 ＿＿＿＿＿ 常 去 博物馆。
   Tā zài Běijīng ＿＿＿＿＿ cháng qù bówùguǎn.

5. 四十 年 ＿＿＿＿＿ 上海 没 有 地铁。
   Sìshí nián ＿＿＿＿＿ Shànghǎi méi yǒu dìtiě.

6. 我 哥哥 下 个 月 ＿＿＿＿＿ 去 电话 公司 工作。
   Wǒ gēge xià ge yuè ＿＿＿＿＿ qù diànhuà gōngsī gōngzuò.

7. _____中国　没　有　美国　银行。现在　有。
_____ Zhōngguó méi yǒu Měiguó yínháng. Xiànzài yǒu.

8. 我 _____ 告诉 你 这 件　事。
Wǒ _____ gàosù nǐ zhè jiàn shì.

9. 她 吃饭 _____ 喜欢　看　电视。
Tā chīfàn _____ xǐhuān kàn diànshì.

10. 电影 _____ 几点　开始 _____?
Diànyǐng _____ jǐ diàn kāishǐ _____?

IV. Insert the time expressions in the parentheses in the proper place in the following sentences:

1. 老师们　每　天　上班。　　　　　　(七点)
Lǎoshīmen měi tiān shàngbān.　　　(qī diǎn)

2. 老师们　每　天　工作。　　　　　　(七个小时)
Lǎoshīmen měi tiān gōngzuò.　　　(qī ge xiǎoshí)

3. 我的　美国　朋友　在广州　　住了。　(三　年)
Wǒde Měiguó péngyou zài Guǎngzhōu zhù le.　(sān nián)

4. 大卫　和 玛丽 结婚。　　　　　　(下 个　月)
Dàwèi hé Mǎlì jiéhūn.　　　　　　(xià ge yuè)

5. 你在　澳门　玩儿　了?　　　　　　(几天)
Nǐ zài Àomén wánr le?　　　　　　(jǐ tiān)

V. Fill in the blanks with the following expressions:

好玩儿 hǎowánr　　好看 hǎokàn　　好听 hǎotīng
好吃 hǎochī　　　好喝 hǎohē

1. 中国　菜很 _____。
Zhōngguó cài hěn _____.

2. 美国　音乐 很 ＿＿＿＿＿＿＿。
Měiguó yīnyuè hěn ＿＿＿＿＿＿＿.

3. 青岛　　啤酒很 ＿＿＿＿＿＿＿。
Qīngdǎo píjiǔ　hěn ＿＿＿＿＿＿＿.

4. 这 本 书 不 ＿＿＿＿＿＿＿。
Zhè běn shū bù ＿＿＿＿＿＿＿.

5. 香港　　不 ＿＿＿＿＿＿＿。
Xiānggǎng bù ＿＿＿＿＿＿＿.

VI. Decide which of the following adjectives must be followed by 的 de when modifying a noun:

新＿＿ 汽车	好吃＿＿菜	短＿＿＿大衣
xīn ＿＿ qīchē	hǎochī ＿＿ cài	duǎn ＿＿ dàyī

不 老＿＿ 人	高兴＿＿＿事	热＿＿＿茶
bù lǎo ＿＿ rén	gāoxìng ＿＿ shì	rè ＿＿＿＿ chá

VII. Translate the following into Chinese:
1. I didn't go to the bank today.

＿＿＿＿＿＿＿＿＿＿＿＿＿

2. Before she came to America, she was a teacher. After she came to America, she was a student.

＿＿＿＿＿＿＿＿＿＿＿＿＿＿＿＿＿＿＿＿＿＿＿＿＿

3. I heard that Suzhou is a fun place.

＿＿＿＿＿＿＿＿＿＿＿＿＿

4. Where did you have lunch today?

＿＿＿＿＿＿＿＿＿＿＿＿＿

5. They have worked at the company for twenty years.

＿＿＿＿＿＿＿＿＿＿＿＿＿＿＿＿＿

6. What are you planning to do tonight?

   _____

7. My younger sister is about to be married.

   _____

8. Besides France, we also went to England and Germany.

   _____

9. Children like to ask a lot of questions when they are at the movies.

   _____

10. She said that she would tell me later.

    _____

VIII. Translate the following into English:

1. 我 姐姐 结婚 以前 住 在 加州。
   Wǒ jiějie jiéhūn yǐqián zhù zài Jiāzhōu.

   _____

2. 这 个地方 以前没 有 大学。
   Zhè ge dìfang yǐqián méi yǒu dàxué.

   _____

3. 现在 很 多 人不 打算 结婚。
   Xiànzài hěn duō rén bù dǎsuan jiéhūn.

   _____

4. 快 下雨 了。
   Kuài xiàyǔ le.

   _____

5. 她 是 三 个 星期 以前 从 中国 回来 的。
   Tā shì sān ge xīngqī yǐqián cóng Zhōngguó huí lái de.

   _____

6. 除了 英语, 我的 老师 还会 说 法语 和 西班牙语。
   Chúle Yīngyǔ, wǒde lǎoshī hái huì shuō Fǎyǔ hé Xībānyáyǔ.

---

7. 我 最近 很 忙, 没 有 时间 学 中文, 但是 以后
   Wǒ zuìjìn hěn máng, méi yǒu shíjiān xué Zhōngwén, dànshì yǐhòu
   我 会 学。
   wǒ huì xué.

---

8. 他们 是 坐飞机 去 华盛顿 的。
   Tāmen shì zuò fēijī qù Huáshèngdùn de.

---

9. 我 这 个 周末 要 参加 我 朋友 的婚礼。
   Wǒ zhè ge zhōumo yào cānjiā wǒ péngyou de hūnlǐ.

---

10. 雪 下 了 两 天。
    Xuě xià le liǎng tiān.

IX. Writing

Write five sentences for things you did in the past and five sentences for things you will do in the future.

ENGLISH TRANSLATION OF THE TEXT

Conversations (*pages 2-5*)

A: Mary, how have you been recently?
B: Sit down. I have something to tell you.
A: What is it?
B: I'm getting married.
A: You will be a bride? Great. Congratulations! Who is the bridegroom?
B: It's David.
A: When did you meet him?
B: I met him last year.
A: Where did you meet him?
B: I met him in Beijing. At that time, we were both studying Chinese in Beijing.
A: What school did you study Chinese at?
B: We studied Chinese at Beijing University.
A: When are you planning to get married?
B: The third of next month. You will soon receive our invitation. You must come to our wedding.
A: I'll definitely come. Where are you going to spend your honeymoon after the wedding?
B: We'll go to Hong Kong.
A: Have you been there before?
B: No. This is the first time. I heard that Hong Kong is an interesting place.
A: Tell me if it is the case after you come back.
B: Sure.

*   *   *   *   *

A: Mary, when did you come back from Hong Kong?
B: We came back last week.
A: How many days did you spend in Hong Kong?
B: We spent a week in Hong Kong.
A: How is Hong Kong?
B: Hong Kong is a fun place. The scenery is also beautiful.
A: Besides Hong Kong, wWhere else did you go?
B: We also went to Macao.
A: Is that so? How did you go to Macao? Did you fly there?
B: We didn't fly. We went there by boat.
A: How long does it take to go from Hong Kong to Macao by boat?
B: Macao is very close to Hong Kong. It takes only an hour by boat.

*   *   *   *   *

A: Mr. Wang, I'd like to ask you a question about a private matter. I wonder if you
     would mind.
B: Go ahead.
A: Are you married?
B: Yes, I am.
A: When did you get married?
B: I got married three years ago. How about you, Mr. Li? Are you married?
A: Not yet.
B: Do you have a girlfriend?
A: Yes. She and I work together.
B: When are you planning to get married?
A: Don't know now. Maybe in two years.

Reading Passage (*page 6*)

My friend David is getting married soon. I'll be attending his wedding next week.
David's bride is Mary. Both David and Mary are Americans. They met when they were
studying Chinese at Beijing University last year. Before they came to Beijing, David
worked at a bank and Mary was an elementary school teacher. They would like to get
married in China. Their parents are coming to Beijing to attend their wedding. After the
wedding, David and Mary are going to teach English at Nanjing University. They will
return to America in a year.

LESSON 2
CHINESE & ENGLISH

CONVERSATIONS

(English translation, page 49)

A: 马丁，听说 你在学 中文？
Mǎdīng, tīngshuō nǐ zài xué Zhōngwén?

B: 对，我 很 喜欢 中文。
Duì, wǒ hěn xǐhuan Zhōngwén.

A: 你学了多 长 时间 了？
Nǐ xué le duō cháng shíjiān le?

B: 我 学了一年 多 了。
Wǒ xué le yì nián duō le.

A: 你学得 怎么样？
Nǐ xué de zěnmeyàng?

B: 我 想 我学 得还 可以。我 现在 已经 能 认识
Wǒ xiǎng wǒ xué de hái kěyǐ.   Wǒ xiànzài yǐjīng néng rènshi
五百 个字，会写 三 百个字了。
wǔbǎi ge zì,   huì xiě sānbǎi ge zì le.

A: 真 不错。你说 中文   说 得也很 好。
Zhēn bú cuò.   Nǐ shuō Zhōngwén shuō de yě hěn hǎo.

B: 哪里，我说 中文   说 得还不太 流利。
Nǎlǐ,   wǒ shuō Zhōngwén shuō de hái bú tài liúlì.

A: 你觉得中文   难不难？
Nǐ juéde Zhōngwén nán bu nán?

B: 有的 地方难，有的 地方不 难。语法 和 发音不 难，
Yǒude dìfang nán, yǒude dìfang bù nán. Yǔfǎ hé fāyīn bù nán,
但是 写字 难 一些。
dànshì xiě zì nán yìxiē.

A: 你 每 天 写 汉字 吗?
Nǐ měi tiān xiě hànzì ma?

B: 我 想　每 天 写，但是 有时 工作　忙，没 有
Wǒ xiǎng měi tiān xiě,　dànshì yǒushí gōngzuò máng, méi yǒu
时间 练习。
shíjiān liànxí.

A: 你 觉得 什么　是 学 中文　　的 最 好 的 办法?
Nǐ juéde　shénme shì xué Zhōngwén de zuì hǎo de bànfǎ?

B: 我 觉得 最 好 的 办法 是 去 中国　　学。你 想　去 吗?
Wǒ juéde zuì hǎo de bànfǎ shì qù Zhōngguó xué.　Nǐ xiǎng qù ma?

A: 当然　想。 可是 我 在 工作，不 能 在 中国　　住
Dāngrán xiǎng. Kěshì wǒ zài gōngzuò, bù néng zài Zhōngguó zhù
很 长　时间。
hěn cháng shíjiān.

B: 你 可以 夏天 去。中国　　的 很 多 学校 有　短期
Nǐ kěyǐ　xiàtiān qù.　Zhōngguó de hěn duō xuéxiào yǒu duǎnqī
中文　班。
Zhōngwén bān.

A: 我 如果 去 中国　学 中文，你想　我 应该 去 哪
Wǒ rúguǒ qù Zhōngguó xué Zhōngwén, nǐ xiǎng wǒ yīnggāi qù nǎ
个 城市?
ge chéngshì?

B: 我 想 你 最好 去 北京。北京　人 都 说　普通话。
Wǒ xiǎng nǐ zuìhǎo qù Běijīng.　Běijīng rén dōu shuō pǔtōnghuà.

*　　*　　*　　*　　*

A: 小　王，你 的 英语　最近 有 很 大 的 进步。
Xiǎo Wáng, nǐde　Yīngyǔ zuìjìn yǒu hěn dà de jìnbù.

B: 谢谢。我 的 英语　还 很 差。
Xièxie.　Wǒde Yīngyǔ hái hěn chà.

A: 你学 英语 学了几年 了？
Nǐ xué Yīngyǔ xué le jǐ nián le?

B: 我 学 英语 已经学了两 年 多了。但是 我 想
Wǒ xué Yīngyǔ yǐjīng xué le liǎng nián duō le. Dànshì wǒ xiǎng
我的 英语 还 不够 好。
wǒde Yīngyǔ hái bú gòu hǎo.

A: 你 为什么 要 学 英语？
Nǐ wèishénme yào xué Yīngyǔ?

B: 我 想 以后 去 英国 上学。 懂 英语，工作 机会
Wǒ xiǎng yǐhòu qù Yīngguó shàngxué. Dǒng Yīngyǔ, gōngzuò jīhuì
也 会多 一些。
yě huì duō yìxiē.

A: 你 觉得学 英语 什么 最难？
Nǐ juéde xué Yīngyǔ shénme zuì nán?

B: 我 觉得说 最难。我 没 有 机会练 口语。
Wǒ juéde shuō zuì nán. Wǒ méi yǒu jīhuì liàn kǒuyǔ.

A: 我 可以 帮助 你。你跟 我练 中文。 你如果有
Wǒ kěyǐ bāngzhù nǐ. Nǐ gēn wǒ liàn Zhōngwén, nǐ rúguǒ yǒu
时间 也可以帮助 我 练 英语。
shíjiān yě kěyǐ bāngzhù wǒ liàn Yīngyǔ.

B: 这 是一个好 主意。
Zhè shì yí ge hǎo zhǔyì.

LESSON 2: CHINESE & ENGLISH

READING PASSAGE

小王在北京的中国银行工作，她在那儿已经工作五年了
。小王的家离单位很远，每天她起得很早，五点半就起
床了。她要坐一个小时的地铁才能到公司。小王每天工
作八个小时，下班后她还去英语学校学英语。她学英语
已经学了两年多了。她学得很好，已经能用英语和外国
朋友交谈了。

Xiǎo Wáng zài Běijīng de Zhōngguó Yínháng gōngzuò, tā zài nàr yǐjīng
gōngzuò le wǔ nián. Xiǎo Wáng de jiā lí dānwèi hěn yuǎn, měi tiān tā qǐ
de hěn zǎo, wǔ diǎn bàn jiù qǐchuáng le. Tā yào zuò yí ge xiǎoshi de dìtiě
cái néng dào gōngsī. Xiǎo Wáng měi tiān gōngzuò bā ge xiǎoshi, xiàbān
hòu tā hái qù Yīngyǔ xuéxiào xué Yīngyǔ. Tā xué Yīngyǔ yǐjīng xué le
liǎng nián duō le. Tā xué de hěn hǎo, yǐjīng néng yòng Yīngyǔ hé wàiguó
péngyou jiāotán le.

(English translation, page 50)

NEW WORDS AND EXPRESSIONS

在	zài	*progressive aspect marker*
得	de	*verb complement marker*
还	hái	fairly; passably; still
可以	kěyǐ	pretty good; not bad
已经	yǐjīng	already
真	zhēn	really; truly
哪里	nǎlǐ	*polite response to a compliment*
流利	liúlì	fluent
语法	yǔfǎ	grammar
发音	fāyīn	pronounce; pronunciation
难	nán	hard; difficult
一些	yìxiē	somewhat; a little
汉字	hànzì	Chinese characters
练习	liànxí	practice (*n./v.*)
办法	bànfǎ	way; means; method
短期	duǎnqī	short-term
班	bān	class
如果	rúguǒ	if
应该	yīnggāi	should; ought to
城市	chéngshì	city
进步	jìnbù	progress (*n./v.*)
差	chà	not good; poor
够	gòu	enough
机会	jīhuì	opportunity
练	liàn	practice (*v.*)
口语	kǒuyǔ	spoken language
帮助	bāngzhù	help (*n./v.*)
跟	gēn	with; and

SUPPLEMENTARY WORDS AND EXPRESSIONS

主意	zhǔyì	idea
就	jiù	as early as; already; then
才	cái	as late as; not until
到	dào	arrive; reach
交谈	jiāotán	converse; chat
阅读	yuèdú	reading
听力	tīnglì	listening comprehension
句子	jùzi	sentence
忘	wàng	forget
复习	fùxí	review (*n./v.*)
听写	tīngxiě	dictation
操练	cāoliàn	drill
光盘	guāngpán	CD-ROM
录音	lùyīn	record (sound); recording
生词	shēngcí	new words
课文	kèwén	text
声调	shēngdiào	tone
念	niàn	read aloud
教材	jiàocái	textbook
书法	shūfǎ	calligraphy

LANGUAGE POINTS

Indication of the progressive aspect

To indicate the progressive or continuous aspect of an action, Chinese uses the aspect marker 在 zài before the verb. The particle 呢 ne can be used optionally at the end of the sentence:

经理 在 打 电话 (呢)。
Jīnglǐ zài dǎ diànhuà (ne).
The manager is making a phone call.

我 先生　在 睡觉 (呢)。
Wǒ xiānsheng zài shuìjiào (ne).
My husband is sleeping.

For emphasis, 在 zài can be preceded by the adverb 正 zhèng (*right then*; *just*):

他 来 的 时候, 我 正　在 学习。
Tā lái de shíhou, wǒ zhèng zài xuéxí.
When he came, I was studying.

When either 正 zhèng or 呢 ne appears in the sentence, 在 zài can be omitted:

他 正　看书 (呢)。
Tā zhèng kànshū (ne).
He is reading.

他们 吃饭 呢。
Tāmen chīfàn ne.
They are eating.

The negative word for the progressive aspect marker is 没有 méiyou instead of 不 bù:

孩子们 没有　在 玩儿。
Háizimen méiyou zài wánr.
The children are not playing.

你学了多长时间的中文了
nǐ xué le duō cháng shíjiān de Zhōngwén le?

Questions may arise as to why there are two 了 le in the sentence. The first 了 le is what we have learned—an aspect marker indicating the completion of an action. As explained earlier, the completion of an action can be in the future as well as the past. We should also note that this completion generally has no bearing on the present, i.e., it does not say anything about the status of the action at the point of speaking. To indicate the relevance, a second 了 le is used at the end of the sentence. This 了 le is grammatically referred to as a modal particle. The distinction is best demonstrated by the following graphs:

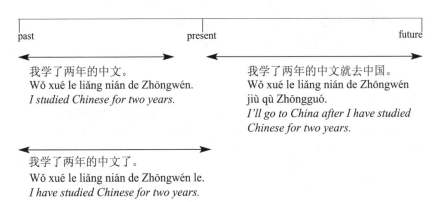

Now let's compare some sentences:

我 学 了 一 年 多 的 中文。
Wǒ xué le yì nián duō de Zhōngwén.
I studied Chinese for more than one year.
(*Sometime in the past, having no bearing on the present.*)

我 学 了 一 年 多 的 中文 了。
Wǒ xué le yì nián duō de Zhōngwén le.
I have been studying Chinese for more than one year.
(*Up to the point of speaking*)

他 在 纽约 住 了 十 年。
Tā zài Niǔyuē zhù le shí nián.
He lived in New York for ten years.
(*Sometime in the past, having no bearing on the present*)

他 在 纽约 住 了 十 年 了。
Tā zài Niǔyuē zhù le shí nián le.
He has lived in New York for ten years.
(*Up to the point of speaking*)

我们 吃了饭 就去看 电影。
Wǒmen chī le fàn jiù qù kàn diànyǐng.
We'll go to see a movie right after we eat dinner.
(*Event [seeing a movie] has not started yet.*)

我们 吃了饭 就 去看 电影 了。
Wǒmen chī le fàn jiù qù kàn diànyǐng le.
We went to see a movie right after we ate dinner.
(*Event [seeing a movie] has taken place.*)

Verb complements

A unique feature of the Chinese language is the verb complement, which
is an adjective, a verb or even a phrase after a main verb indicating the
degree, result, direction, and potential of the main verb. This contrasts
with English in that such functions are usually served by an adverb or an
adverbial phrase. We have seen the directional complements 来 lái and
去 qù in the previous lesson. Sentences below in this lesson are examples
of complements of degree:

你 说 中文 说 得 很 好。
Nǐ shuō Zhōngwén shuō de hěn hǎo.
You speak Chinese very well.

她起得很 早。
Tā qǐ de hěn zǎo.
She gets up very early.

As with the other types of complements, the complement of degree follows
the verb, but unlike most of the other types of complements, it is always
introduced by the particle 得 de. Additional examples of complements
of degree are:

他 写 得 好。
Tā xiě de hǎo.
He writes well.

火车　今天　到 得 早。
Huǒchē jīntiān dào de zǎo.
The train arrived early today.

When the sentence takes the negative form, 不 bù is placed after 得 de instead of before the verb:

他 写 得 不 好。
Tā xiě de bù hǎo.
He doesn't write well.

火车　今天　到 得 不 早。
Huǒchē jīntiān dào de bù zǎo.
The train did not arrive early today.

If the verb takes an object, the object needs to be placed immediately after the verb, thus creating a conflict with the complement introduced by 得 de, which should also be placed immediately after the verb. To satisfy both conditions, the object is placed after the verb, but the verb needs to be repeated after the object so that it can immediately precede the complement:

他 说 中文　　说 得 很 流利。
Tā shuō Zhōngwén shuō de hěn liúlì.
He speaks Chinese fluently.

There are two ways commonly used in Chinese to avoid the repetitiveness:

Leave out the initial verb:

他 中文　　说 得 很 流利。
Tā Zhōngwén shuō de hěn liúlì.

Shift the object to the beginning of the sentence:

中文　　他 说 得 很 流利。
Zhōngwén tā shuō de hěn liúlì.

There are two ways to ask a question about the verb complement: 1) using 怎么样 zěnmèyang, and 2) using one of the two Yes/No question formats. For example, *how does he speak Chinese* can be expressed in one of the following ways:

他 说 中文　　说 得 怎么样?
Tā shuō Zhōngwén shuō de zěnmèyang?

他 说　中文　　说　得 流利 吗?
Tā shuō Zhōngwén shuō de liúlì　ma?

他 说　中文　　说　得 流利不流利?
Tā shuō Zhōngwén shuō de liúlì　bu liúlì?

我现在已经 能认识五百个字，会写三百个字了
wǒ xiànzài yǐjīng néng rènshi wǔbǎi ge zì, huì xiě sānbǎi ge zì le

When the adverb 已经 yǐjīng appears in the sentence, the modal particle 了 le must be used at the end of the sentence to indicate that the event has taken place.

你学英语学了几年了 nǐ xué Yīngyǔ xué le jǐ nián le

It was mentioned in Lesson 1 that words and expressions that indicate a duration of time should follow the verb instead of preceding it:

我 在北京　住了五年 了。
Wǒ zài Běijīng zhù le wǔ nián le.
I have lived in Beijing for five years.

However, there is a complication when the verb takes an object. The verb needs to be repeated after the object, just as the verb needs to be repeated after the object before it precedes a verb complement introduced by 得 de (*see above*):

学生们　　看 书 看 了一个 小时。
Xuéshengmen kàn shū kàn le yí ge xiǎoshi.
The students read (books) for an hour.

他学 中文　　学了两 年 了。
Tā xué Zhōngwén xué le liáng nián le.
He has been studying Chinese for two years.

To avoid the repetition of the verb, Chinese often turns the duration of time into an attribute of the object:

学生们　　看了一个 小时　的 书。
Xuéshengmen kàn le yí ge xiǎoshi de shū.

他 学 了 两　年 的 中文　　了。
Tā xué le liǎng nián de　Zhōngwén le.

This is quite comparable to the convertibility of the following sentences in English:

I can commit to teaching for one year.

I can commit to one year of teaching.

Response to compliments in Chinese

There is a propensity among the Chinese to respond to a compliment not by acknowledging it in the form of a *thank you,* but by declining it. It is considered in Chinese culture too presumptuous to readily accept a compliment. The most commonly used expression in responding to a compliment is 哪 里　nǎlǐ, which literally means *where,* used here with the implied meaning of *where is the connection between what I did and what you complimented.* Alternatively, speakers of Chinese would simply deny by saying that the compliment is not true and couple the denial with a self-effacing statement:

A: 你的 中文　　很　流利。
　Nǐde　Zhōngwén hěn liúlì.
　Your Chinese is very fluent.

B: 哪里，我的 中文　　不 流利，我的 中文　　很
　Nǎlǐ,　　wǒde　Zhōngwén bù liúlì,　　wǒde Zhōngwén hěn
　差。
　chà.
　No, my Chinese is not fluent. My Chinese is very poor.

This propensity is also reflected in other aspects of Chinese social life. For example, it is not proper for a Chinese to open a gift in the presence of the giver. To do so would reveal that the recipient is too greedy. In receiving a present, one should never say, "*this is exactly what I want.*" If anything, he or she probably should show disinterest and say, *"this is something that I don't need."* The idea is that one feels guilty for causing someone to spend money or time. So don't be offended when you give your Chinese friend a gift, but he or she shows little interest. Your Chinese friend is probably feeling guilty for causing you the trouble.

一些 yìxiē

Unlike most other verb modifiers, 一些 yìxiē in the sense of *somewhat, a few,* or *a little* follows the verb instead of preceding it. This is also true of expressions such as 一下儿 yìdiǎn (*slightly, a while*), 一会儿 yíhuìr (*a little while*), and 极了 jíle (*extremely*).

两年多了 liǎng nián duō le *and* 十多年 shí duō nián

To indicate the idea of *over* (*a certain amount*) or *more than*, Chinese uses 多 duō. Note that the positioning of 多 duō is different depending on the actual number. If the number is less than ten, 多 duō is placed after the classifier, whereas if the number is greater than ten, 多 duō is placed before the classifier. Compare:

五 个 多 星期
wǔ ge duō xīngqī
more than five weeks

二十 多 个 小时
èrshí duō ge xiǎoshi
more than twenty hours

学中文的最好的办法 xué Zhōngwén de zuì hǎo de bànfǎ

It is time for us to be reminded of the modifier-preceding-modified principle in Chinese. The verbal phrase 学中文 xué Zhōngwén (*to learn Chinese*) modifies 办法 bànfǎ (*method*). As such, it is placed before 办法 bànfǎ. The modifier-modified relationship is marked by the particle 的 de. Similar examples are:

练习 口语 的 机会
liànxí kǒuyǔ de jīhuì
opportunity to practice spoken language

要 参加 的 婚礼
yào cānjiā de hūnlǐ
wedding to attend

去 过 的 地方
qù guo de dìfang
places visited

能 认识 的 汉字
néng rènshi de hànzì
Chinese characters that (one) can recognize

学习的时间
xuéxí de shíjiān
time to study

五点半就起床了 wǔ diǎn bàn jiù qǐchuáng le *and* **坐一个小时的地铁才能到公司 zuò yí ge xiǎoshí de dìtiě cái néng dào gōngsī**

就 jiù in the first sentence means *earlier than expected* or *better than expected*: "get up as early as 5:30." In this sense 就 jiù is often opposed to 才 cái, which means *later than expected* or *worse than expected*: "take the subway for as long as an hour before getting to work." Compare:

九点 上课，他八点 就 来了。
Jiǔ diǎn shàngkè, tā bā diǎn jiù lái le.
Class started at 9, but he came as early as 8.

九点 上课，他十点 才 来。
Jiǔ diǎn shàngkè, tā shí diǎn cái lái.
Class started at 9, but he didn't come until 10.

Note that the aspect marker 了 le must be used with 就 jiù, but it cannot be used with 才 cái.

EXERCISES

Answer key, pages 271-273

I. Answer the following questions:

1. 你 在 我们的 城市 住 了 几 年 了？
   Nǐ zài wǒmende chéngshì zhù le jǐ nián le?

2. 你 学 中文 学 了 几 年 了？
   Nǐ xué Zhōngwén xué le jǐ nián le?

3. 你 写 汉字 写 得 怎么样？
   Nǐ xiě hànzì xiě de zěnmeyàng?

4. 你 做 饭 做 得 怎么样？
   Nǐ zuò fàn zuò de zěnmeyàng?

5. 你 工作 吗？你 工作 了 几 年 了？
   Nǐ gōngzuò ma? Nǐ gōngzuò le jǐ nián le?

6. 你 每 天 学 多 长 时间 的 中文？
   Nǐ měi tiān xué duō cháng shíjiān de Zhōngwén?

7. 你 每 天 起 得 早 不 早？ 睡 得 晚 不 晚 ？
   Nǐ měi tiān qǐ de zǎo bu zǎo? Shuì de wǎn bu wǎn?

8. 你 现在 能 认识 多少 汉字？ 能 写 多少 汉字？
   Nǐ xiànzài néng rènshi duōshao hànzì? Néng xiě duōshao hànzì?

9. 别人 说 你的 中文 好，你 怎么 回答？
   Biérén shuō nǐde Zhōngwén hǎo, nǐ zěnme huídá?

10. 你 昨天 晚上 八 点 在 做 什么？
    Nǐ zuótiān wǎnshang bā diǎn zài zuò shénme?

II. Describe what people are doing in the following pictures, using one of the following indicators:

在 zài   正在 zhèng zài   在 zài   呢 ne

1.

_____。

2.

_____。

3.

_____。

4.

_____。

5.

_____。

6.

_____。

III. Complete the following sentences:

1. 你 法语 说 得 _____ 。
   Nǐ Fǎyǔ shuō de _____ .

2. 汽车 开 得 _____ 。
   Qìchē kāi de _____ .

3. 我 太太 起床 起 得 _____ 。
   Wǒ tàitai qǐchuáng qǐ de _____ .

4. 外国 学生 写 字 写 得 _____ ?
   Wàiguó xuésheng xiě zì xiě de _____ ?

5. 雨 下 得 _____ ?
   Yǔ xià de _____ ?

IV. Change the following into negative sentences:

1. 老师 来 得 很 早。
   Lǎoshī lái de hěn zǎo.

   _____

2. 我 妈妈 做 饭 做 得 很 好。
   Wǒ māma zuò fàn zuò de hěn hǎo.

   _____

3. 他 开 车 开 得 很 快。
   Tā kāi chē kāi de hěn kuài.

   _____

4. 那 个 老 人 走 得 很 慢。
   Nà ge lǎo rén zǒu de hěn màn.

   _____

5. 他们 在 北京 玩儿 得很 高兴。
Tāmen zài Běijīng wánr de hěn gāoxìng.

_____

V. How do you say the following:

1. more than five days; more than twenty people

_____

2. long enough, not high enough

_____

3. easy in some respects and difficult in other respects

_____

4. the best way to learn a foreign language

_____

5. opportunity to practice spoken language

_____

6. married for ten years

_____

7. study Chinese with a Chinese friend

_____

8. know a few Chinese characters

_____

9. rapid progress

_____

10. talk with foreign friends in English

_____

VI. Fill in the blanks with 就 jiù or 才 cài:

1. 她 从　大学 毕业 以后 ＿＿＿ 结婚 了。
   Tā cóng dàxué bìyì　yǐhòu ＿＿＿＿ jiéhūn le.

2. 电影　已经 开始 了半 个 小时 他 ＿＿＿ 来。
   Diànyǐng yǐjīng kāishǐ le bàn ge xiǎoshí tā ＿＿＿＿ lái.

3. 我 爸爸 每 天 五 点 ＿＿＿ 起床　了。
   Wǒ bàba měi tiān wǔ diǎn ＿＿＿＿ qǐchuáng le.

4. 我们　坐 了 两 个小时 的 汽车 ＿＿＿ 到 飞机场。
   Wǒmen zuò le liǎng ge xiǎoshí de qìchē ＿＿＿＿ dào fēijīchǎng.

5. 马丁　来 中国　＿＿＿ 一 个 星期。
   Mǎdīng lái Zhōngguó ＿＿＿＿ yí ge xīngqī.

6. 一 个星期 后，暑假 ＿＿＿ 开始 了。
   Yí ge xīngqī hòu, shǔjià ＿＿＿＿ kāishǐ le.

VII. Translate the following into Chinese:

1. We ate for two hours.

   ＿＿＿＿＿＿＿＿＿＿＿＿＿＿＿＿＿

2. He has been driving for more than five hours.

   ＿＿＿＿＿＿＿＿＿＿＿＿＿＿＿＿＿

3. Students are attending a class.

   ＿＿＿＿＿＿＿＿＿＿＿＿＿＿＿＿＿

4. What was your mother doing when you went home yesterday?

   ＿＿＿＿＿＿＿＿＿＿＿＿＿＿＿＿＿

5. The American teacher made a thirty-minute phone call to America.

   ＿＿＿＿＿＿＿＿＿＿＿＿＿＿＿＿＿

6. Did you sleep well last night?

   ＿＿＿＿＿＿＿＿＿＿＿＿＿＿＿＿＿

7. I'm so busy with my work that I don't have an opportunity to travel.

   _____

8. I have been learning English for more than ten years, but my English is not good enough.

   _____

9. It snowed heavily.

   _____

10. She goes to bed late, but gets up early.

   _____

VIII. Translate the following into English:

1. 这 本 书 你 只 能 看 三 天。
   Zhè běn shū nǐ zhǐ néng kàn sān tiān.

   _____

2. 我 太太 在 中学 工作 了 二十 年。
   Wǒ tàitai zài zhōngxué gōngzuò le èrshí nián.

   _____

3. 他 开车 开 了 三十 多 个 小时 才 开 到 加州。
   Tā kāi chē kāi le sānshí duō ge xiǎoshí cái kāi dào Jiāzhōu.

   _____

4. 我 每 天 坐 一个小时 的 汽车 去 上班。
   Wǒ měi tiān zuò yí ge xiǎoshí de qìchē qù shàngbān.

   _____

5. 学生们 写 了 三十 分钟 的 字。
   Xuéshengmen xiě le sānshí fēnzhōng de zì.

   _____

6. 老师 说 得很 慢。
Lǎoshī shuō de hěn màn.

_____

7. 美国 朋友 在北京 玩儿 得 很 高兴。
Měiguó péngyou zài Běijīng wánr de hěn gāoxìng.

_____

8. 孩子们 看 电视 看 了 两 个 小时。
Háizimen kàn diànshì kàn le liǎng ge xiǎoshí.

_____

9. 没 有 人 跟 我 练 中文。
Méi yǒu rén gēn wǒ liàn Zhōngwén.

_____

10. 我们 只 坐 了一个 小时 的 火车 就 从 上海 到 了
Wǒmen zhǐ zuò le yí ge xiǎoshí de huǒchē jiù cóng Shànghǎi dào le
苏州。
Sūzhōu.

_____

IX. Topics for discussion and writing:

1. 你 觉得 中文 难 不 难？什么 地方 难？什么
Nǐ juéde Zhōngwén nán bu nán? Shénme dìfang nán? Shénme
地方 不 难？
dìfang bù nán?

2. 你 是 怎么 学 汉字、语法、发音 和 生词 的？
Nǐ shì zěnme xué hànzì, yǔfǎ, fāyīn hé shēngcí de?

3. 你 觉得 什么 是 学 中文 的 最 好 的 方法？
Nǐ juéde shénme shì xué Zhōngwén de zuì hǎo de fāngfǎ?

ENGLISH TRANSLATION OF THE TEXT

Conversations (*pages 28-31*)

A: Martin, I heard that you are learning Chinese?
B: Yes. I like Chinese very much.
A: How long have you been studying it?
B: I have been studying it for more than a year.
A: How have you been doing?
B: I think I'm fine. By now, I can recognize five hundred characters and write three hundred.
A: That's great. You also speak Chinese very well.
B: I'm not sure about that. I don't speak Chinese very fluently.
A: Do you think Chinese is difficult?
B: In some aspects, it is; in other aspects, it is not. Grammar and pronunciation are not difficult, but writing characters is a little hard.
A: Do you write characters every day?
B: I would like to, but sometimes I just don't have time to practice because of my work.
A: What do you think is the best way to learn Chinese?
B: I think the best way is to study it in China. Would you like to go?
A: Of course I would. But I'm working, so I can't spend a long time in China.
B: You can go there during the summer. Many schools in China have short-term Chinese language classes.
A: If I go to China to study Chinese, which city do you think I should go?
B: I think you should go to Beijing. People in Beijing all speak Mandarin.

          *   *   *
  *   *

A: Xiao Wang, you have made a lot of progress in English recently.
B: Thank you, but my English is still very poor.
A: How many years have you studied English?
B: I have studied English for more than two years, but I don't think my English is good enough.
A: Why do you want to study English?
B: I would like to study in England in the future. Besides, there will be more work opportunities if I know English.
A: What do you think is the most difficult thing in learning English?
B: I found that speaking is the most difficult. I don't have opportunities to practice spoken English.
A: I can help you with that. You can practice Chinese with me. If you have time, I can also practice English with you.
B: This is a good idea.

Reading Passage (*page 31*)

Xiao Wang works at Bank of China in Beijing. She has worked there for five years. Xiao Wang's home is far from her work. She gets up very early every day. She gets up as early as 5:30. She needs to take the subway for an hour before she can get to work. Xiao Wang works for eight hours every day. She also goes to an English school after work to study English. She has been learning English for more than two years. She is doing well in her study and can already conduct conversations in English with her foreign friends.

LESSON 3
CALLING &
ANSWERING

CONVERSATIONS

(English translation, page 70)

A: 喂!
Wèi!

B: 您 找 谁?
Nín zhǎo shuí?

A: 我 找 你们的 经理。他 在 不 在?
Wǒ zhǎo nǐmende jīnglǐ.   Tā zài bu zài?

B: 请 等 一下儿,我 去 看看。… 对 不 起,他 在 开 会。
Qǐng děng yíxiàr ,   wǒ qù kànkan. … Duìbuqǐ,   tā zài kāi huì.
你 过 一会儿 打 来,好 吗?
Nǐ guò yíhuìr   dǎ lai,   hǎo ma?

A: 我 能 不 能 给 他 留 个 话?
Wǒ néng bu néng gěi tā   liú ge huà?

B: 当然 可以。您 贵 姓?
Dāngrán kěyǐ.   Nín guì xìng?

A: 我 姓 张, 我 叫 张 明。
Wǒ xìng Zhāng, wǒ jiào Zhāng Míng.

B: 您的 电话 号码 是 多少?
Nínde diànhuà hàomǎ shì duōshao?

A: 我的 号码 是 212—734—8659。
Wǒde hàomǎ shì 212—734—8659.

B: 请问, 您 要 留 什么 话?
Qǐngwèn, nín yào liú shénme huà?

A: 你们的 经理 回 来 后，请 他 给 我 打 电 话。
Nǐmende jīnglǐ huí lai hòu, qǐng tā gěi wǒ dǎ diànhuà.

B: 好，张　先生。　　我 一定 让 他 给 您 回 话。
Hǎo, Zhāng Xiānsheng. Wǒ yídìng ràng tā gěi nín huí huà.

*　　*　　*　　*　　*

A: 我 昨天　晚上　给 你 打 电话，没 有 人 接。
Wǒ zuótiān wǎnshang gěi nǐ dǎ diànhuà, méi yǒu rén jiē.
你 去 哪儿 了？
Nǐ qù nǎr le?

B: 我 哪儿 也 没 去。你 是 几点 给 我 打 的 电话？
Wǒ nǎr yě méi qù. Nǐ shì jǐ diǎn gěi wǒ dǎ de diànhuà?

A: 我 是 八 点 给 你 打 的 电话。
Wǒ shì bā diǎn gěi nǐ dǎ de diànhuà.

B: 我的 手机 那个 时候 关 掉 了。对不起，你 找
Wǒde shǒujī nà ge shíhou guān diào le. Duìbuqǐ, nǐ zhǎo
我 有 事 吗？
wǒ yǒu shì ma?

A: 没　有 大 事，只 是 想　和 你 聊聊。
Méi yǒu dà shì, zhǐ shì xiǎng hé nǐ liáoliao.

B: 你 星期六 能　来 我 这儿 坐坐　吗？
Nǐ xīngqīliù néng lái wǒ zhèr zuòzuo ma?

A: 可以，星期六 什么　时间 对 你 方便？
Kěyǐ, xīngqīliù shénme shíjiān duì nǐ fāngbiàn?

B: 我 一 天　都 在 家。你 什么　时间 来 都 可以。
Wǒ yì tiān dōu zài jiā. Nǐ shénme shíjiān lái dōu kěyǐ.

*　　*　　*　　*

A: 中国　餐馆 吗？
Zhōngguó cānguǎn ma?

B: 是，这 是 中国　餐馆。
Shì, zhè shì Zhōngguó cānguǎn.

A: 你们 送 不 送 饭？
Nǐmen sòng bu sòng fàn?

B: 送，您 要 什么 饭？
Sòng, nín yào shénme fàn?

A: 请 给 我 送 一个 炒饭 和一个 豆腐。
Qǐng gěi wǒ sòng yí ge chǎofàn hé yí ge dòufu.

B: 什么　时候 要 送 到？
Shénme shíhou yào sòng dào?

A: 请 在 七 点 前 送 到。
Qǐng zài qī diǎn qián sòng dào.

B: 没 问题。请　告诉 我 您的 地址。
Méi wèntí.　Qǐng gàosu wǒ nínde dìzhǐ.

A: 我的 地址 是 公园　路 530号。
Wǒde dìzhǐ shì Gōngyuán Lù 530 hào.

B: 您的 电话　号码 是 多少？
Nínde diànhuà hàomǎ shì duōshao?

A: 我的 电话　号码 是 754-3698。
Wǒde diànhuà hàomǎ shì 754-3698.

B: 好，一会儿 见。
Hǎo, yíhuìr jiàn.

A: 谢 谢。
Xièxie.

READING PASSAGE

现在手机越来越普通。好像什么人都有一部。手机给我
们带来很多方便。我们用手机除了可以打电话，还可以
上网、听音乐，等等。在用手机的时候，我们要尊重别
人。有的人在电影院和上课的时候也不关掉手机，这是
很不好的。还有的人一边开车一边打电话，这样是很不
安全的。人们说得对□有一利就有一弊。

Xiànzài shǒujī yuèláiyuè pǔtōng. Hǎoxiàng shénme rén dōu yǒu yí bù.
Shǒujī gěi wǒmen dài lái hěn duō fāngbiàn. Zài yòng shǒujī de shíhou,
wǒmen yào zūnzhòng biérén. Yǒude rén zài diànyǐngyuàn hé shàngkè de
shíhou yě bù guān diào shǒujī, zhè shì hěn bù hǎo de. Hái yǒude rén yìbiān
kāichē yìbiān yòng shǒujī dǎ diànhuà, zhèyàng shì hěn bù ānquán de.
Rénmen shuō de duì, yǒu yí lì jiù yǒu yí bì.

(*English translation, page 71*)

利 弊 皆 存

NEW WORDS AND EXPRESSIONS

喂	wéi; wèi	hello
开会	kāi huì	attend a meeting
一会儿	yíhuìr	a little while
打	dǎ	make (a phone call); hit
给	gěi	to; give
留	liú	leave (a message)
号码	hàomǎ	(telephone) number
让	ràng	ask (sb. to do sth.); let
接	jiē	pick up; answer (a phone call)
手机	shǒujī	cell phone
关掉	guān diào	turn off (a device)
只是	zhǐshì	merely; only; just
聊	liáo	chat
对	duì	to; for; regarding
方便	fāngbiàn	convenient; convenience
送	sòng	deliver; take sb. or sth. to
炒饭	chǎofàn	fried rice
豆腐	dòufu	tofu
地址	dìzhǐ	(mailing) address
越来越	yuèláiyuè	more and more; increasingly
部	bù	*classifier*
普通	pǔtōng	common; ordinary
上网	shàng wǎng	get on the internet
等等	děngdeng	so on
联系	liánxì	contact (*v./n.*)
尊重	zūnzhòng	respect
别人	biérén	other people
一边 ... 一边	yìbiān … yìbiān	simultaneously; at the same time

安全	ānquán	safe
利	lì	benefit; advantage
弊	bì	drawback; disadvantage

SUPPLEMENTARY WORDS AND EXPRESSIONS

公用电话	gōngyòng diànhuà	public phone; pay phone
国际电话	guójì diànhuà	international call
国内电话	guónèi diànhuà	domestic call
智能电话	zhìnéng diànhuà	smart phone
区号	qūhào	area code
电话号码本	diànhuà hàomǎ běn	phone book
电话卡	diànhuàkǎ	telephone card
拨	bō	dial
发	fā	send (email, text messages)
短信	duǎnxìn	text message

LANGUAGE POINTS

喂 wéi, wèi

The word is pronounced in two ways in a telephone conversation depending on who is the caller and who is the answerer. The person who answers the phone would greet the caller by saying 喂 wéi, whereas the caller would pronounce it as 喂 wèi to attract attention. Additionally, the greeting convention in a telephone conversation in China is such that callers would have to identify themselves first sometimes even when their calls are made to a business.

一会儿 yíhuìr, 一下儿 yíxiàr, *and* 一点儿 yìdiǎnr

These are often confused. Let's compare them:

一会儿 yíhuìr *a little while*; always used after a verb:

老师 现在 很 忙。你 过 一会儿 再 问 他吧。
Lǎoshī xiànzài hěn máng. Nǐ guò yíhuìr   zài wèn tā ba.
The teacher is busy now. Please ask him in a little while.

一下儿 yíxiàr; always used after a verb to suggest that the action is brief, tentative, or informal (see *Beginner's Chinese*, Lesson 7):

我 能 不 能 看 一下儿 你的 中文   书?
Wǒ néng bu néng kàn yíxiàr   nǐde Zhōngwén shū?
Can I take a look at your Chinese book?

一点儿 yìdiǎnr *a little bit*; used both as an adjective before a noun and a complement after a verb, e.g.:

A: 你 会 说 法语 吗?
Nǐ huì shuō Fǎyǔ ma?
Do you speak French?

B: 会 一点儿。
Huì yìdiǎnr.
A little.

A: 你 会 说 什么 语言？
Nǐ huì shuō shénme yǔyán?
What languages do you speak?

B: 我 会 说 英语，西班牙语 和 一点儿中文。
Wǒ huì shuō Yīngyǔ, Xībānyáyǔ hé yìdiǎnr Zhōngwén.
I speak English, Spanish and a little Chinese.

给 gěi

给 gěi can be used as a verb as well as a preposition. As a verb, it means *to give* and is usually followed by two objects:

我 妈妈 给 我 一 百 块 钱。
Wǒ māma gěi wǒ yì bǎi kuài qián.
My mother gave me $100.

学校 给 我们 班 一台电脑。
Xuéxiào gěi wǒmen bān yì tái diànnǎo.
The school gave our class a computer.

As a preposition, it is used with a noun to mean *to* or *for*. Since it is used to modify the verb of the sentence, the phrase is placed before the verb:

给 电话 公司 工作
gěi diànhuà gōngsī gōngzuò
work for a telephone company

给 学校 买 书
gěi xuéxiào mǎi shū
buy books for the school

给 我 妈妈 打 电话
gěi wǒ māma dǎ diànhuà
call my mother

给 我 朋友 写信
gěi wǒ péngyou xiě xìn
write a letter to my friend

请他给我打电话 qǐng tā gěi wǒ dǎ diànhuà *and* 让他给您回话 ràng tā jìngkuài gěi nín huí huà

Both 让 ràng and 请 qǐng can be used to mean *ask sb. to do sth*. Whether to use 让 ràng or 请 qǐng depends on who makes the request. If you ask someone to do something for you, you should generally use 请 qǐng, which is more polite. If someone asks you to do something, you should generally use 让 ràng. Compare:

我 请 他 给 我 买 报纸。
Wǒ qǐng tā gěi wǒ mǎi bàozhǐ.
I asked him to buy me a newspaper.

他 让 我 给 他买 报纸。
Tā ràng wǒ gěi tā mǎi bàozhǐ.
He asked me to buy him a newspaper.

哪儿也没有去 nǎr yě méiyou qù

This structure emphasizes that what is stated applies to any situation. It takes one of the following forms:

S + Wh-Q Word + 也 yě / 都 dōu (+ neg) + V
or
S + Wh-Q Word + V + S 也 yě / 都 dōu + V

The difference between them is that the second structure involves two sentences.

The following examples illustrate the use of these two structures:

我们的 老师 什么 都 知道。
Wǒmende lǎoshī shénme dōu zhīdào.
Our teacher knows everything.

她 妈妈 什么 菜 都 会 做。
Tā māma shénme cài dōu huì zuò.
Her mother knows how to cook any dish.

汽车 哪儿 都 不 能 停。
Qìchē nǎr dōu bù néng tíng.
The car can't be parked anywhere.

我 怎么 说 她也不 听。

Wǒ zěnme shuō tā yě bù tīng.
No matter what I say, she won't listen.

在 上海　他 谁　都 不 认识。
Zài Shànghǎi tā shuí dōu bú rènshi.
He doesn't know anyone in Shanghai.

我 今天 什么　电话　也 没有 打。
Wǒ jīntiān shénme diànhuà yě méiyou dǎ.
I didn't make any phone calls today.

我 什么　时候 给 他 打 电话 他 都 不 在。
Wǒ shénme shíhou gěi tā dǎ diànhuà tā dōu bú zài.
He is never home whenever I call him.

来我这儿坐坐 **lái wǒ zhèr zuòzuo**

The object to 来 lái or 去 qù, if there is any, must be a place word. Ideas such as *please come to me* or *go to your mother* are expressed in Chinese by using either 这儿 zhèr or 那儿 nàr after the pronoun or the noun:

请 来 我 这儿。
Qǐng lái wǒ zhèr.

去 你妈妈 那儿。
Qù nǐ māma nàr.

这儿 zhèr is used when the movement is toward the speaker (e.g. 我 wǒ) and 那儿 nàr is used when the movement is away from the speaker (e.g. 你妈妈 nǐ māma).

星期六什么时间对你方便 **xīngqīliù shénme shíjiān duì nǐ fāngbiàn?**

对 duì is used as a preposition meaning *to, regarding,* or *concerning*. Since the phrase modifies the verb or the predicate adjective of the sentence, it is placed before it. The 对 duì-phrase is often used with the following verbs and predicate adjectives:

他 对 我 说。
Tā duì wó shuō.
He said to me.

英语　对我的帮助　很大。
Yīngyǔ duì wǒde bāngzhù hěn dà.
English is a great help to me.

她对音乐没有兴趣。
Tā duì yīnyuè méi yǒu xìngqù.
She is not interested in music.

他们对我很好。
Tāmen duì wǒ hěn hǎo.
They are very nice to me.

一天都在家　yì tiān dōu zài jiā
Used in certain expressions, 一 yī means *all, entire,* or *whole* (for the tonal
variations of the word, please refer to *Beginner's Chinese*, page 100):

我们　一家人昨天　去了博物馆。
Wǒmen yì jiā rén zuótiān qù le bówùguǎn.
Our whole family went to the museum yesterday.

他有一房子的书。
Tā yǒu yì fángzi de shū.
He has a roomful of books.

As an adverb, 都 dōu is often used after such words as 每 měi (*every*),
全 quán (*entire*), 各 gè (*each*), and 任何 rènhé (*any*) to emphasize non-
exclusiveness:

他们全家都去了博物馆。
Tāmen quán jiā dōu qù le bówùguǎn.
Their whole family went to the museum.

各个大学都给外国人开中文　课。
Gè ge dàxué dōu gěi wàiguórén kāi Zhōngwén kè.
Each (every) university offers Chinese classes to foreigners.

你每天都看报吗?
Nǐ měi tiān dōu kàn bào ma?
Do you read newspapers everyday?

Another example in this lesson is:

好像　什么　人　都　有　一部　手机。
Hǎoxiàng shénme rén dōu yǒu yí bù shǒujī.
It seems that everyone has a cell phone.

什么时候要送到 shénme shíhou yào sòng dào

到 dào in the sense of *arrive* or *reach* is used after another verb as a complement to indicate a place or a time that the action extends to: 寄到中国 jì dào Zhōngguó (*mail to China*); 玩儿到十点 wánr dào shí diǎn (*play till ten o'clock*); 走到学校 zǒu dào xuéxiào (*walk to school*).

部 bù as a classifier

As a classifier, 部 bù is used for such machinery or devices as cars, telephones, and machines.

别人 biérén

别 bié in 别人 biérén means *other*, however other than in 别人 biérén and a few other set expressions, it takes the form of 别的 biéde: 别的学校 biéde xuéxiào (*other schools*), 别的国家 biéde guójiā (*other countries*), 别的公司 biéde gōngsī (*other companies*).

还有的人一边开车一边用手机打电话
hái yǒude rén yìbiān kāichē yìbiān yòng shǒujī dǎ diànhuà

Used in pairs, 一边 … 一边 … yìbiān … yìbiān … indicates that two actions are taking place simultaneously:

他　喜欢　一边　看书　一边　听　音乐。
Tā xǐhuan yìbiān kànshū yìbiān tīng yīnyuè.
He likes to listen to music while reading.

很　多　大学生　一边　工作，一边　上学。
Hěn duō dàxuéshēng yìbiān gōngzuò, yìbiān shàngxué.
Many college students go to school while they work.

EXERCISES

Answer key, pages 273-275

I. Answer the following questions:

1. 你有 手机 吗？你的 手机 号码 是 多少？
Nǐ yǒu shǒujī ma? Nǐde shǒujī hàomǎ shì duōshao?
我有手机. 我的号码是六一零九六五八

2. 今天 什么 时候 给 你 打电话 方便？
Jīntiān shénme shíhou gěi nǐ dǎ diànhuà fāngbiàn?
八点给我打电话（哥哥打电话了）

3. 你 今天 有 没有 打电话？给 谁 打了电话？
Nǐ jīntiān yǒu méiyou dǎ diànhuà? Gěi shuí dǎ le diànhuà?
我今天给我

4. 手机 很 方便，你觉得手机 有 没 有 不 好 的 地方？
Shǒujī hěn fāngbiàn, nǐ juéde shǒujī yǒu méi yǒu bù hǎo de dìfang?
我觉得手机有一点儿不好的地方例如有些人手机成病气

5. 有 人 给 你 妈妈 打电话，但是 她 不 在 家。
Yǒu rén gěi nǐ māma dǎ diànhuà, dànshì tā bú zài jiā.
你怎么 说？
Nǐ zěnme shuō?

_____

6. 你去 过 中国 吗？你 在 中国 的 时候 有 没有
Nǐ qù guo Zhōngguó ma? Nǐ zài Zhōngguó de shíhou yǒu méiyou
用 过 公用 电话？你 会 用 吗？
yòng guo gōngyòng diànhuà? Nǐ huì yòng ma?

_____

7. 除了 打 电话，你 用 手机 做 什么？
Chúle dǎ diànhuà, nǐ yòng shǒujī zuò shénme?

_____

8. 在 你们那儿，开汽车的时候 能 不能 用 手机
   Zài nǐmen nàr,   kāi qìchē de shíhou néng bu néng yòng shǒujī
   打 电话?
   dǎ diànhuà?

   开汽车的时候我们 都 不能用手机
   or   *gèng*
                                     更

9. 你喜欢打 电话 还是 发 短信?
   Nǐ xǐhuan dǎ diànhuà háishi fā duǎnxìn?

   我 更喜欢 发短信 因为 很方便.

10. 你常常   请 中国   餐馆 给你送 饭吗?
    Nǐ chángchang qǐng Zhōngguó cānguǎn gěi nǐ sòng fàn ma?

   _____

II. How do you say the following:

1. make a phone call; answer a phone call; return a phone call

   _____

2. She is very nice to me.

   _____

3. What did he say to you?

   _____

4. 7 pm is not good for me.

   _____

5. Can I leave a message for her?

   _____

6. I'll take someone to the airport this afternoon.

   _____

7. Our whole family was home last night.

   _____

8. Our manager is at a meeting.

   _____

9. Please come to me if you have questions.

_____

10. More and more people are learning Chinese.

_____

III. Fill in the blanks with the following expressions:

一会儿 yíhuìr   一下儿 yíxiàr   一点儿 yìdiǎnr

1. 老师 现在 很 忙，你 过 ___一下儿___ 再 来 吧。
   Lǎoshī xiànzài hěn máng, nǐ guò _____ zài lái ba.

2. 我 能 不 能 试 ___一点___ 这件 衣服?
   Wǒ néng bu néng shì _____ zhè jiàn yīfu?

3. 昨天 只 下 了 _____ 雨。 一会儿
   Zuótiān zhǐ xià le _____ yǔ.

4. 我 不 饿，我 吃 了 _____ 东西。 一点
   Wǒ bú è, wǒ chī le _____ dōngxi.

5. 他 每 天 中午 都 要 睡 _____。 一会儿?
   Tā měi tiān zhōngwǔ dōu yào shuì _____.

6. 我 能 不 能 用 _____ 你的 电话?
   Wǒ néng bu néng yòng _____ nǐde diànhuà?

IV. Translate the following into Chinese, using the patterns:

S + Wh-Q Word + 也 yě / 都 dōu (+ neg) + V
or
S + Wh-Q Word + V + S 也 yě / 都 dōu + V

1. You can buy a phone card in any store.

_____

2. I didn't see any movies this year.

_____

3. She didn't eat anything yesterday. Today, she doesn't want to eat anything either.

_____

4. Whenever I call her, her phone is always busy.

_____

5. The child wouldn't listen however her father talked to her.

_____

V. Translate the following into Chinese:
1. It is not safe to make phone calls while driving.

_____

2. Sorry, our manager is not in yet. Would you like to leave a message?

_____

3. If you can't make it to school tomorrow, please give me a call.

_____

4. Someone from Peking University called you this afternoon. She left a message asking you to call her back.

_____

5. If you need to tell me something, please call my cell phone.

_____

6. The teacher asked me to tell you that there is no class tomorrow.

_____

7. I asked the teacher to take a look at my homework.

_____

8. It is not good to study while watching TV at the same time.

_____

9. Excuse me, could you tell me where I can find a pay phone?

_____

10. Can you call me a little later on?

_____

VI. Translate the following into English:

1. 她 让 我 给 她 打 电话，可是 忘 了 告诉 我 她的电话
号码。
Tā ràng wǒ gěi tā dǎ diànhuà, kěshì wàng le gàosù wǒ tāde diànhuà
hàomǎ.

_____

2. 我 最 不 喜欢 别人 在 我 吃饭 的 时候 给 我 打 电话。
Wǒ zuì bù xǐhuan biérén zài wǒ chīfàn de shíhou gěi wǒ dǎ diànhuà.

_____

3. 他说 他给 我发了短信，但是 我 没有 收到。
Tā shuō tā gěi wǒ fā le duǎnxìn, dànshì wǒ méiyou shōudào.

_____

4. 以前，中国 的大学生 只学习，不工作， 现在
Yǐqián, Zhōngguó de dàxuéshēng zhǐ xuéxí, bù gōngzuò, xiànzài
越来越 多 的 大学生 一边 学习，一边 工作。
yuèláiyuè duō de dàxuéshēng yìbiān xuéxí, yìbiān gōngzuò.

_____
_____

5. 三十年前， 大多数中国人的家里都没有电话， 很不方
便。去看朋友不能先约 (*set up; appoint*) 时间。有时走很
远的路去看一个朋友，到了他家才知道他不在家。
今天大多数中国人都有了手机，很方便。
Sānshí nián qián, dàduōshù Zhōngguórén de jiā lǐ dōu méi yǒu
diànhuà, hěn bù fāngbiàn. Qù kàn péngyou bù néng xiān yuē shíjiān.
Yǒushí zǒu hěn yuǎn de lù qù kàn yí ge péngyou, dào le tā jiā cái
zhīdào tā bú zài jiā. Jīntiān dàduōshù Zhōngguórén dōu yǒu le
shǒujī, hěn fāngbiàn.

_____
_____
_____
_____

VII. Write and say your home and office phone numbers in Chinese.

Home: _____

Office: _____

VIII. Make a phone call to a Chinese restaurant to order food in Chinese.

ENGLISH TRANSLATION OF THE TEXT

Conversations (*page 52-54*)

A: Hello!
B: Who would you like to speak to?
A: I'd like to speak to your manager. Is he there?
B: Just a minute. Let me check. ... Sorry, he is at a meeting. Could you call back a little later on?
A: Can I leave him a message?
B: Sure. What's your family name?
A: My family name is Wang.
B: What's your telephone number?
A: My number is 212-734-8659.
B: What's your message?
A: Please ask your manger to give me a call when he is back.
B: Sure, Mr. Wang. I'll definitely ask him to return your call.

*   *   *   *   *

A: I called you last night, but no one answered the phone. Where were you?
B: I didn't go anywhere. What time did you call me?
A: I called at 8.
B: My cell phone was turned off at that time. Sorry about that. Was there something you needed to talk to me about?
A: Nothing major. I only wanted to have a chat with you.
B: Could you stop by my place this Saturday?
A: Sure. What time on Saturday is good for you?
B: I'll be home the whole day. You can come anytime.

*   *   *   *   *

A: Is this the Chinese restaurant?
B: Yes, this is the Chinese restaurant.
A: Do you deliver?
B: Yes, we do. What would you like?
A: Please deliver a fried rice and a tofu dish.
B: When would you like to have them?
A: Please have the food delivered by 7.
B: No problem. Please tell me your address.
A: My address is 530 Park Road.
B: What's your phone number?
A: My number is 754-3698.
B: Okay, see you in a little while.
A: Thank you.

Reading Passages (*page 55*)

Cell phones are getting more and more common. It seems that everyone has one. The cell phone brings us a lot of convenience. Besides using it to make calls, we can also use it to get on the internet, listen to music and so on. When using the cell phone, we should respect other people. There are people who don't even turn off their cell phones in movie theaters and in class. This is not very good. There are also people who make calls on their cell phones while driving. This is very dangerous. It is well said that a benefit always comes with a drawback.

LESSON 4

HERE & THERE

CONVERSATIONS

(English translation, pages 96-97)

A: 词典 在 哪儿？
Cídiǎn zài nǎr?

B: 词典 在 书架 的 上边。
Cídiǎn zài shūjià de shàngbian.

A: 报纸 在 哪儿？
Bàozhǐ zài nǎr?

B: 报纸 在 手表 的下边。
Bàozhǐ zài shǒubiǎo de xiàbian.

A: 汽车 在 哪儿？
Qìchē zài nǎr?

B: 汽车 在 学校 的 前边。
Qìchē zài xuéxiào de qiánbian.

A: 椅子 在 哪儿？
Yǐzi zài nǎr?

B: 椅子 在 桌子 的 后边。
Yǐzi zài zhuōzi de hòubian.

A: 猪 在 哪儿？
Zhū zài nǎr?

B: 猪 在 牛 的 旁边。
Zhū zài niú de pángbiān.

A: 刀 在 哪儿?
Dāo zài nǎr?

B: 刀 在 盘子 的 右边。
Dāo zài pánzi de yòubian.

A: 叉子 在 哪儿?
Chāzi zài nǎr?

B: 叉子 在 盘子 的 左边。
Chāzi zài pánzi de zuǒbian.

A: 中文 书 在 哪儿?
Zhōngwén shū zài nǎr?

B: 中文 书 在 书包 的 里面。
Zhōngwén shū zài shūbāo de lǐmiàn.

A: 自行车 在 哪儿?
Zìxíngchē zài nǎr?

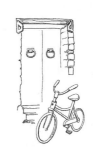

B: 自行车 在 门 的 外边。
Zìxíngchē zài mén de wàibian.

A: 餐馆 在 哪儿?
Cānguǎn zài nǎr?

B: 餐馆 在 银行 的 对面。
Cānguǎn zài yínháng de duìmiàn.

A: 船　在 哪儿？
Chuán zài nǎr?

B: 船　在河的中间。
Chuán zài hé de zhōngjiān.

A: 书店　在 哪儿？
Shūdiàn zài nǎr?

B: 书店　在 银行 和 餐馆　的
Shūdiàn zài yínháng hé cānguǎn de
中间。
zhōngjiān.

A: 左边　是 什么？右边　是
Zuǒbian shì shénme? Yòubian shì
什么？
shénme?

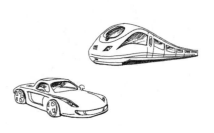

B: 左边　是 汽车。右边　是
Zuǒbian shì qìchē.　Yòubian shì
火车。
huǒchē.

A: 对面　有 什么？
Duìmiàn yǒu shénme?

B: 对面　有 电影院　和 面包店。
Duìmiàn yǒu diànyǐngyuàn hé miànbāodiàn.

A: 日本 在 哪儿?
Rìběn zài nǎr?

B: 日本 在 中国　 的 东边。
Rìběn zài Zhōngguó de dōngbian.

A: 韩国　 在 哪儿?
Hánguó zài nǎr?

B: 韩国　 在 中国　　 的 东北边。
Hánguó zài Zhōngguó de dōngběibian.

A: 中国　　 的 北边 有 什么 国家?
Zhōngguó de běibian yǒu shénme guójiā?

B: 中国　　 的 北边 有 蒙古　 和
Zhōngguó de běibian yǒu Ménggǔ hé
俄国。
Éguó.

A: 上海　 在 中国　 的 哪儿?
Shànghǎi zài Zhōngguó de nǎr?

B: 上海　 在 中国　 的 东部。
Shànghǎi zài Zhōngguó de dōngbù.

　　　　*　　*　　*　　*　　*

老师：今天 是 新 学期 的 第一 天。我们 把 教室
Lǎoshī：Jīntiān shì xīn xuéqī de dì yī tiān.　Wǒmen bǎ jiàoshì
　　　重新　 布置 一下儿，好 不 好?
　　　chóngxīn bùzhì yíxiàr,　　hǎo bu hǎo?

学生: 好，老师。请 告诉我们 怎么 做。
Xuésheng: Hǎo, lǎoshī.   Qǐng gàosù wǒmen zěnme zuò.

老师: 先 把这些新书 放 在书架上。
Lǎoshī: Xiān bǎ zhè xiē xīn shū fàng zài shūjià shang.

学生: 书架还 放 在老地方 吗?
Xuésheng: Shūjià hái fàng zài lǎo dìfang ma?

老师: 我们 把书架 换 个地方，把它放 在两 个
Lǎoshī: Wǒmen bǎ shūjià huàn ge dìfang, bǎ tā fàng zài liǎng ge
窗子 的中间， 你们 觉得好 不好?
chuāngzi de zhōngjiān, nǐmen juéde hǎo bu hǎo?

学生: 我 觉得很 好。
Xuésheng: Wǒ juéde hěn hǎo.

老师: 我 买了一张 中国 地图。请 把它挂 在
Lǎoshī: Wǒ mǎi le yì zhāng Zhōngguó dìtú.   Qǐng bǎ tā guà zài
教室 后面 的墙 上。
jiàoshì hòumiàn de qiáng shang.

学生: 我 有 一张 世界地图，我 能 不能 把它挂
Xuésheng: Wǒ yǒu yì zhāng shìjiè dìtú, wǒ néng bu néng bǎ tā guà
在中国 地图 的旁边?
zài Zhōngguó dìtú de pángbiān?

老师: 好 主意。
Lǎoshī: Hǎo zhǔyì.

学生: 老师，电脑 放 在哪儿? 放 在你的桌子
Xuésheng: Lǎoshī, diànnǎo fàng zài nǎr?   Fàng zài nǐde zhuōzi
上 吗?
shang ma?

老师：　不，学校　给我们　买　了一张　　电脑　　桌子。
Lǎoshī:　Bù,　xuéxiào gěi wǒmen mǎi le yì　zhāng diànnǎo zhuōzi.

我们　可以　把　电脑　放　在　电脑　桌子　上。
Wǒmen kěyǐ　bǎ　diànnǎo fàng zài diànnǎo zhuōzi shang.

学生：　太　好　了！电脑　　桌子　在　哪儿？
Xuésheng: Tài hǎo leō! Diànnǎo zhuōzi zài　nǎr?

老师：　在　教室　外面。　请　把它拿　进来。
Lǎoshī:　Zài jiàoshì wàimiàn. Qǐng bǎ　tā　ná　jìn　lai.

学生：　电脑　　桌子拿　进来了。你要我把它放　在
Xuésheng: Diànnǎo zhuōzi ná jìn　lai le.　　Nǐ yào wǒ bǎ tā fàng zài

哪儿？
nǎr?

老师：　请　把它放　在　教室　的　后面。
Lǎoshī:　Qǐng bǎ　tā fàng zài jiàoshì de　hòumiàn.

READING PASSAGE

中国在亚洲的东部，是世界上第三大国家。中国从北到南有5500公里，从东到西有5000公里。长江是中国最长的河，长城是中国最有名的景点。中国的周围有14个国家，它们在中国的北边、西边和南边。中国的东边是太平洋。

Zhōngguó zài Yàzhōu de dōngbù, shì shìjiè shang dìsān dà guójiā. Zhōngguó cóng béi dào nán yǒu wǔqiān wǔbai gōnglǐ, cóng dōng dào xǐ yǒu wǔqiān gōnglǐ. Chángjiāng shì Zhōngguó zuì cháng de hé, Chángchéng shì Zhōngguó zuì yǒumíng de jǐngdiǎn. Zhōngguó de zhōuwéi yǒu shísì ge guójiā, tāmen zaì Zhōngguó de běibian, xībian he nánbian. Zhōngguó de dōngbian shì Tàipíngyáng.

(*English translation, page 98*)

NEW WORDS AND EXPRESSIONS

词典	cídiǎn	dictionary
书架	shūjià	bookshelf
椅子	yǐzi	chair
桌子	zhuōzi	table; desk
刀	dāo	knife
叉子	chāzi	fork
盘子	pánzi	plate
书包	shūbāo	book bag
门	mén	door; gate
沙发	shāfā	sofa
韩国	Hánguó	(South) Korea
国家	guójiā	country
蒙古	Ménggǔ	Mongolia
俄国	Éguó	Russia
部	bù	part; section
学期	xuéqī	semester
把	bǎ	*preposition*
教室	jiàoshì	classroom
重新	chóngxīn	again; anew
布置	bùzhì	arrange (furniture); decorate
先	xiān	first
放	fàng	put; lay
窗子	chuāngzi	window
地图	dìtú	map
挂	guà	hang
墙	qiáng	wall
电脑	diànnǎo	computer
世界	shìjiè	world

拿	ná	take; hold; fetch
进	jìn	enter; come in
公里	gōnglǐ	kilometer
长江	Chángjiāng	Yangtze River
长城	Chángchéng	the Great Wall
景点	jǐngdiǎn	scenic spot; tourist attraction
周围	zhōuwéi	area around; surroundings
太平洋	Tàipíngyáng	the Pacific Ocean

SUPPLEMENTARY WORDS AND EXPRESSIONS

附近	fùjìn	nearby; vicinity
房间	fángjiān	room
公寓	gōngyù	apartment
卧室	wòshì	bedroom
厨房	chúfáng	kitchen
客厅	kètīng	living room
饭厅	fàntīng	dining room
卫生间	wèishēngjiān	bathroom
车库	chēkù	garage
楼上	lóushàng	upstairs
楼下	lóuxià	downstairs
黑板	hēibǎn	blackboard
加拿大	Jiā'nádà	Canada
墨西哥	Mòxīgē	Mexico
大西洋	Dàxīyáng	the Atlantic Ocean

LANGUAGE POINTS

Indication of locations

To indicate relative locations or positions, Chinese uses position words. These words differ from English prepositions *in*, *on*, and *so on* in that they are nouns used in conjunction with the preposition 在 zài to indicate locations. The following is a complete list of position nouns:

上边	shàngbian	on; over; above
下边	xiàbian	under; below; underneath
前边	qiánbian	in front of; ahead of
后边	hòubian	behind; at the back of
旁边	pángbiān	beside; next to
里边	lǐbian	in; inside
外边	wàibian	outside
左边	zuǒbian	left of; on the left
右边	yòubian	right of; on the right
对面	duìmiàn	across from; opposite
中间	zhōngjiān	in the middle of; between; among
东边	dōngbian	east of; in the east
南边	nánbian	south of; in the south
西边	xībian	west of; in the west
北边	běibian	north of; in the north

边 biān in 上边 shàngbian, 下边 xiàbian, 前边 qiánbian, 后边 hòubian, 里边 lǐbian, and 外边 wàibian can be replaced by 面 miàn or 头 tóu.

边 biān in 左边 zuǒbian, 右边 yòubian, 东边 dōngbian, 南边 nánbian, 西边 xībian, and 北边 běibian can be replaced by 面 miàn.

Additionally, 边 biān (or 面 miàn or 头 tóu) is often left out altogether in 里边 lǐbian and 上边 shàngbian.

Similar to the patterns we learned in Lesson 3 in *Beginner's Chinese* that indicate locations, the position words introduced in this lesson are used in the following three patterns:

1. S + 在 zài (N) + (的 de) + position word

书 在 桌子 的 上边。
Shū zài zhuōzi de shàngbian.
The book is on the table.

船　在桥 的下边。
Chuán zài qiáo de xiàbian.
The boat is under the bridge.

中国　在日本 的西边。
Zhōngguó zài Rìběn de xībian.
China lies to the west of Japan.

学生们　　在外边。
Xuéshengmen zài wàibian.
The students are outside.

Note that the subject in the pattern must be definite or specified. Also when a noun is present after 在 zài, it can be optionally followed by 的 de to indicate the attributive relationship. Note also that when 边 biān is left out from the position word, 的 de cannot be used. Compare:

学校　(的) 里边 有 商店。
Xuéxiào de lǐbian yǒu shāngdiàn.
There is a store in the school.

学校　里有 商店。
Xuéxiào lǐ yǒu shāngdiàn.

2. (N) + (的 de) + position word + 有 yǒu + S

桌子 上 有 书。
Zhuōzi shang yǒu shū.
There is a book on the table.

桥 下 有 船。

Qiáo xià yǒu chuán.

There is a boat under the bridge.

美国 的北边 有 一个 国家。

Měiguó de běibian yǒu yí ge guójiā.

There is a country north of the United States.

里边 有 商店。

Lǐbian yǒu shāngdiàn.

There is a store inside.

These are so-called existential sentences, where the subject is indefinite or unspecified. If the subject is definite or specified, 是 shì should generally be used instead of 有 yǒu:

香港 的北边 是 广州。

Xiānggǎng de běibian shì Guǎngzhōu.

North of Hong Kong is Guangzhou.

张 先生 的 左边 是 张 太太。

Zhāng Xiānsheng de zuǒbian shì Zhāng Tàitai.

Left of Mr. Zhang is Mrs. Zhang.

There is supposed to be a 在 zài before N + position word, but it is invariably left out when it appears at the beginning of an existential sentence.

Please note that position words are not necessary after nouns that indicate a place:

曼哈顿 在 纽约。

Mànhādùn zài Niǔyuē.

Manhattan is in New York.

我 在 学校 工作。

Wǒ zài xuéxiào gōngzuò.

I work in a school.

教室后面的墙上 jiàoshì hòumiàn de qiáng shang

Mention was made in *Beginner's Chinese* that modifiers always precede modified in Chinese, whether they are individual words or phrases or sentences. In this case, 教室后面 jiàoshì hòumiàn (*at the back of the classroom*) modifies or defines 墙 qiáng (*wall*) to mean *wall at the back of the classroom*. It is therefore placed before 墙 qiáng. When the modifier is a phrase or a sentence, it is always marked at the end by the particle 的 de to indicate the attributive relationship. Similar examples are:

桌子 上 的 电脑
zhuōzi shang de diànnǎo
the computer on the table

图书馆 里 的书
túshūguǎn lǐ de shū
books in the library

公园 外 的河
gōngyuán wài de hé
the river outside the park

边 biān 和 部 bù

In indicating the relative position of two locations, directional words 东 dōng, 南 nán, 西 xī, and 北 běi used with 边 biān (东边 dōngbian, 西边 xībian, etc.) suggest that the two locations are outside of each other. Whereas those used with 部 bù (东部 dōngbù, 西部 xībù, etc.), which means *section*, suggest that one location is part of the other. Compare:

日本 在 中国 的东边。
Rìběn zài Zhōngguó de dōngbian.
Japan is to the east of China.

上海 在 中国 的 东部。
Shànghǎi zài Zhōngguó de dōngbù.
Shanghai is in the eastern part of China.

Points of the compass

When we enumerate the four points of the compass (north, south, east and west) in Chinese, the conventional order is to follow the clockwise direction starting from the east: 东 dōng (*east*), 南 nán (*south*), 西 xī (*west*), and 北 běi (*north*).

Additionally, 东 dōng (*east*) and 西 xī (*west*) serve as the cardinal points when we indicate points such as northeast, northwest, southeast, and southwest, which is exactly the reverse of the order in English: 东南 dōngnán (*southeast*), 东北 dōngběi (*northeast*), 西南 xīnán (*southwest*), and 西北 xīběi (*northwest*). See the illustration of the following graph:

The 把 bǎ-construction

Frequently used in Chinese, 把 bǎ is a grammatical device used to shift the object before the verb. The 把 bǎ-construction takes the following form:

S + 把 bǎ + O + V + other elements

Several conditions must be met in using the 把 bǎ-construction:

1. For an object to be shifted to the front, it must be a definite or specified one. We can say 把这本书看完了 bǎ zhè běn shū kàn wán le (*finish reading the book*), but we can't say 把一本书看完了 bǎ yì běn shū kàn wán le (*finish reading a book*).

2. The verb must be one that can produce a tangible result in the object, such as causing it to change hands, location, form, state, or to disappear and so on. We can say 把书放在桌上 bǎ shū fàng zài zhuō shang (*put the book on the table*), but we can't say 把这件事知道 bǎ zhè jiàn shì zhīdào (*to know the matter*). Verbs that cannot be used in the 把 bǎ-construction include 认识 rènshi (*know*), 喜欢 xǐhuan (*like*), 开始 kāishǐ (*begin*), 来 lái (*come*), 回 huí (*go back to*), 坐 zuò (*sit*), 进 jìn (*enter*), 有 yǒu (*have*), 是 shì (*be*), and so on.

3. The verb must be a complex one, i.e. it must be followed by another element. This element can be a verb complement such as 完 wán or a particle such as 了 le.

When there is a choice, the sentence that uses the 把 bǎ-construction differs in meaning from the one that doesn't. Although both 他吃了饭 tā chī le fàn and 他把饭吃了 tā bǎ fàn chī le can be translated as *he ate the food*, the foci of the sentences are different. 他吃了饭 tā chī le fàn answers the question *what did he do*, whereas 他把饭吃了 tā bǎ fàn chī le answers the question *what did he do to the food*.

The use of the 把 bǎ-construction is obligatory when a change (of location, form or shape) is suggested such as: move the table out of the room, change US dollars to Renminbi, cut the pizza into 4 slices and translate English into Chinese.

If the 把 bǎ-construction takes the negative form, the negative word should precede 把 bǎ:

老师　没有　把 电脑　　放　在 她的　桌子　上。
Lǎoshī méiyou bǎ diànnǎo fàng zài tāde　zhuōzi shang.
The teacher didn't put the computer on her desk.

有的　学生　　上课　的 时候 也 不把手机 关　　掉。
Yǒude xuésheng shàngkè de shíhou yě bù bǎ shǒujī guān diào.
Some students don't even turn off their cell phones in class.

EXERCISES

Answer key, pages 275-277

I. Answer the following questions:

(For questions 1-6, please refer to the pictures given.)

1. 狗 在 哪儿?
   Gǒu zài nǎr?

   _____

2. 刀 在 哪儿?
   Dāo zài nǎr?

   _____

3. 盘子 在 哪儿?
   Pánzi zài nǎr?

   _____

4. 电脑 在 哪儿?
   Diànnǎo zài nǎr?

   _____

5. 教室 里 有 什么?
   Jiàoshì lǐ yǒu shénme?

   _____

6. 餐馆　在 银行　的 左边　吗？
   Cānguǎn zài yínháng de zuǒbian ma?

_____

7. 你的 书包 里有　什么？
   Nǐde　shūbāo lǐ yǒu shénme?

_____

8. 你家 附近 有 中国　　餐馆　吗？
   Nǐ jiā fùjìn　yǒu Zhōngguó cānguǎn ma?

_____

9. 俄国 在 中国　　的 南边　吗？
   Éguó zài Zhōngguó de nánbian ma?

_____

10. 美国　的 北边　是 加拿大 吗？
    Měiguó de běibian shì Jiā'nádà ma?

_____

II. How do you say the following?

1. East Asia　　　_____

2. Southeast Asia　_____

3. South America　_____

4. North America　_____

5. North Africa　　_____

6. South Africa   _____

7. Central Africa   _____

8. Central Asia   _____

9. Western Europe   _____

10. Eastern Europe   _____

11. Northern Europe   _____

12. Southern Europe   _____

III. Fill in the blanks with 在 (zài), 是 (shì), or 有 (yǒu):

1. 医院 ____ 我们 公司 的 对面。
   Yīyuàn ____ wǒmen gōngsī de duìmiàn.

2. 学校 里 ____老师 和 学生。
   Xuéxiào lǐ ____ lǎoshī hé xuésheng.

3. 我 家的 东边 ____ 中国 银行。
   Wǒ jiā de dōngbian ____ Zhōngguó Yínháng.

4. 加拿大 ____ 美国 的北边。
   Jiā'nádà ____ Měiguó de běibian.

5. 中国 的北边 ____ 俄国 和 蒙古。
   Zhōngguó de běibian ____ Éguó hé Ménggǔ.

6. 电影院 ____学校 和 银行 的中间。
   Diànyǐngyuàn ____ xuéxiào hé yínháng de zhōngjiān.

7. 桌子 上 ____ 书 和 词典。
   Zhuōzi shang ____ shū hé cídiǎn.

8. 南边 ____北京 火车站。
   Nánbian ____ Běijīng Huǒchēzhàn.

9. 他的女朋友　坐 _____　他 左边。
Tāde nǚpéngyou zuò _____ tā zuǒbian.

10. 冰箱　里 _____　很 多 菜。
Bīngxiāng lǐ _____ hěn duō cài.

IV. Tell the differences between the following pairs:

1. 汽车 的后面
   qìchē de hòumiàn

   _____

   后面　的 汽车
   hòumiàn de qìchē

   _____

2. 学校　的 前面
   xuéxiào de qiánmiàn

   _____

   前面　的学校
   qiánmiàn de xuéxiào

   _____

3. 书 的 上边
   shū de shàngbian

   _____

   上边　的书
   shàngbian de shū

   _____

4. 商店　的 东边
   shāngdiàn de dōngbian

   _____

   东边　的 商店
   dōngbian de shāngdiàn

   _____

5. 银行　的 对面
   yínháng de duìmiàn

   _____

   对面　的 银行
   duìmiàn de yínháng

   _____

V. Say where the following countries are in relation to those in the brackets:

1. 英国 Yīngguó   [法国 Fǎguó]
2. 印度 Yìndù   [中国 Zhōngguó]
3. 墨西哥 Mòxīgē   [美国 Měiguó]
4. 日本 Rìběn   [韩国 Hánguó]
5. 波兰 Bōlán   [俄国 Éguó]
6. 埃及 Āijí   [苏丹 Sūdān]

VI. The 把 ba-construction.

A. Change the following sentences using the 把 ba-construction:

1. 他 卖 了他的 汽车。
   Tā mài le tāde qìchē.

   _____

2. 我 关 掉 了我的 手机。
   Wǒ guān diào le wǒde shǒujī.

   _____

3. 他们 喝 了茶。
   Tāmen hē le chá.

   _____

4. 妈妈 洗了那 件 毛衣。
   Māma xǐ le nà jiàn máoyī.

   _____

5. 公司 换 了我的 工作。
   Gōngsī huàn le wǒde gōngzuò.

   _____

B. How do you say the following:

1. put your book in your book bag

   _____

2. forgot my wallet at home

   _____

3. deliver the food to the school

   _____

4. bring your friend home

   _____

5. write your name on the paper

   _____

VII. Translate the following into Chinese:

1. The cat (猫 māo) is under the bed.

_____

2. The Atlantic Ocean is to the east of the United States.

_____

3. Our school is between the hospital and the bank.

_____

4. The map is behind the door.

_____

5. My home is next to a store.

_____

6. There are three bookshelves in the classroom.

_____

7. Children are playing outside the building.

_____

8. The liquor store is across from the restaurant.

_____

9. There are two countries north of China.

_____

10. California is in the western part of the United States.

_____

VIII. Translate the following into English:

美国在北美洲，是世界第四大国家（第一大国家是俄国，第二大国家是加拿大，第三大国家是中国）。美国的北边是加拿大，南边是墨西哥，东边和西边没有国家。东边是大西洋，西边是太平洋。

Měiguó zài Běi Měizhōu, shì shìjiè dì sì dà guójiā (dì yī dà guójiā shì Éguó, dì èr dà guójiā shì Jiā'nádà, dì sān dà guójiā shì Zhōngguó).
Měiguó de běibian shì Jiā'nádà, nánbian shì Mòxīgē, dōngbian hé xībian méi yǒu guójiā. Dōngbian shì Dàxīyáng, xībian shì Tàipíngyáng.

_____
_____
_____
_____
_____
_____

IX. Discussion and writing topics:

1. Describe your home or apartment.

2. Describe your community.

3. Describe a geographical area.

ENGLISH TRANSLATION OF THE TEXT

Conversations (*pages 74-79*)

A: Where is the dictionary?
B: The dictionary is on the bookshelf.

A: Where is the newspaper?
B: The newspaper is under the watch.

A: Where is the bus?
B: The bus is in front of the school.

A: Where is the chair?
B: The chair is behind the desk.

A: Where is the pig?
B: The pig is next to the cow.

A: Where is the knife?
B: The knife is to the right of the plate.

A: Where is the fork?
B: The fork is to the left of the plate.

A: Where is the Chinese book?
B: The Chinese book is in the book bag.

A: Where is the bike?
B: The bike is outside the door.

A: Where is the restaurant?
B: The restaurant is across from the bank.

A: Where is the boat?
B: The boat is in the middle of the river.

A: Where is the bookstore?
B: The bookstore is between the bank and the restaurant.

A: What is on the left? What is on the right?
B: The car is on the left and the train is on the right.

A: What's opposite here?
B: Opposite here are a movie theater and a bakery.

A: Where is Japan?
B: Japan is to the east of China.

A: Where is Korea?
B: Korea is to the northeast of China.

A: What countries lie to the north of China?
B: Mongolia and Russia are to the north of China.

A: What part of China is Shanghai in?
B: Shanghai is in the eastern part of China.

*   *   *   *   *

Teacher:	Today is the first day of the new semester. Let's rearrange the classroom, shall we?
Student:	Good, teacher. Please tell us what to do.
Teacher:	First put these new books on the bookshelf.
Student:	Shall we put the bookshelf in the old place?
Teacher:	Let's put the bookshelf in a different place. Put it between the two windows. What do you think?
Student:	I think it is good.
Teacher:	I bought a map of China. Please hang it up on the wall at the back of the classroom.
Student:	I have a map of the world. Can I hang it next to the map of China?
Teacher:	Good idea.
Student:	Teacher, where should the computer go? Shall I put it on your desk?
Teacher:	No. The school bought a computer table for us. We can put the computer on the computer table.
Student:	That's great. Where is the computer table?
Teacher:	It's outside the classroom. Please bring it in.
Student:	I got it in. Where should I put it?
Teacher:	Please put it at the back of the classroom.

Reading Passage (*page 80*)

China is in the east of Asia and it is the third largest country in the world. China extends 5,500 kilometers from north to south and 5,000 kilometers from east to west. The Yangtze River is the longest river in China and the Great Wall is the most famous tourist attraction of the country. There are 14 countries around China to its north, west and south. East of China is the Pacfiic Ocean.

LESSON 5

SCHOOL & SCHOOL LIFE

CONVERSATIONS

(English translation, pages 119-120)

A: 你在 哪儿上学？
Nǐ zài nǎr   shàngxué?

B: 我 在 第 五 中学   上学。
Wǒ zài Dì Wǔ Zhōngxué shàngxué.

A: 你上   初中   还是 高中？
Nǐ shàng chūzhōng háishi gāozhōng?

B: 我 上   高中。
Wǒ shàng gāozhōng.

A: 你 现在 是 几年级？
Nǐ xiànzài shì jǐ niánjí?

B: 我 现在 是 高中   一 年级。
Wǒ xiànzài shì gāozhōng yì niánjí.

A: 你们 班 有 多少   学生？
Nǐmen bān yǒu duōshao xuésheng?

B: 我们   班 有 四十个学生。
Wǒmen bān yǒu sìshí ge xuésheng.

A: 你们 有 些 什么 课？
Nǐmen yǒu xiē shénme kè?

B: 我们   有 中文、   数学，外语，历史，体育，音乐、
Wǒmen yǒu Zhōngwén, shùxué, wàiyǔ,   lìshǐ,   tǐyù,   yīnyuè,
自然 科学 和 美术   等等。
zìrán kēxué hé měishù děngdeng.

A: 你们 有 什么 外语 课?
Nǐmen yǒu shénme wàiyǔ kè?

B: 我们 有 英语、法语和 日语, 但是 大多数 学生
Wǒmen yǒu Yīngyǔ, Fǎyǔ hé Rìyǔ,   dànshì dàduōshù xuésheng
都 选 英语。
dōu xuǎn Yīngyǔ.

A: 你们 有 没 有 外国 老师?
Nǐmen yǒu méi yǒu wàiguó lǎoshī?

B: 有,我们 有 两 个外国 老师, 一个是 英国人,
Yǒu, wǒmen yǒu liǎng ge wàiguó lǎoshī,   yí ge shì Yīngguórén,
一 个是 日本人。他们 教 我们 英语 和日语。
yí ge shì Rìběnrén.   Tāmen jiāo wǒmen Yīngyǔ hé Rìyǔ.

*   *   *   *   *

A: 你 在哪儿上学?
Nǐ zài nǎr   shàngxué?

B: 我 不上学 了。我 毕业了。
Wǒ bú shàngxué le.   Wǒ bìyè le.

A: 你 已经毕业了? 真 快。你有 没有 找 到 工作?
Nǐ yǐjīng bìyè le?   Zhēn kuài. Nǐ yǒu méiyou zhǎo dào gōngzuò?

B: 我 没有 找 工作,我 想 读研究生。
Wǒ méiyou zhǎo gōngzuò, wǒ xiǎng dú yánjiūshēng.

A: 你想 读 什么?
Nǐ xiǎng dú shénme?

B: 我 想 读 历史。
Wǒ xiǎng dú lìshǐ.

A: 读 研究生　要 几年？
Dú yánjiūshēng yào jǐ nián?

B: 读 硕士　要 两　年，读 博士一般 要　五 年。
Dú shuòshì yào liǎng nián, dú bóshì yìbān yào wǔ nián.

A: 你 要 读 硕士　还是 博士？
Nǐ yào dú shuòshì háishi bóshì?

B: 我 现在　还 不 知道。我 想　　先 读 硕士，以后 再
Wǒ xiànzài hái bù zhīdào. Wǒ xiǎng xiān dú shuòshì, yǐhòu zài
决定　要 不 要 读 博士。你 呢？你还 在 上学　　吗？
juédìng yào bu yào dú bóshì.　Nǐ ne?　Nǐ hái zài shàngxué ma?

A: 不，我 也 毕业了，正　　在 找　工作。
Bù,　wǒ yě bìyè le,　zhèng zài zhǎo gōngzuò.

B: 你 想　　做 什么？
Nǐ xiǎng zuò shénme?

A: 我 学 的是 英语，我 想　　当 英语　老师。
Wǒ xué de shì Yīngyǔ, wǒ xiǎng dāng Yīngyǔ lǎoshī.

B: 听说　很 多 学校　现在 要 老师，你 一定 能　找
Tīngshuō hěn duō xuéxiào xiànzài yào lǎoshī,　nǐ yídìng néng zhǎo
到 老师 的 工作。
dào lǎoshī de gōngzuò.

A: 那就 太 好 了。
Nà jiù tài hǎo le.

　　　　　　*　　*　　*　　*　　*

A: 小　王，有　人 说　在 中国　　进 大学 难，出 大学
Xiǎo Wáng, yǒu rén shuō zài Zhōngguó jìn dàxué nán, chū dàxué
容易，在 美国　进 大学容易，出 大学 难。你 觉得 是
róngyì, zài Měiguó jìn dàxué róngyì, chū dàxué nán. Nǐ juéde shì
这样　吗？
zhèyang ma?

B: 是 这样。中国　　每 年 有 很 多 高中　　毕业生，
Shì zhèyang. Zhōngguó měi nián yǒu hěn duō gāozhōng bìyèshēng,
他们 都 想　进一流 的 大学，但是 没 有 那么 多
tāmen dōu xiǎng jìn yīliú de dàxué, dànshi méi yǒu nàme duō
一流的 大学，所以 不是 每 个人 都 能　进最好 的
yīliú ge dàxué, suǒyǐ bú shì měi ge rén dōu néng jìn zuìhǎo de
大学。
dàxué.

A: 一般 怎么 进 大学 呢？
Yìbān zěnme jìn dàxué ne?

B: 你要 通过　很 严格 的 考试。如果 成绩 不 好，就
Nǐ yào tōngguò hěn yángé de kǎoshì. Rúguǒ chéngjī bù hǎo, jiù
不 能　进 大学或 不 能　进很 好 的 大学。
bù néng jìn dàxué huò bù néng jìn hěn hǎo de dàxué.

A: 在 美国 上　大学不要 通过　考试，但是 要 进好
Zài Měiguó shàng dàxué bú yào tōngguò kǎoshì, dànshì yào jìn hǎo
的 大学也 不 容易。
de dàxué yě bù róngyì.

READING PASSAGE

中国的学校分小学、中学和大学。孩子们一般在六岁或七岁开始上小学。中学又分初中和高中。小学六年，初中三年，高中三年，大学四年。每个孩子必须上小学和初中，大多数人也上高中和大学。大学毕业后，大多数人开始工作，也有人去读研究生。以前，学生一个星期要上六天的课，现在一个星期上五天的课，星期六和星期天不上学。中国的小学生和中学生很辛苦，他们每天要做很多作业，很少有时间玩儿。

Zhōngguó de xuéxiào fēn xiǎoxué, zhōngxué hé dàxué. Háizimen yìbān zài liù suì huò qī suì kāishǐ shàng xiǎoxué. Zhōngxué yòu fēn chūzhōng hé gāozhōng. Xiǎoxué liù nián, chūzhōng sān nián, gāozhōng sān nián, dàxué sì nián. Měi ge háizi bìxū shàng xiǎoxué hé chūzhōng, dàduōshù rén yě shàng gāozhōng hé dàxué. Dàxué bìyè hòu, dàduōshù rén kāishǐ gōngzuò, yě yǒu rén jìxù xuéxí, dú yánjiūshēng. Yǐqián, xuésheng yí ge xīngqī yào shàng liù tiān de kè, xiànzài yí ge xīngqī shàng wǔ tiān de kè, xīngqīliù hé xīngqītiān bú shàngxué. Zhōngguó de xiǎoxuésheng hé zhōngxuésheng hěn xīnkǔ, tāmen měi tiān yào zuò hěn duō zuòyè, hěn shǎo yǒu shíjiān wánr.

(English translation, page 120)

NEW WORDS AND EXPRESSIONS

初	chū	beginning (of a time period); primary
高	gāo	high; tall
年级	niánjí	(of school) grade; year
数学	shùxué	mathematics
外语	wàiyǔ	foreign language
体育	tǐyù	physical education
自然科学	zìrán kēxué	natural sciences
美术	měishù	fine art
大多数	dàduōshù	majority; most of
选	xuǎn	select; choose
毕业	bìyè	graduate (v.)
毕业生	bìyèshēng	graduate (n.)
研究生	yánjiūshēng	graduate student
读	dú	study; read aloud
硕士	shuòshì	master's degree; master's degree holder
博士	bóshì	doctoral degree; doctoral degree holder
先 … 再	xiān … zài	first … then
决定	juédìng	decide; decision
出	chū	go out; exit
容易	róngyì	easy
所以	suǒyǐ	therefore
一流	yīliú	first-rate; first-class
那么	nàme	so; to such degree
通过	tōngguò	pass
严格	yángé	rigorous; strict; tough
考试	kǎoshì	exam (v.); examination
成绩	chéngjī	grade; result; achievement
或	huò	or

分	fēn	divide; separate; distinguish
又	yòu	further
必须	bìxū	must
辛苦	xīnkǔ	hard (*adj.*); toilsome
很少	hěn shǎo	seldom; rarely

SUPPLEMENTARY WORDS AND EXPRESSIONS

教育	jiàoyù	educate; education
专业	zhuānyè	major; profession; specialty
学位	xuéwèi	(academic) degree
学士	xuéshì	bachelor's degree; bachelor's degree holder
幼儿园	yòu'éryuán	kindergarten
本科生	běnkēshēng	undergraduate student
暑假	shǔjià	summer vacation
寒假	hánjià	winter vacation
课外活动	kèwài huódòng	extracurricular activity
回答	huídá	answer (*n./v.*)
翻译	fānyì	translate; translation
作业	zuòyè	(of school) assignment
作文	zuòwén	composition
测验	cèyàn	test; quiz
词汇	cíhuì	vocabulary

LANGUAGE POINTS

中学 zhōngxué

The term 中学 zhōngxué literally means "middle school", but it is not the same thing as the middle school in the U.S. In the U.S. "middle school" usually refers to the junior high school or the intermediate school, but in China, 中学 zhōngxué actually refers to the secondary school, comprising both the junior high school and the high school.

你们有些什么课 nǐmen yǒu xiē shénme kè?

些 xiē in the sentence is short for 一些 yì xiē. It is a suffix used after 一 yī and demonstrative pronouns 这 zhè, 那 nà, and 哪 nǎ to indicate an indeterminate or unspecified amount: 一些 yìxiē (*some*); 这些 zhèxiē (*these*), 那些 nàxiē (*those*), and 哪些 nǎxiē (*which ones*). Note that 些 xiē is not a plural suffix. If what follows 这 zhè or 那 nà is a specific number, 些 xiē cannot be used:

> 这 三本 书
> zhè sān běn shū
> these three books

> 那 五 个 人
> nà wǔ ge rén
> those five people

初 chū

初 chū in the sense of *beginning* or *primary* is only used in certain set expressions such as 初中 chūzhōng (*junior high school*), 年初 niánchū (*beginning of the year*), and 月初 yuèchū (*beginning of the month*).

我不上学了 wǒ bú shàngxué le

This 了 le is different from the aspect particle 了 le we discussed in *Beginner's Chinese* (Lesson 10). Instead of indicating the completion of an action, it indicates a change of condition, suggesting a contrast to the previous state or action:

天　冷　了。
Tiān lěng le.
It is getting cold. (*implying that it is no longer warm*)

他　有　工作　了。
Tā yǒu gōngzuò le.
He has a job now. (*implying that he didn't have a job before*)

Compare the following two sentences:

我　没　有　钱。
Wǒ méi yǒu qián.
I don't have money. (*a statement of fact*)

我　没　有　钱　了。
Wǒ méi yǒu qián le.
I don't have money now. (*a new situation implying that I had money before*)

In this usage, 了 le can be used with cognitive and non-action verbs such as 喜欢 xǐhuan (*like*) and 是 shì (*to be*):

我　太太　现在　喜欢　吃　豆腐　了。
Wǒ tàitai xiànzài xǐhuan chī dòufu le.
My wife likes to eat tofu now. (*implying that she didn't like it before*)

我们　是 公民　了。
Wǒmen shì gōngmín le.
We are now citizens. (*implying that we were not before*)

The negative form of this usage of 了 le is 不 bù instead of 没有 méiyou unless the verb is 有 yǒu, when 没 méi should be used:

我　不吸烟　了。
Wǒ bù xīyān le.
I no longer smoke.

他 没　有　汽车了。
Tā méi yǒu qìchē le.
He no longer has a car.

This use of 了 le can also suggest the emergence of a new situation:

现在 四点 了, 我们 上 课 吧。
Xiànzài sì diǎn le, wǒmen shàng kè ba.
It's four o'clock now; let's begin our class.

我 三十 岁 了。
Wǒ sānshí suì le.
I'm thirty years old now.

你有没有找到工作 nǐ yǒu méiyou zhǎo dào gōngzuò?

Used after a verb as a complement, 到 dào suggests the successful accomplishment of an action that involves a certain amount of difficulty and effort. Compare:

买 了电影 票
mǎi le diànyǐng piào
bought the movie ticket (*no difficulty or effort suggested*)

买 到 了电影 票
mǎi dào le diànyǐng piào
succeeded in buying the movie ticket (*difficulty or effort suggested*)

吃了北京 烤鸭
chī le Běijīng kǎoyā
ate Peking Duck (*no difficulty suggested; it was easily available*)

吃 到 了北京 烤鸭
chī dào le Běijīng kǎoyā
managed to eat Peking Duck (*difficulty suggested; there may have been many people waiting in line*)

There are two negative forms for this use of 到 dào: 1) 没有 méiyou + V + 到 dào for the unsuccessful completion of an action, and 2) V + 不 到 bú dào for a projected failure to succeed:

现在 是 冬天， 吃 不 到 西瓜。
Xiànzài shì dōngtiān, chī bú dào xīguā.
It is winter now. We can't find watermelons to eat.

我 去 晚 了，没有 看 到 他。
Wǒ qù wǎn le,   méiyou kàn dào tā.
I got there late, so I didn't get to see him.

我学的是英语 wǒ xué de shì Yīngyǔ

The noun modified by a sentence is often left out, as in this instance, resulting in a nominal construction. This often happens when the noun has occurred in the prior speech context or is understood. The missing noun in the sentence cited is 专业 zhuānyè (*major* or *subject*). Other examples are:

好 的 (人) 多，坏 的 (人) 少。
hǎo de (rén) duō, huài de (rén) shǎo.
There are more good people than bad people.

我 说 的 (话)，你懂 不懂？
Wǒ shuō de (huà), nǐ dǒng bu dǒng?
Do you understand what I say?

如果 rúguǒ ... 就 jiù ...

There are three major differences between 如果 rúguǒ (*if*) ... 就 jiù (*then*) ... in Chinese and *if* ..., (*then*) ... in English:

1. The 如果 rúguǒ (*if*) clause always precedes the 就 jiù (*then*) clause.

2. The subject in the 如果 rúguǒ (*if*) clause can either precede 如果 rúguǒ or follow it. We can say both of the following:

   如果 你 不来，我 就 不 去。
   Rúguǒ nǐ bù lái,   wǒ jiù bú qù.

   你 如果不来，我 就 不 去。
   Nǐ rúguǒ bù lái,   wǒ jiù bú qù.
   If you don't come, I won't go.

3. 就 jiù is an adverb. As such, it occurs before the verb and after the subject. This is different from *then* in English, where it is placed before the subject.

或 huò and 还是 háishi

Although both are translated as *or*, they differ significantly in usage. While 或 huò is used between two alternatives in declarative sentences, 还是 háishi is used between two alternatives in interrogative sentences. For example:

你今天 来 或 明天　来 都 可以。
Nǐ jīntiān lái huò míngtiān lái dōu kěyǐ.
It's okay whether you come today or tomorrow.

你今天 来还是 明天　来？
Nǐ jīntiān lái háishi míngtiān lái?
Are you coming today or tomorrow?

你 喜欢 米饭 还是 面条？
Nǐ xǐhuan mǐfàn háishi miàntiáo?
Do you like rice or noodles?

如果 成绩 不 好，就 不 能 进大学 或 不能　进
Rúguǒ chéngjī bù hǎo,　jiù bù néng jìn dàxué huò bù néng jìn
很 好 的大学。
hěn hǎo de dàxué.
If your grades are not good, you can't get into a college or you can't get into a good college.

或 huò can alternatively be expressed as 或者 huòzhě.

EXERCISES

Answer key, pages 277-279

I. Answer the following questions:

1. 你是 学生　吗？你 在 哪儿上学？
   Nǐ shì xuésheng ma?　Nǐ zài nǎr　shàngxué?

2. 你是 在 哪儿上　的大学？
   Nǐ shì zài nǎr　shàng de dàxué?

3. 你 在 大学 时，读 的 是 什么　专业？
   Nǐ zài dàxué shí,　dú de shì shénme zhuānyè?

4. 你有 什么　学位？
   Nǐ yǒu shénme xuéwèi?

5. 你们 学校　有 没 有 外国 老师？他们 教 什么 课？
   Nǐmen xuéxiào yǒu méi yǒu wàiguó lǎoshī? Tāmen jiāo shénme kè?

6. 你们 上　星期 有 没 有 中文　作业？有 什么
   Nǐmen shàng xīngqī yǒu méi yǒu Zhōngwén zuòyè? Yǒu shénme
   作业？
   zuòyè?

7. 你们的 中文　课要不要 考试？什么　时候 考？
   Nǐmende Zhōngwén kè yào bu yào kǎoshì? Shénme shíhou kǎo?

8. 这 学期 什么　时候 结束？
   Zhè xuéqī shénme shíhou jiéshù?

9. 你 在 大学的时候，最 喜欢 什么 课？最 不 喜欢
   Nǐ zài dàxué de shíhou,　zuì xǐhuan shénme kè? Zuì bù xǐhuan
   什么 课？
   shénme kè?

10. 现在 什么　工作 好 找？什么 工作　不好 找？
    Xiànzài shénme gōngzuò hǎo zhǎo? Shénme gōngzuò bù hǎo zhǎo?

II. How do you say the following, using 了 le?

1. We have become teachers now.

_____

2. It's getting hot.

_____

3. She can drive a car now.

_____

4. My father no longer works.

_____

5. Students in this class have a computer now.

_____

III. How do you say the following, using the nominal contruction?

1. what our teacher said

_____

2. what we read

_____

3. what the company did

_____

4. what you want

_____

5. what they can't do

_____

IV. Fill in the blanks with one of the verbs listed below with the complement 到 dào:

看　　　找　　　买　　　吃
kàn　　 zhǎo　　mǎi　　 chī

1. 孩子们 去博物馆 _____ 了很 多 有意思 的 东西。
　 Háizimen qù bówùguǎn _____ le hěn duō yǒuyìsī de dōngxī.

2. 我 去 了很 多 书店，但是 没有 _____ 这 本 书。
　 Wǒ qù le hěn duō shūdiàn, dànshì méiyǒu _____ zhè běn shū.

3. 街上 的 餐馆 都 关门 了。他们 没有 _____
　 Jiē shang de cānguǎn dōu guānmén le.　Tāmen méiyou _____
　 饭。
　 fàn.

4. 他 刚 毕业 就 _____ 了工作。
　 Tā gāng bìyè jiù _____ le gōngzuò.

5. 很 多 人 想 看 这 个 电影，我 没有 _____ 票。
　 Hěn duō rén xiǎng kàn zhè ge diànyǐng, wǒ méiyou _____ piào.

V. Fill in the blanks with either 或 (者) huò (zhě) or 还是 háishi:

1. 你 在家 吃 中饭 _____ 在 公司 吃 中饭?
　 Nǐ zài jiā chī zhōngfàn _____ zài gōngsī chī zhōngfàn?

2. 我 想 请 你 _____ 你的 朋友 做 这件 事。
　 Wǒ xiǎng qǐng nǐ _____ nǐde péngyou zuò zhè jiàn shì.

3. 大卫 和他太太想 去香港 _____ 澳门 度
　 Dàwèi hé tā tàitai xiǎng qù Xiānggǎng _____ Àomén dù
　 蜜月。
　 mìyuè.

4. 学生们 问 老师这星期 有 考试 _____ 下
　 Xuéshengmen wèn lǎoshī zhè xīngqī yǒu kǎoshì _____ xià
　 星期 有 考试。
　 xīngqī yǒu kǎoshì.

5. 日本 在 中国　　 的东边 ＿＿＿＿ 西边？
   Rìběn zài Zhōngguó de dōngbian ＿＿＿＿ xībian?

VI. Each sentence below contains an error. Find and correct it:

1. 这些 五 本 书 都 是 我的。
   Zhèxiē wǔ běn shū dōu shì wǒde.

   ＿＿＿＿＿＿＿＿＿＿＿＿＿＿＿＿＿

2. 我 想　 星期六 还是 星期天 去 看 电影。
   Wǒ xiǎng xīngqīliù háishi xīngqītiān qù kàn diànyǐng.

   ＿＿＿＿＿＿＿＿＿＿＿＿＿＿＿＿＿

3. 今年 夏天 很 多人 去 中国　 旅行，我不买 到
   Jīnnián xiàtiān hěn duō rén qù Zhōngguó lǔxíng, wǒ bú mǎi dào
   飞机票。
   fēijīpiào.

   ＿＿＿＿＿＿＿＿＿＿＿＿＿＿＿＿＿

4. 如果 不能 去 英国，就 我们 去 法国。
   Rúguǒ bù néng qù Yīngguó, jiù wǒmen qù Fǎguó.

   ＿＿＿＿＿＿＿＿＿＿＿＿＿＿＿＿＿

5. 我 爸爸 妈妈 四十 年　 结婚 了。
   Wǒ bàba māma sìshí nián jiéhūn le.

   ＿＿＿＿＿＿＿＿＿＿＿＿＿＿＿＿＿

6. 汽车 在 前面　 的 房子。
   Qìchē zài qiánmiàn de fángzi.

   ＿＿＿＿＿＿＿＿＿＿＿＿＿＿＿＿＿

7. 老师 很 好 对 我们。
   Lǎoshī hěn hǎo duì wǒmen.

   ＿＿＿＿＿＿＿＿＿＿＿＿＿＿＿＿＿

8. 你的 美国　 朋友 说 中文　 很 好。
   Nǐde Měiguó péngyou shuō Zhōngwén hěn hǎo.

   ＿＿＿＿＿＿＿＿＿＿＿＿＿＿＿＿＿

9. 你 昨天 怎么 来 学校？
Nǐ zuótiān zěnme lái xuéxiào?

_____

10.他学 中文   学了两 多 年 了。
Tā xué Zhōngwén xué le liǎng duō nián le.

_____

VII. Translate the following into Chinese:

1. I didn't go to college after I graduated from high school.

_____

2. There are twenty-eight students in my son's class.

_____

3. The students were very happy because the teacher said that there would be no homework.

_____

4. I'm sorry I can't go to see the movie with you tonight. I need to study because there is a test tomorrow.

_____

5. Many parents want their children to be lawyers or doctors after they graduate from college.

_____

6. Our summer vacation starts at the beginning of July.

_____

7. The teacher asked the students to hand in their homework the following Monday.

_____

8. Students must pass these exams before they can be admitted to college.

_____

9. Many college students don't want to go to graduate school.

_____

10. Have you found a job?

_____

VIII. Translate the following into English:

1. 这 个 学校　从　小学　 到　高中　 有 十二 个 年级。
Zhè ge xuéxiào cóng xiǎoxué dào gāozhōng yǒu shí'èr ge niánjí.

_____
_____

2. 每 个 研究生 都 要 学 两 种 外语。
Měi ge yánjiūshēng dōu yào xué liǎng zhǒng wàiyǔ.

_____
_____

3. 高中　 毕业生 在 进 大学 前必须 通过 外语 考试。
Gāozhōng bìyèshēng zài jìn dàxué qián bìxū tōngguò wàiyǔ kǎoshì.

_____
_____

4. 现在　美国　越来越 多 的 中学　 开 中文　 课。
Xiànzài Měiguó yuèláiyuè duō de zhōngxué kāi Zhōngwén kè.

_____
_____

5. 他 能　找　到　工作，但是 他 没有　找。
Tā néng zhǎo dào gōngzuò, dànshì tā méiyou zhǎo.

_____
_____

6. 英语 专业　又 分 英国　语言 和 英国　文学。
Yīngyǔ zhuānyè yòu fēn Yīngguó yǔyán hé Yīngguó wénxué.

_____
_____

7. 在 中国，　学生　必须 先 读 硕士　才 能　读博士。
Zài Zhōngguó, xuésheng bìxū xiān dú shuòshì cái néng dú bóshì.
在 美国，读 博士不 一定 先　读 硕士。
Zài Měiguó, dú bóshì bù yídìng xiān dú shuòshì.

_____
_____

8.　很　多 大学 毕业生 如果 找　不 到 工作　就 去 读
　　Hěn duō dàxué bìyèshēng rúguǒ zhǎo bú dào gōngzuò jiù qù dú
　　研究生。
　　yánjiūshēng.

　　_____

　　_____

9.　我 觉得 在 美国　进 大学 和 出 大学 都 不 容易。
　　Wǒ juéde zài Měiguó jìn dàxué hé chū dàxué dōu bù róngyì.

　　_____

　　_____

10.　大多数 外国　学生　来美国 上　大学 或 读
　　Dàduōshù wàiguó xuésheng lái Měiguó shàng dàxué huò dú
　　研究生　都 要 先　通过　英语 考试。
　　yánjiūshēng dōu yào xiān tōngguò Yīngyǔ kǎoshì.

　　_____

　　_____

　　_____

IX. Discussion and writing topics:

1.　有 人 说 在 美国　进大学 容易，出 大学 难，
　　Yǒu rén shuō zài Měiguó jìn dàxué róngyì, chū dàxué nán,
　　你 同意 不 同意？
　　nǐ tóngyì bu tóngyì?

2.　你 觉得 学生　进大学 应该 不 应该 通过
　　Nǐ juéde xuésheng jìn dàxué yīnggāi bu yīnggāi tōngguò
　　严格 的 考试?
　　yángé de kǎoshì?

3.　谈谈 你的 国家 的 教育 制度 (system)。
　　Tántan nǐde guójiā de jiàoyù zhìdù.

ENGLISH TRANSLATION OF THE TEXT

Conversations (*pages 100-103*)

A: What school do you go to?

B: I go to Middle School Number Five.

A: Are you in junior middle school or senior middle school?

B: I'm in senior middle school (high school).

A: What year are you in?

B: I'm in the first year.

A: How many students are there in your class?

B: There are forty students in my class.

A: What classes do you have?

B: We have Chinese, mathematics, foreign language, history, physical education, music, natural sciences, fine arts and so on.

A: What foreign languages do you have?

B: We have English, French and Japanese, but most students choose English.

A: Do you have foreign teachers?

B: Yes, we do. We have two foreign teachers, one British and one Japanese. They teach us English and Japanese.

*   *   *   *   *

A: What school are you attending?

B: I don't go to school any more. I graduated.

A: You already graduated? Time goes by so fast. Have you found a job?

B: I didn't look for one. I'm planning to go to graduate school.

A: What would you like to study?

B: I would like to study history.

A: How many years will your graduate study take?

B: It takes two years to get an M.A. It usually takes five years to get a Ph.D.

A: Are you going to get an M.A. or Ph.D.?

B: I don't know yet. I would like to get an M.A. first and then decide if I should go for a Ph.D. How about you? Are you still in school?

A: No, I also graduated. I'm looking for a job.

B: What would you like to do?

A: I studied English and I would like to become an English teacher.

B: I heard that many schools are now looking for teachers. You can definitely find a teaching job.

A: That would be great.

*   *   *   *   *

A: Xiao Wang, I heard that it is difficult to get into a college, but it is easy to get out of it in China. Do you think so?

B: I do. There are many students who graduate from high schools every year and all of them want to go to top universities. but there are not enough top universities. So not every high school graduate can go to the best universities.

A: So what does one usually need to do in order to get into college?

B: You need to pass very tough exams. If your grades are not good, you can't get into a college or you can't get into a good one.

A: You don't have to pass an exam to get into a college in America, but it is not easy to get into a good one either.

Reading Passage (*page 104*)

Schools in China are divided into elementary schools, middle schools and universities. Children usually start elementary school at 6 or 7. Middle school is further divided into junior middle school and senior middle school. Elementary school is six years, junior middle school is three years, senior middle school is three years and college is four years. Every child must attend elementary school and junior middle school, but most people also attend senior middle school and college. After college, most people start working, but there are also people who go to graduate school. In the past, students went to school six days a week, but now they go to school five days a week. There is no school on Saturday and Sunday. Elementary and middle school students in China live a very hard life because they have to do a lot of homework and don't have much time to enjoy themselves.

LESSON 6

HEALTH & FITNESS

CONVERSATIONS

(English translation, pages 144-145)

A: 你是不是不舒服？你的脸色不太好。
Nǐ shì bu shì bù shūfu?　Nǐde liǎnsè bú tài hǎo.

B: 我是有点儿不舒服。
Wǒ shì yǒudiǎnr bù shūfu.

A: 你有什么感觉？
Nǐ yǒu shénme gǎnjué?

B: 我头疼。我想我今天不能去上班了。
Wǒ tóu téng. Wǒ xiǎng wǒ jīntiān bù néng qù shàngbān le.

A: 你是不应该去上班。你应该去看医生。
Nǐ shì bù yìnggāi qù shàngbān. Nǐ yìnggāi qù kàn yīshēng.

*　　*　　*　　*　　*

A: 你哪儿不舒服？
Nǐ nǎr　bù shūfu?

B: 医生，我有点儿头疼，感觉很累。
Yīshēng, wǒ yǒudiǎnr tóu téng, gǎnjué hěn lèi.

A: 你是什么时候开始头疼的？
Nǐ shì shénme shíhou kāishǐ tóu téng de?

B: 昨天晚上。
Zuótiān wǎnshang.

A: 发不发烧？
Fā bu fāshāo?

B: 我想不发烧，但是我咳嗽。
Wǒ xiǎng bù fāshāo,　dànshì wǒ késòu.

A: 我 给 你 检查 一下儿吧。
Wǒ gěi nǐ jiǎnchá yíxiàr   ba.

*   *   *   *   *

A: 医生   怎么 说？
Yīshēng zěnme shuō?

B: 他说 我 感冒 了。
Tā shuō wǒ gǎnmào le.

A: 他有没有   说   怎么 治？
Tā yǒu méiyou shuō zěnme zhì?

B: 他给 我 做 了检查，说   不要紧。
Tā gěi wǒ zuò le jiǎnchá, shuō bú yàojǐn.

A: 他有 没有 给你 开 药？
Tā yǒu méiyou gěi nǐ kāi yào?

B: 开了。医生   说 我 吃 一个星期 的药 就 会 好 的。
Kāi le.   Yīshēng shuō wǒ chī yí ge xīngqī de yào jiù huì hǎo de.
如果 药 吃 完 后 病   还不好，他 要 我 去看 他。
Rúguǒ yào chī wán hòu bìng hái bù hǎo, tā yào wǒ qù kàn tā.

*   *   *   *   *

A: 你 昨天   怎么 没 来 上课？
Nǐ zuótiān zěnme méi lái shàngkè?

B: 我 病 了。
Wǒ bìng le.

A: 你 怎么 了？
Nǐ zěnme le?

B: 我 有点儿 发烧。
Wǒ yǒudiǎnr fāshāo.

A: 你的病 现在 有 没有 好？
Nǐde bìng xiànzài yǒu méiyou hǎo?

B: 今天 比 昨天 好 多 了，但是 还 没有 全 好。
Jīntiān bǐ zuótiān hǎo duō le, dànshì hái méiyou quán hǎo.

A: 你有没有 去 看 医生？
Nǐ yǒu méiyou qù kàn yīshēng?

B: 没有，我 想 是 小 病，不要紧。
Méiyou, wǒ xiǎng shì xiǎo bìng, bú yàojǐn.

A: 你要 多 休息。
Nǐ yào duō xiūxi.

B: 我 会 的。
Wǒ huì de.

*   *   *   *   *

A: 听说 你 最近 身体 不 好，常常 去 看 医生。
Tīngshuō nǐ zuìjìn shēntǐ bù hǎo, chángcháng qù kàn yīshēng.
你怎么 了？
Nǐ zěnme le?

B: 我 过敏。
Wǒ guòmǐn.

A: 你 对 什么 过敏？
Nǐ duì shénme guòmǐn?

B: 我 不 知道，医生们 也 不 知道，所以 谁 都 治 不
Wǒ bù zhīdào, yīshēngmen yě bù zhīdào, suǒyǐ shuí dōu zhì bù
好 我的 病。
hǎo wǒde bìng.

A: 你 可以 试试 中医。
Nǐ kěyǐ shìshi zhōngyī.

B: 你觉得 中医　能　治 好 西医治不好 的 病　吗？
Nǐ juéde zhōngyī néng zhì hǎo xīyī　zhì bù hǎo de bìng ma?

A: 有　可能。
Yǒu kěnéng.

B: 这 是 好 主意。你 认识 一个 好 中医　吗？
Zhè shì hǎo zhǔyì.　Nǐ rènshi yí ge hǎo zhōngyī ma?

A: 我的 中医　林　医生　不错。你 可以 去 看 他。
Wǒde zhōngyī Lín Yīshēng bú cuò.　Nǐ kěyǐ qù kàn tā.

READING PASSAGE

中国人很喜欢锻炼。他们一般起得很早，特别是老年人。很多人早上五点就起床了。大多数人喜欢在公园，或在街旁锻炼。中国人的锻炼方式各种各样，有的慢跑，有的打太极拳，还有的散步。中国有很多自行车，但是人们骑自行车不是为了锻炼，而是把自行车作为交通工具。你如果去中国，早上去公园或街上看别人锻炼、骑自行车上班是一件很有意思的事。

Zhōngguórén hěn xǐhuan duànliàn. Tāmen yìbān qǐ de hěn zǎo, tèbiéshì lǎoniánrén. Hěn duō rén zǎoshàng wǔ diǎn jiù qǐchuáng le. Dàduōshù rén xǐhuan zài gōngyuán, huò zài jiē shang duànliàn. Zhōngguórén de duànliàn fāngshì gèzhònggèyàng, yǒude mànpǎo, yǒude dǎ tàijíquán, hái yǒude sànbù. Zhōngguó yǒu hěn duō zìxíngchē, dànshì rénmen qí zìxíngchē bú shì wèile duànliàn, érshì bǎ zìxíngchē zuò wéi jiāotōng gōngjù. Nǐ rúguǒ qù Zhōngguó, zǎoshàng qù gōngyuán huò jiē shang kàn biérén duànliàn, qí zìxíngchē qù shàngbān shì yí jiàn hěn yǒuyìsi de shì.

(*English translation, page 145*)

NEW WORDS AND EXPRESSIONS

舒服	shūfu	feeling well; comfortable
脸色	liǎnsè	look (*n.*); complexion
感觉	gǎnjué	feeling
头	tóu	head
疼	téng	hurt; pain (*v.*)
医生	yīshēng	(medical) doctor
感冒	gǎnmào	cold; have a cold
发烧	fāshāo	have a fever
咳嗽	késòu	cough (*n./v.*)
检查	jiǎnchá	exam; inspect; examination; inspection
治	zhì	treat (a disease)
不要紧	bú yàojǐn	doesn't matter; not important
开药	kāi yào	prescribe medicine
好	hǎo	become well; recover (from a sickness)
完	wán	finish
病	bìng	become sick; sickness
全	quán	completely; entirely
休息	xiūxi	rest; relax
身体	shēntǐ	health; body
过敏	guòmǐn	allergic
中医	zhōngyī	Chinese medicine; doctor of Chinese medicine
西医	xīyī	Western medicine; doctor of Western medicine
锻炼	duànliàn	physical exercise; workout
特别	tèbié	especially; particularly
老年人	lǎoniánrén	old people

慢跑	mànpǎo	jogging; jog
方式	fāngshì	method; form; way
各种各样	gèzhǒnggèyàng	various; all kinds of
太极拳	tàijíquán	taiji (taichi)
散步	sànbù	take a walk
人们	rénmen	people
为了	wèile	for; for the sake of; in order to
把 ... 作为	bǎ ... zuòwéi	treat ... as
交通工具	jiāotōng gōngjù	means of transportation
不是 ... 而是	bú shì ... ér shì ...	not ... but rather ...

SUPPLEMENTARY WORDS AND EXPRESSIONS

炎症	yánzhèng	infection
嗓子	sǎngzi	throat; voice
牙	yá	tooth
肚子	dùzi	stomach
背	bèi	back
腿	tuǐ	leg
针灸	zhēngjiū	acupuncture
病人	bìngrén	patient; sick person
药房	yàofáng	pharmacy
医疗保险	yīliáo bǎoxiǎn	medical insurance
运动	yùndòng	exercise (v./n.); sports
健身房	jiànshēnfáng	gym
游泳	yóuyǒng	swim; swimming
足球	zúqiú	soccer
打球	dǎ qiú	play a ballgame

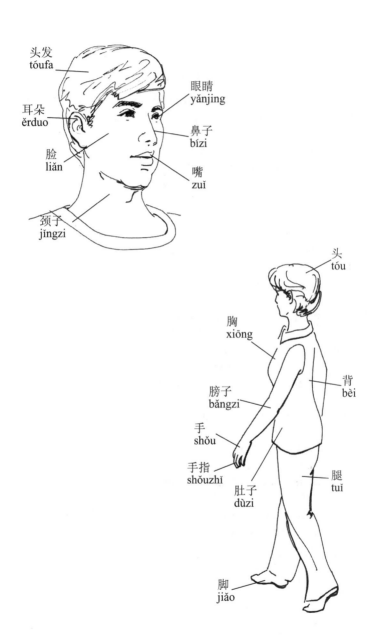

头发
tóufa

眼睛
yǎnjing

耳朵
ěrduo

鼻子
bízi

脸
liǎn

嘴
zuǐ

颈子
jǐngzi

头
tóu

胸
xiōng

背
bèi

膀子
bǎngzi

手
shǒu

手指
shǒuzhǐ

肚子
dùzi

腿
tuǐ

脚
jiǎo

LANGUAGE POINTS

我是有点儿不舒服 wǒ shì yǒudiǎnr bù shūfu

是 shì is used here to emphasize the following verb or the predicate adjective. It often suggests a strong assertion or strong denial:

你是不应该去上班。
Nǐ shì bù yīnggāi qù shàngbān.
You definitely shouldn't go to work.

我是去过中国。
Wǒ shì qù guo Zhōngguó.
I definitely have been to China.

火车是比汽车快。
Huǒchē shì bǐ qìchē kuài.
The train is indeed faster than the car.

他是不住在纽约。
Tā shì bú zhù zài Niǔyuē.
It is true that he does not live in New York.

This usage is similar to *do*/*does* or *did* in emphasizing verbs in English:

It *did* rain yesterday.
She *does* have a college degree.
We *do* accept credit card payment.

In a question, the use of 是 shì suggests that the speaker is positive about the answer and is seeking a confirmation:

你是不是不舒服?
Nǐ shì bu shì bù shūfu?
You are not feeling well, are you?

我头疼 wǒ tóu téng

This is a typical example of the topic-comment construction in Chinese, which accounts for a large percentage of sentences in Chinese. In such a sentence, there is a binary division of two parts between *topic* and *comment*. The topic is what the speaker takes as his/her point of departure and the comment is a statement on that topic. The comment is often in the form of a sentence as in the sentence cited, where the topic is 我 wǒ (*I*), and 头疼 tóu téng (*head hurts*) is the comment. Other examples include:

象　鼻子长。

Xiàng bízi　cháng.

The elephant has a long trunk. (*literally*: Elephant trunk long.)

树　叶子多。

Shù yèzi　duō.

The tree has a lot of leaves. (*literally*: Tree leaves many.)

你哪儿不舒服 nǐ nǎr bù shūfu and 你怎么了 nǐ zěnme le

These are the two most common expressions used by doctors and other people in inquiring about someone who appears to be sick. 你哪儿不舒服 nǐ nǎr bù shūfu literally means *what part of your body troubles you* and 你怎么了 nǐ zěnme le means *what's wrong*.

舒服 shūfu in the sense of *feeling well* is only used in the negative sentence. In an affirmative sentence, 舒服 shūfu means *comfortable*.

医生说我吃一个星期的药就会好的
yīshēng shuō wǒ chī yí ge xīngqī de yào jiù huì hǎo de

就 jiù is a frequently used word in Chinese with multiple meanings. The following is the summary of the various meanings of the word that we have come across so far:

1. adverb used for emphasis:

银行　就在那儿。

Yínháng jiù zài nàr.

The bank is right there.

2. adverb with the meaning of *earlier than expected* or *better than expected*:

他只上 了三年 的大学 就 毕业了。

Tā zhǐ shàng le sān nián de dàxué jiù bìyè le.

He graduated from college after only three years.

3. *then*, often used in conjunction with 如果 rúguǒ (*if*):

如果 天不好，我 就 不 去 野餐。

Rúguǒ tiān bù hǎo, wǒ jiù bú qù yěcān.

If the weather is not good, then I won't go to the picnic.

4. adverb indicating that an action closely follows another:

他们 下 了班 就 去飞机场。

Tāmen xià le bān jiù qù fēijīchǎng.

They will go to the airport as soon as they get off work.

5. *just about*, often used with 要 yào and/or 了 le:

天 就要 下雨了。

Tiān jiù yào xiàyǔ le.

It is about to rain.

饭 十分钟 就 好 了。

Fàn shí fēnzhōng jiù hǎo le.

The meal will be ready in ten minutes.

药吃完后 yào chī wán hòu and 治好病 zhì hǎo bìng

Both 完 wán (*finish*) and 好 hǎo (*get well*; *become ready*) are verbs used after another verb as a complement indicating the result of an action expressed by the preceding verb. While 完 wán indicates the completion of an action, 好 hǎo suggests a satisfactory condition or readiness resulting from the action of the preceding verb. Similar examples include:

吃 完 饭

chī wán fàn

finish eating the meal

看 完 书
kàn wán shū
finish reading the book

修 好 车
xiū hǎo chē
fix the car

做 好 饭
zuò hǎo fàn
get the meal ready

Unlike past-tense verbs in English that usually indicate a result such as *the meal was cooked* and *the watch was repaired*, verbs in Chinese do not automatically indicate a result, even with a past reference. To indicate a result, a complement is needed. Compare:

车修了 chē xiū le
(*only says that repair work was performed on the car, but does not suggest that the car is now in working order*)
and
车修好了 chē xiū hǎo le
(*says that the car has been fixed and is in working order*)

饭做了 fàn zuò le
(*only says that the process of cooking has started, but does not say if the meal is ready*)
and
饭做好了 fàn zuò hǎo le
(*says that the meal is ready*)

To suggest a negative result that has already been produced, 没有 méiyou is used before the verb:

我 没有 看 完 这 本 书。
Wǒ méiyou kàn wán zhè běn shū.
I didn't finish reading the book.

你的 车 没有 修 好。
Nǐde chē méiyou xiū hǎo.
Your car has not been fixed.

To suggest a potential negative result, 不 bù is used. It is placed after the verb and before the complement:

我 今天 看 不 完 这 本 书。
Wǒ jīntiān kàn bù wán zhè běn shū.
I can't finish reading the book today.

他 修 不 好 我的 车。
Tā xiū bù hǎo wǒde chē.
He can't fix my car.

怎么 zěnme and 为什么 wèishénme

Both of them can be used to mean *why*. Whereas 怎么 zěnme usually suggests surprise or implies criticism, 为什么 wèishénme is quite neutral. Compare:

你 为什么 来 晚 了?
Nǐ wèishénme lái wǎn le?
Why are you late? (*an innocent question inquiring about the reason*)

你 怎么 来 晚 了?
Nǐ zěnme lái wǎn le?
How come you are late? (*implying you shouldn't have been late*)

中医能治好西医治不好的病吗?
zhōngyī néng zhì hǎo xīyī zhì bù hǎo de bìng ma?

西医治不好 xīyī zhì bù hǎo is a sentence functioning as the attribute of the noun 病 bìng. Since it is a modifier, it is placed before the modified word 病 bìng. 的 de is used between them to mark the relationship. Other examples are:

这 是 我 昨天 买 的 书。
Zhè shì wǒ zuótiān mǎi de shū.
This is the book I bought yesterday.

我们 住 的 地方 很 小。
Wǒmen zhù de dìfang hěn xiǎo.
The place where we live is very small.

不是 bú shì … 而是 ér shì

They are always used in conjunction with each other to mean *not … but rather*:

他去 中国　　不 是 工作，而是 玩儿。

Tā qù Zhōngguó bú shì gōngzuò, ér shì wánr.

He is going to China not to work, but for pleasure.

我 不 是 美国人，而是 英国人。

Wǒ bú shì Měiguórén, ér shì Yīngguórén.

I'm not American, rather I'm English.

EXERCISES

Answer key, pages 279-282

I. Answer the following questions:

1. 你身体 好 吗? 最近 有 没有 看 过 医生?
Nǐ shēntǐ hǎo ma? Zuìjìn yǒu méiyǒu kàn guo yīshēng?
_____

2. 你 学 中文　是 为了 去 中国　　吗?
Nǐ xué Zhōngwén shì wèile qù Zhōngguó ma?
_____

3. 你 有 没有　看 过 中医? 你 觉得 中医　怎么样?
Nǐ yǒu méiyou kàn guo zhōngyī? Nǐ juéde zhōngyī zěnmeyàng?
_____

4. 你每 天 锻炼　吗? 你 怎么　锻炼?
Nǐ měi tiān duànliàn ma?　Nǐ zěnme duànliàn?
_____

5. 你 有 自行车 吗? 你 把 自行车　作为　锻炼　的 工具
Nǐ yǒu zìxíngchē ma? Nǐ bǎ zìxíngchē zuòwéi duànliàn de gōngjù
还是 交通　工具?
háishi jiāotōng gōngjù?

6. 你 一般 在 哪儿 锻炼?
Nǐ yìbān zài nǎr duànliàn?

7. 你 过敏 吗? 你 对 什么　过敏?
Nǐ guòmǐn ma? Nǐ duì shénme guòmǐn?
_____

8. 医生　见 到 病人　时 会 怎么 说?
Yīshēng jiàn dào bìngrén shí huì zěnme shuō?
_____

9. 一个人 如果 感冒，会 有 什么　感觉？
   Yí ge rén rúguǒ gǎnmào, huì yǒu shénme gǎnjué?

   _____

10. 在 中国，　　病人 在 医院 的 药房 拿 药。在 美国，
    Zài Zhōngguó, bìngrén zài yīyuàn de yàofáng ná yào. Zài Měiguó,
    病人 在 哪儿 拿 药？
    bìngrén zài nǎr   ná yào?

    _____

II. How do you say the following in Chinese?
1. the doctor who works in Shanghai

   _____

2. the place where we exercise

   _____

3. the time when they begin their class

   _____

4. the teacher who teaches us English

   _____

5. things that need to be done today

   _____

6. open the door

   _____

7. turn on the TV

   _____

8. drive

   _____

9. prescribe medicine

   _____

10. attend a meeting

    _____

III. Fill in the blanks with the complements 好 hǎo or 完 wán:

1. 我 这 个 周末 很 忙，看 不 _____ 这 本 书。

   Wǒ zhè ge zhōumò hěn máng, kàn bù _____ zhè běn shū.

2. 他 用 _____ 了钱。

   Tā yòng _____ le qián.

3. 西医没有 治 _____ 我的 病，中医 治 _____

   Xīyī méiyou zhì _____ wǒde bìng, zhōngyī zhì _____

   了我的 病。

   le wǒde bìng.

4. 今天 老师 让 学生们 写 一百个字，但是 他们 写

   Jīntiān lǎoshī ràng xuéshengmen xiě yìbǎi ge zì, dànshì tāmen xiě

   不 _____。

   bù _____.

5. 爸爸 没有 听 _____ 孩子 的话 就 说 他不 能 出

   Bàba méiyou tīng _____ háizi de huà jiù shuō tā bù néng chū

   去 玩儿。

   qù wánr.

IV. Rewrite the following sentences, using 是 shì to emphasize the verb and then turn them into questions:

1. 我 家 我 爸爸 做 饭。

   Wǒ jiā wǒ bàba zuò fàn.

   _____

   _____

2. 他 在 北京 大学 学习。

   Tā zài Běijīng Dàxué xuéxí.

   _____

   _____

3. 我 太太 不 喜欢 看 电影。

   Wǒ tàitai bù xǐhuan kàn diànyǐng.

   _____

   _____

4. 大多数 中国人 起得 很 早。
Dàduōshù Zhōngguórén qǐ de hěn zǎo.

_____

_____

5. 打 太极拳 对 身体 有 帮助。
Dǎ tàijíquán duì shēntǐ yǒu bāngzhù.

_____

_____

V. Express the following using the words in the supplementary vocabulary list:
1. I had a stomachache yesterday.

_____

2. My husband has a toothache.

_____

3. He has a sore throat.

_____

4. That gentleman has a backache.

_____

5. The patient has a pain in her leg.

_____

VI. Decide which of the following are topic-comment sentences:
1. 那 个 老年人 身体 不 好。
Nà ge lǎoniánrén shēntǐ bù hǎo.

2. 桂林 的 风景 很 美。
Guìlín de fēngjǐng hěn měi.

3. 他的 美国 朋友 名字 叫 麦克。
Tāde Měiguó péngyou míngzi jiào Màikè.

4. 我 觉得 英国 的 英语 比 美国 的 英语 好听。
Wǒ juéde Yīngguó de Yīngyǔ bǐ Měiguó de Yīngyǔ hǎotīng.

5. 我们的 老师 工作 很 忙。
   Wǒmende lǎoshī gōngzuò hěn máng.

6. 公司 的经理在 打电话。
   Gōngsī de jīnglǐ zài dǎ diànhuà.

7. 我 头 不 疼，但是 肚子 疼。
   Wǒ tóu bù téng, dànshì dùzi téng.

8. 美国 的 北边 是 加拿大。
   Měiguó de běibian shì Jiā'nádà.

9. 男 学生 数学 好，女 学生 英语 好。
   Nán xuésheng shùxué hǎo, nǚ xuésheng Yīngyǔ hǎo.

10. 你 一 定 能 找 到 老师 的工作。
    Nǐ yídìng néng zhǎo dào lǎoshī de gōngzuò.

VII. Explain what 就 jiù in each of the following sentences means:

1. 如果 找 不 到 工作，我 就 去 读 研究生。
   Rúguǒ zhǎo bú dào gōngzuò, wǒ jiù qù dú yánjiūshēng.

   _____

2. 前面 就 是 火车站。
   Qiánmiàn jiù shì huǒchēzhàn.

   _____

3. 他们 就 要 结婚 了。
   Tāmen jiù yào jiéhūn le.

   _____

4. 老师 打 完 电话 就 去 教室 了。
   Lǎoshī dǎ wán diànhuà jiù qù jiàoshì le.

   _____

5. 她 用 了半 个 小时 就把 作业 做 完 了。
   Tā yòng le bàn ge xiǎoshí jiù bǎ zuòyè zuò wán le.

   _____

VIII. Translate the following into Chinese:

1. Is it true that China is in East Asia?

   _____

2. I do live in New York.

   _____

3. Please put the newspaper on the table.

   _____

4. It is Sunday today. How come you are still at work?

   _____

5. When did you begin to have a fever?

   _____

6. Many people believe in (信 xìn) Chinese medicine because they think Chinese medicine can cure some diseases that Western medicine can't.

   _____

   _____

7. The doctor said that you have to be on medication for a month.

   _____

8. It doesn't matter if you don't speak Chinese.

   _____

9. Are you allergic to seafood?

   _____

10. I've seen many doctors, but none could cure my disease.

   _____

IX. Translate the following into English:

1. 中国　　没有私人 (private) 医生。人们　有　病　的
   Zhōngguó méi yǒu sīrén　　yīshēng. Rénmen yǒu bìng de
   时候要去医院看医生。
   shíhou yào qù yīyuàn kàn yīshēng.

   _____

   _____

2. 医生　没有给我检查就说我没有病。
   Yīshēng méiyou gěi wǒ jiǎnchá jiù shuō wǒ méi yǒu bìng.

   _____

   _____

3. 我妈妈很会作菜，特别是中国　　菜。
   Wǒ māma hěn huì zuò cài,　tèbié　shì Zhōngguó cài.

   _____

   _____

4. 他今天来上班　了，但是病还没有全好。
   Tā jīntiān lái shàngbān le,　dànshì bìng hái méiyou quán hǎo.

   _____

   _____

5. 你的脸色不是不好，是很不好。
   Nǐde　liǎnsè bú shì bù hǎo, shì hěn bù hǎo.

   _____

   _____

6. 很多人在西医治不好他们的病的时候，才去
   Hěn duō rén zài xīyī　zhì bù hǎo tāmende bìng de shíhou, cái qù
   看中医。
   kàn zhōngyī.

   _____

   _____

7. 发烧是很多病的症状 (symptom)。
   Fāshāo shì hěn duō bìng de zhèngzhuàng.

   _____

   _____

8. 这 只 是 一点儿小 病，不要紧。吃 点儿 药 就 会
   Zhè zhǐ shì yìdiǎnr   xiǎo bìng, bú yàojǐn.   Chī diǎnr yào jiù huì
   好 的。
   hǎo de.

   _____

   _____

9. 每 天 慢跑 是 很 好 的 锻炼 方式。
   Měi tiān mànpǎo shì hěn hǎo de duànliàn fāngshì.

   _____

   _____

10. 我 学 中文   不 是 为了 和 中国人   说话，而是
    Wǒ xué Zhōngwén bú shì wèile hé Zhōngguórén shuōhuà, ér shì
    为了 看 书。
    wèile kàn shū.

   _____

   _____

X. Topics for discussion/writing:

1. 你 锻炼 不 锻炼？ 你 喜欢 什么 运动？
   Nǐ duànliàn bu duànliàn? Nǐ xǐhuan shénme yùndòng?

2. 谈谈 你看 医生 的一次经历 (experience)。
   Tántan nǐ kàn yīshēng de yí cì jīnglì.

ENGLISH TRANSLATION OF THE TEXT

Conversations (*pages 122-125*)

A: Are you feeling sick? You don't look well.
B: It's true that I'm not feeling well.
A: What bothers you?
B: I have a headache. I don't think I can go to work today.
A: You shouldn't go to work. You should go to see a doctor.

        *   *   *   *   *

A: What bothers you?
B: Doctor, I have a headache. I'm feeling very tied.
A: When did you develop this headache?
B: Last night.
A: Do you have a fever?
B: I don't think so, but I cough.
A: Let me examine you.

        *   *   *   *   *

A: What did the doctor say?
B: He said that I had caught a cold.
A: Did he say how he is going to treat it?
B: He examined me and said that it was nothing major.
A: Did he prescribe any medicine for you?
B: Yes, he did. The doctor said that I would get well after taking the medicine for a week. He asked me to see him if I don't get well after finishing the medicine.

        *   *   *   *   *

A: Why didn't you come to class yesterday?
B: I was sick.
A: What was wrong?
B: I had a little fever.
A: Are you well now?
B: It's much better today than yesterday, but I've not completely recovered.
A: Did you go to see a doctor?
B: No. I think it is a minor thing, not a big deal.

A: You should take it easy.
B: I will.

*   *   *   *   *

A: I heard that you have not been in good health recently. What's wrong?
B: I have an allergy.
A: What are you allergic to?
B: I don't know and the doctors don't know either. That's why no one can cure me.
A: You may want to try Chinese medicine.
B: Do you think Chinese medicine can cure what Western medicine can't?
A: It's possible.
B: This is a good idea. Do you know a good doctor of Chinese medicine?
A: My Chinese doctor Dr. Lin is very good. You may go to see him.

Reading Passage (*page 126*)

Chinese people like to exercise very much. They usually get up very early, especially the old people. Many people get up as early as five o'clock in the morning. Most people like to exercise in parks or by the street side. There are various types of exercises that Chinese people do. Some go jogging, others do taiji or take a walk. There are lots of bicycles in China, but people ride bicycles not as exercise, but rather as a means of transportation. If you go to China, it would be an interesting thing to go to the parks or the streets in the morning to see people exercise and ride the bicycle to go to work.

LESSON 7

HOLIDAYS & FESTIVALS

CONVERSATIONS

(English translation, pages 166-167)

A: 你能 不 能 给 我 介绍 一下儿 中国 的节日？
Nǐ néng bu néng gěi wǒ jièshào yíxiàr Zhōngguó de jiérì?

B: 当然 能。可是 中国 的节日很 多，我们 只 能
Dāngrán néng. Kěshì Zhōngguó de jiérì hěn duō, wǒmen zhǐ néng
说 重要 的。
shuō zhòngyào de.

A: 好。我 想 先 问问 中国人 过不过 元旦。
Hǎo. Wǒ xiǎng xiān wènwen Zhōngguórén guò bu guò yuándàn.

B: 过。但是 对中国人 来说，元旦 不是最重要
Guò. Dànshì duì Zhōngguórén lái shuō, yuándàn bú shì zuì zhòngyào
的节日。最 重要 的节日是 中国 新 年。
de jiérì. Zuì zhòngyào de jiérì shì Zhōngguó Xīn Nián.

A: 中国 新年 是几月几号？
Zhōngguó Xīn Nián shì jǐ yuè jǐ hào?

B: 每 年 不 一样。有时 在一月，有时 在二月。
Měi nián bù yíyàng. Yǒushí zài yíyuè, yǒushí zài èryuè.

A: 除了中国 新年，还有 什么 重要 的节日？
Chúle Zhōngguó Xīn Nián, hái yǒu shénme zhòngyào de jiérì?

B: 十月 一号 是国庆节。全 国 都 放假。
Shíyuè yī hào shì Guóqìngjié. Quán guó dōu fàngjià.

A: 中国 有 没有 圣诞节？
Zhōngguó yǒu méi yǒu Shèngdànjié?

B: 没 有。虽然 圣诞节 不是中国人 的节日，但是
Méi yǒu. Suīrán Shèngdànjié bú shì Zhōngguórén de jiérì, dànshì
现在 有的人 也 过 这个节日。
xiànzài yǒude rén yě guò zhè ge jiérì.

A: 我 听说 有 一个 中秋节。 这 是 什么 节？
Wǒ tīngshuō yǒu yí ge Zhōngqiūjié. Zhè shì shénme jié?

B: "中" 的意思是 *middle*，"秋" 的意思是 *autumn*。
"Zhōng" de yìsi shì *middle*, "qiū" de yìsi shì *autumn*.
"中秋节" 的意思就 是 *Mid-Autumn Festival*。
"Zhōngqiūjié" de yìsi jiù shì *Mid-Autumn Festival*.
这 一 天 月亮 最 圆。人们 吃 月饼， 全 家 团聚。
Zhè yì tiān yuèliàng zuì yuán. Rénmen chī yuèbǐng, quán jiā tuánjù.

A: 中秋节 是 什么 时候？
Zhōngqiūjié shì shénme shíhou?

B: 中秋节 和 新 年 一样，每 年 不同，但是 一般 在
Zōngqiūjié hé Xín Nián yíyàng, měi nián bùtōng, dànshì yìbān zài
十月。
shíyuè.

* * * * *

A: 你 知道 明年 的中国 新 年 是 哪 一 天 吗？
Nǐ zhīdào míngnián de Zhōngguó Xīn Nián shì nǎ yì tiān ma?

B: 明年 的 中国 新 年 是 二月十 号。
Míngnián de Zhōngguó Xīn Nián shì èryuè shí hào.

A: 中国人 一般 怎么 过 年？
Zhōngguórén yìbān zěnme guò nián?

B: 除夕 的 晚上， 全 家 人 团聚，做 很 多 菜，吃 很
Chúxī de wǎnshang, quán jiā rén tuánjù, zuò hěn duō cài, chī hěn
多 菜。新 年 的 那天，大人 还 要 给 小孩子 红包。
duō cài. Xīn Nián de nà tiān, dàrén hái yào gěi xiǎoháizi hóngbāo.

A: 什么 是 红包？
Shénme shì hóngbāo?

B: 红包 里装 着 钱，是 给 小孩子 的 礼物。
Hóngbāo lǐ zhuāng zhe qián, shì gěi xiǎoháizi de lǐwù.

A: 新 年 的 时候 大家 交换 礼物吗？
Xīn Nián de shíhou dàjiā jiāohuàn lǐwù ma?

B: 中国人 没 有 这 个 习惯。
Zhōngguórén méi yǒu zhè ge xíguàn.

A: 中国人 过 年 一般 吃 些 什么？
Zhōngguórén guò Nián yìbān chī xiē shénme?

B: 各种各样 的 东西，但是 大多数 人 都 要 吃 饺子。
Gèzhǒnggèyàng de dōngxī, dànshì dàduōshù rén dōu yào chī jiǎozi.

* * * * *

A: 明年 是 什么 年？
Míngnián shì shénme nián?

B: 明年 是 鸡年。明年 生 的 孩子 都 属 鸡。
Míngnián shì jī nián. Míngnián shēng de háizi dōu shǔ jī.

A: 我 不 知道 我 属 什么。你 能 告诉 我 吗？
Wǒ bù zhīdào wǒ shǔ shénme. Nǐ néng gàosù wǒ ma?

B: 可以。你 今年 多 大？
Kěyǐ. Nǐ jīnnián duō dà?

A: 我 今年 二十岁，我 是 一九九七年 生 的。
Wǒ jīnnián èrshí suì, wǒ shì yī jiǔ jiǔ qī nián shēng de.

B: 你 比 我 小 两 岁。我 属猪。你 是 牛 年 生 的，
Nǐ bǐ wǒ xiǎo liǎng suì. Wǒ shǔ zhū. Nǐ shì niú nián shēng de,
你 属 牛。
nǐ shǔ niú.

A: 我 知道 了，如果 你 知道 一个 人 属 什么，你 就 能
Wǒ zhīdào le, rúguǒ nǐ zhīdào yí ge rén shǔ shénme, nǐ jiù néng
猜 到 他 有 多 大。
cāi dào tā yǒu duō dà.

B: 你 说 得 不错。一般 是 这样。
Nǐ shuō de bú cuò. Yìbān shì zhèyàng.

READING PASSAGE

对很多美国人来说，圣诞节是一年中最重要的节日。孩子们特别喜欢这个节日，因为他们能得到很多礼物。很多人在家里放圣诞树，树上摆着各种各样的装饰品。圣诞节的除夕，全家人要团聚，做很多的菜，吃很多的菜。美国人过圣诞节和中国人过中国新年有一个很大的不同，这就是美国人要交换礼物，他们在圣诞节前要花很多时间去商店选礼物、买礼物。

Duì hěn duō Měiguórén lái shuō, Shèngdànjié shì yì nián zhōng zuì zhòngyào de jiérì. Háizimen tèbié xǐhuan zhè ge jiérì, yīnwéi tāmen néng dédào hěn duō lǐwù. Hěn duō rén zài jiā lǐ fàng Shèngdànshù, shù shang bǎi zhe gèzhònggèyàng de zhuāngshìpǐn. Shèngdànjié de chúxī, quán jiā rén yào tuánjù, zuò hěn duō de cài, chī hěn duō de cài. Měiguórén guò Shèngdànjié hé Zhōngguórén guò Zhōngguó Xīn Nián yǒu yí ge hěn dà de bù tóng, zhè jiù shì Měiguórén yào jiāohuàn lǐwù, tāmen zài Shèngdànjié qián yào huā hěn duō shíjiān qù shāngdiàn xuǎn lǐwù, mǎi lǐwù.

(*English translation, page 167*)

NEW WORDS AND EXPRESSIONS

介绍	jièshào	say sth. about; introduce; introduction
节日	jiérì	holiday; festival
重要	zhòngyào	important
元旦	Yuándàn	(Western/Gregorian) New Year
一样	yíyàng	the same
对 ... 来说	duì ... lái shuō	as far as ... is concerned; for
放假	fàngjià	have a vacation; have a day off
国庆节	Guóqìngjié	National Day; Independence Day
中秋节	Zhōngqiūjié	Mid-Autumn Festival
月亮	yuèliang	moon
圆	yuán	round; circular
月饼	yuèbǐng	moon cake
不同	bùtóng	difference; different
除夕	chúxī	eve
团聚	tuánjù	get together
大人	dàrén	adult; grown-up
包	bāo	bag
装	zhuāng	hold; load; install
着	zhe	*aspect marker*
大家	dàjiā	everyone; people
交换	jiāohuàn	exchange (*v./n.*)
礼物	lǐwù	gift; present
习惯	xíguàn	habit; custom
饺子	jiǎozi	dumplings
猜	cāi	guess
属	shǔ	born in the Chinese zodiac year of
生	shēng	give birth to; be born; produce

因为	yīnwéi	because
得到	dédào	receive; obtain; acquire
树	shù	tree
摆	bǎi	place (*v*.); put; arrange
装饰品	zhuāngshìpǐn	decorative objects; decorations
花	huā	spend (time or money)

SUPPLEMENTARY WORDS AND EXPRESSIONS

传统	chuántǒng	tradition; traditional
庆祝	qìngzhù	celebrate; celebration
情人节	Qíngrénjié	Valentine's Day
母亲节	Mǔqinjié	Mother's Day
父亲节	Fùqinjie	Father's Day
万圣节	Wànshèngjié	Halloween
感恩节	Gǎn'ēnjié	Thanksgiving Day
鼠	shǔ	mouse; rat
虎	hǔ	tiger
兔	tù	rabbit
蛇	shé	snake
龙	lóng	dragon
马	mǎ	horse
猴	hóu	monkey
狗	gǒu	dog

LANGUAGE POINTS

节日 jiérì and 假 jià

节日 jiérì is equivalent to *holiday* or *festival* in English. It is often shortened to 节 jié, particularly when used with a descriptive word as in 春节 Chūnjié (*Chinese New Year*) and 中秋节 Zhōngqiūjié (*Mid-Autumn Festival*). The names of all the holidays and festivals in China and the translations of most foreign holidays and festivals end in 节 jié.

假 jià, on the other hand, refers to *vacation, days off,* or *leave* such as 暑假 shǔjià (*summer vacation*), 寒假 hánjià (*winter vacation*), 事假 shìjià (*personal day*), 病假 bìngjià (*sick leave*). The verb usually used in collocation with 假 jià in the sense of *have a vacation* is 放 fàng, which literally means *set free* or *release*:

> 你们 国庆节 放 不 放 假?
> Nǐmen Guóqìngjié fàng bu fàng jià?
> Are you getting a day off for the National Day?

> 我们 国庆节 放 两 天 假。
> Wǒmen Guóqìngjié fàng liǎng tiān jià.
> We are getting two days off for the National Day.

我们只能说重要的 wǒmen zhǐ néng shuō zhòngyào de

The noun that follows 的 de is often left out when its antecedent (节日 jiérì, in this case) has appeared in the prior context or is understood. Other examples include:

> A: 你 要 坐 八 点 的火车 还是 九 点 的火车?
> Nǐ yào zuò bā diǎn de huǒchē háishi jiǔ diǎn de huǒchē?
> Are you going to take the 8 o'clock train or the 9 o'clock train.

> B: 我 要 坐 九 点 的。
> Wǒ yào zuò jiǔ diǎn de.
> I'm going to take the ī o'clock's.

A: 那 是 谁的 书？
Nà shì shuíde shū?
Whose book is that?

B: 那 是 我 朋友 的。
Nà shì wǒ péngyou de.
That's my friend's.

我想先问问中国人过不过元旦
wǒ xiǎng xiān wènwen Zhōngguórén guò bu guò yuándàn

如果 rúguǒ is equivalent to *if* when used to indicate a condition, but 如果 rúguǒ can't be used where *if* indicates a form of yes/no question, meaning *whether* as in the sentence cited. The whole sentence means *I'd like to ask if the Chinese celebrate the (Western) New Year.* Similar examples include:

我 想 知道 你明天 来不来。
Wǒ xiǎng zhīdào nǐ míngtiān lái bu lái.
I'd like to know if you are coming tomorrow.

学生们 问 老师 这 个 星期 有 没 有 考试。
Xuéshengmen wèn lǎoshī zhè ge xīngqī yǒu méi yǒu kǎoshì.
Students ask the teacher if there is an exam this week.

In both of the above sentences, 如果 rúguǒ can't be used. The question is indicated by the yes/no question format: 来不来 lái bu lái and 有没有 yǒu méi yǒu.

虽然圣诞节不是中国人的节日，但是现在有的人也过这个节日
Suīrán Shèngdàn jié yě bú shì Zhōngguórén de jiérì, dànshì xiànzài yǒude rén yě guò zhè ge jiérì

It is ungrammatical in English to use *although* in one clause (subordinate clause) when *but* appears in the other clause (main clause), but it is perfectly grammatical to use 虽然 suīrán in conjunction with 但是 dànshì in Chinese. In fact, they are usually used in the same sentence such as:

虽然 大家都 很 累， 但是 没 有 人 想 休息。
Suīrán dàjiā dōu hěn lèi, dànshì méi yǒu rén xiǎng xiūxi.
Although everyone was tired, no one wanted to rest.

虽然 情人节 不 是 中国　　　的节日，但是 越来越
Suīrán Qíngrénjié bú shì Zhōngguó de jiérì,　　dànshì yuèláiyuè
多 的年轻人　　现在 过这 个 节日。
duō de niánqīngrén xiànzài guò zhè ge jiérì.
Although Valentine's Day is not a Chinese festival, more and
more young people are now celebrating it.

When the 虽然 suīrán clause and the 但是 dànshì clause share the same
subject, the subject in the 但是 dànshì clause is usually left out:

他们　虽然 离了婚，但是 还 是 好 朋友。
Tāmen suīrán lí le hūn, dànshì hái shì hǎo péngyou.
Although they are divorced, they remain good friends.

她 虽然 只学 了 半 年 的 中文，　　但是 已经 说
Tā suīrán zhǐ xué le bàn nián de Zhōngwén, dànshì yǐjīng shuō
得很 流利了。
de hěn liúlì le.
Although she has only studied Chinese for half a year, she
already speaks it fairly fluently.

红包里装着钱 hóngbāo lǐ zhuāng zhe qián

着 zhe in the sentence indicates the continuous state of an action:

门　开 着。
Mén kāi zhe.
The door is open.

杯子 在 桌子 上　 放 着。
Bēizi zài zhuōzi shang fàng zhe.
The cups are lying on the table.

树 上　 摆 着 各种各样　 的装饰品。
Shù shang bǎi zhe gèzhònggèyàng de zhuāngshìpǐn.
On the tree decorations are displayed.

Contrast these with:

门　开 了。
Mén kāi le.
The door was opened.

他 把 杯子 放 在 桌子 上。
Tā bǎ bēizi fàng zài zhuōzi shang.
He put the cups on the table.

我 太太 把 装饰品　 摆 在 树 上。
Wǒ tàitai bǎ zhuāngshìpǐn bǎi zài shù shang.
My wife put decorations on the tree.

In these three sentences, the verbs indicate pure actions.

The negative form of a verb followed by 着 zhe is 没有 méiyǒu + verb:

门 没有 开 着。
Mén méiyou kāi zhe.
The door is not open.

杯子 没有 在 桌子 上　 放 着。
Bēizi méiyou zài zhuōzi shang fàng zhe.
The cup is not lying on the table.

树 上　 没有 摆 着 装饰品。
Shù shang méiyou bǎi zhe zhuāngshìpǐn.
On the tree decorations are not displayed.

Chinese zodiac signs

Each Chinese lunar year is associated with a zodiac animal. People who
are born in the same year share the same animal sign. There are altogether
twelve animals that form a cycle. See the graph on the following page for
the twelve animals and the lunar years that are associated with them.

Another easy way to find your zodiac sign is to enter your date of birth at
this website and it will tell you what your sign is:

http://www.chinesezodiac.com/calculator.php

Like the Western zodiac signs, Chinese zodiac animals are associated with
certain attributes. For example, people who are born in the year of the
horse are said to be youthful, intellectual and charming, but also impatient
and reckless at times. The above website also lists the attributes for all the
animal signs.

你今年多大 nǐ jīnnián duō dà?

There are a number of ways in Chinese to ask someone's age depending on who you ask. The most common and useful question form is 你多大 nǐ duō dà (*how old are you*) or 你今年多大 nǐ jīnnián duō dà (*how old are you this year*), which can be used for almost anyone. There are two other forms used when we ask the age of children and old people. For children, the question form is 你几岁 nǐ jǐ suì, and that for old people is 你多大年纪 nǐ duō dà niánjì. Since 你多大年纪 nǐ duō dà niánjì suggests an advanced age, it is not appropriate to use for people of other age groups.

Snake	Horse	Goat	Monkey
2001 1989	2002 1990	2003 1991	2004 1992
1977 1965	1978 1966	1979 1967	1980 1968
1953 1941	1954 1942	1955 1943	1956 1944
1929 1917	1930 1918	1931 1919	1932 1920
Rooster	**Dog**	**Pig**	**Rat**
2005 1993	2006 1994	2007 1995	2008 1996
1981 1969	1982 1970	1983 1971	1984 1072
1957 1945	1958 1946	1959 1947	1960 1948
1933 1921	1934 1922	1935 1923	1936 1924
Ox	**Tiger**	**Rabbit**	**Dragon**
2009 1997	2010 1998	2011 1999	2000 1988
1985 1973	1986 1974	1987 1975	1976 1964
1961 1949	1962 1950	1963 1951	1952 1940
1937 1925	1938 1926	1939 1927	1928 1916

EXERCISES

Answer key, pages 282-284

I. Answer the following questions:

1. 对 中国人　来说，什么 节日最 重要？
   Duì Zhōngguórén lái shuō, shénme jiérì　zuì zhòngyào?

   _____

2. 对 你来 说，什么　节日最 重要？
   Duì nǐ　lái shuō, shénme jiérì　zuì zhòngyào?

   _____

3. 你知道 明年　的中国　　新 年 是几月几号 吗？
   Nǐ zhīdào míngnián de Zhōngguó Xīn Nián shì jǐ yuè jǐ　hào ma?

   _____

4. 中国人　　过 年 时，一般 做 什么？
   Zhōngguórén guò nián shí,　yìbān zuò shénme?

   _____

5. 你过不过 圣诞节？　怎么 过？
   Nǐ guò bu guò Shèngdànjié? Zěnme guò?

   _____

6. 中国　的国庆节　是什么　时候？
   Zhōnguó de Guóqìngjié shì shénme shíhou?

   _____

7. 你们 元旦　放 不 放 假？放 几天 假？
   Nǐmen Yuándàn fàng bu fàng jià?　Fàng jǐ tiān jià?

   _____

8. 中秋节　时，中国人　都 要 吃什么？ 为什么？
   Zhōngqiūjié shí,　Zhōngguórén dōu yào chī shénme? Wèishénme?

   _____

9. 你 知道 明年　的中国　　新 年 是什么　年 吗?
　　Nǐ zhīdào míngnián de Zhōngguó Xīn Nián shì shénme nián ma?

_____

10. 你 属 什么?
　　Nǐ shǔ shénme?

_____

II. How do you say the following in Chinese?:

1. Five characters are written on the blackboard.

_____

2. The dinner is laid on the table.

_____

3. Ten books are being carried in the bag.

_____

4. A map of the world is hanging on the wall.

_____

5. A lot of cups and plates are loaded in the car.

_____

6. Please ask him if he is a student.

_____

7. Could you tell me if there is a hospital here?

_____

8. Do you know if she will be upset if we don't go?

_____

9. If Christmas falls on a Sunday, we'll also have Monday off.

_____

10. I want to know if I can exchange money at the hotel.

_____

III. In what months do the following holidays fall?
Write in Chinese in the blanks the months that the following holidays fall
in. If a holiday can be in one of two months, write both months.

1. 圣诞节   在   _____
   Shèngdànjié   zài

2. 中国   国庆节   在   _____
   Zhōngguó Guóqìngjié   zài

3. 美国   国庆节   在   _____
   Měiguó Guóqìngjié   zài

4. 元旦   在   _____
   Yuándàn   zài

5. 情人节   在   _____
   Qíngrénjié   zài

6. 中国   新 年   在   _____
   Zhōngguó Xīn Nián   zài

7. 感恩节   在   _____
   Gǎn'ēnjié   zài

8. 美国   劳动节   在   _____
   Měiguó Láodòngjié   zài

9. 中国   劳动节   在   _____
   Zhōngguó Láodòngjié   zài

10. 中秋节   在   _____
    Zhōngqiūjié   zài

IV. Write the zodiac signs of your family members, using the following pattern:

我 太太 属 鸡。
Wǒ tàitai shǔ jī.
My wife was born in the year of the chicken.

_____

_____

_____

_____

_____

V. Translate the following into Chinese:

1. For most people in America, Christmas is the most important holiday.

_____

_____

2. My favorite holiday is Thanksgiving, because our whole family will get together.

_____

_____

3. Let me say something about our company first.

_____

_____

4. Can you guess how old I am?

_____

_____

5. Can you tell me something about holidays in your country?

_____

_____

6. The Chinese food in the restaurants in America is not the same as that in the restaurants in China.

_____

_____

7. I'm not in the habit of drinking.

_____

_____

8. Chinese New Year is also called Spring Festival (春节 Chūnjié).

_____

_____

9. Many people in China now celebrate Christmas, although it is not a Chinese holiday.

_____

_____

10. Children in China especially like the New Year, because they can receive a lot of red envelopes that day.

_____

_____

VI. Translate the following into English:

1. 我 弟弟比 我 小 十二 岁，我们 都 属羊。
   Wǒ dìdi bǐ wǒ xiǎo shíèr suì,   wǒmen dōu shǔ yáng.

_____

_____

2. 中国人   过 年 的 时候，没 有 交换 礼物的 习惯。
   Zhōngguórén guò nián de shíhou,   méi yǒu jiāohuàn lǐwù de xíguàn.

_____

_____

3. 以前 中国   新 年 时，人们 都 说 "恭喜 发财"。
   Yǐqián Zhōngguó Xīn Nián shí,   rénmen dōu shuō "Gōngxǐ fācái."
   现在 人们 常 说 "新 年 好"。它们的 意思都
   Xiànzài rénmen cháng shuō "Xīn Nián hǎo." Tāmende yìsī dōu
   一样。
   yíyàng.

_____

_____

4. 中国　　的劳动节　在五月一号。美国　的劳动节
Zhōngguó de Láodòngjié zài wǔ yuè yī hào. Měiguó de Láodòngjié
在九月的第一个星期一。
zài jiǔ yuè de dì yī ge xīngqī yī.

_____

_____

5. 在中国，　以前中秋节　不放假，现在　放一天
Zài Zhōngguó, yǐqián Zhōngqiūjié bú fàngjià, xiànzài fàng yì tiān
假。
jià.

_____

_____

6. 美国人　庆祝　各种各样　的节日。
Měiguórén qìngzhù gèzhònggèyàng de jiérì.

_____

_____

7. 我最喜欢九月。九月的节日最多。
Wǒ zuì xǐhuān jiǔ yuè. Jiǔ yuè de jiérì zuì duō.

_____

_____

8. 节日时，中国人　喜欢进城，美国人喜欢出
Jiérì shí, Zhōngguórén xǐhuan jìn chéng, Měiguórén xǐhuan chū
城。
chéng.

_____

_____

9. 亚洲的很多国家也庆祝中国　新年。
Yàzhōu de hěn duō guójiā yě qìngzhù Zhōngguó Xīn Nián.

_____

_____

10. 我已经用完了今年的假了。
Wǒ yǐjīng yòng wán le jīnnián de jià le.

_____

_____

VII. Topics for discussion/writing:

1. 请 介绍 一下儿你最 喜欢 的节日。

   Qǐng jièshào yíxiàr　　nǐ zuì xǐhuan de jiérì.

2. 请 介绍 一下儿 你们 国家 最 重要　的节日。

   Qǐng jièshào yíxiàr　　nǐmen guójiā zuì zhòngyào de jiérì.

ENGLISH TRANSLATION OF THE TEXT

Conversations (*pages 148-150*)

A: Can you tell me something about holidays in China?
B: Sure, but there are many holidays in China. We can only talk about the important ones.
A: Okay. I'd like to first ask if Chinese people celebrate the (Western) New Year.
B: Yes, they do. But to the Chinese, the (Western) New Year is not the most important holiday. The most important holiday is the Chinese New Year.
A: When is the Chinese New Year?
B: It's different every year. Sometimes it is in January and sometimes it is in February.
A: Besides the Chinese New Year, what are some of the other important holidays?
B: October 1 is the National Day. The entire country gets a day off.
A: Is Christmas celebrated in China?
B: No, but although Christmas is not a Chinese holiday, some people are now celebrating it.
A: I heard that there is a Zhōngqiūjié. What kind of festival is it?
B: "Zhōng" means *middle*, "qiū" means *autumn*. "Zhōngqiūjié" means *Mid-Autumn Festival*. The moon is the fullest on this day. People eat moon cake and families get together.
A: When is the Mid-Autumn Festival?
B: Like the New Year, the date for the Mid-Autumn Festival is different every year, but it usually falls in October.

*   *   *   *   *

A: Do you know when the Chinese New Year is next year?
B: The Chinese New Year next year is February 10.
A: How do the Chinese celebrate the Chinese New Year?
B: On the New Year's Eve, the whole family would get together, cooking and eating a lot of food. On New Year's Day, grown-ups will also give children red envelopes.
A: What is the red envelope?
B: The red envelopes contain money. It is a gift for children.
A: Do people exchange gifts during the New Year?
B: Chinese people do not have this custom.
A: What do Chinese people eat when they celebrate the New Year?
B: All kinds of things, but most people eat dumplings.

*   *   *   *   *

A: What (zodiac) year is next year?
B: Next year is the year of the rooster. Children born next year all have the zodiac
     sign of the rooster.
A: I don't know my sign. Could you tell me?
B: Sure. How old are you this year?
A: I'm twenty this year. I was born in 1997.
B: You are two years younger than I am. My sign is the pig. You were born in the year
     of the ox. Your sign is the ox.
A: Now I know. If you know a person's sign, you will be able to guess his age.
B: You are right. It is generally the case.

Reading Passage (*page 151*)

To many Americans, Christmas is the most important holiday of the year. Children particularly like the day because they will receive a lot of gifts. Many people place a Christmas tree in their homes. Various kinds of decorated items will then be displayed on the tree. On Christmas Eve, the whole family will get together, cooking and eating a lot of food. There is a major difference in the way Americans celebrate Christmas and the Chinese celebrate the Chinese New Year. That is, Americans have the custom of exchanging gifts. They spend a lot of time in the stores before Christmas choosing and buying presents.

LESSON 8

JOB HUNTING & INTERVIEWING

CONVERSATIONS

(English translation, pages 190-191)

A: 你 今天 怎么 没有 去上班？
Nǐ jīntiān zěnme méiyou qù shàngbān?

B: 上　个月 我 被解雇了。我 没 有 工作 了。
Shàng ge yuè wǒ bèi jiěgù le.　Wǒ méi yǒu gōngzuò le.

A: 你被解雇了？这 怎么 可能？
Nǐ bèi jiěgù le?　Zhè zěnme kěnéng?

B: 我们　公司 的 生意 不 好，所以 解雇了 很 多 人。
Wǒmen gōngsī de shēngyì bù hǎo,　suǒyǐ jiěgù le hěn duō rén.

A: 你 有 没有　找　到 新 的 工作？
Nǐ yǒu méiyou zhǎo dào xīn de gōngzuò?

B: 我 找 了一 个月，但是 还 没有　找　到。你 知道
Wǒ zhǎo le yí ge yuè,　dànshì hái méiyou zhǎo dào.　Nǐ zhīdào
哪儿要 人 吗？
nǎr　yào rén ma?

A: 你想　找 什么样　的 工作？
Nǐ xiǎng zhǎo shénmeyàng de gōngzuò?

B: 我 做 的 是秘书。我 还 想　找 秘书 的 工作。
Wǒ zuò de shì mìshū.　Wǒ hái xiǎng zhǎo mìshū de gōngzuò.
你 能　帮　我的忙　吗？
Nǐ néng bāng wǒde máng ma?

A: 我 试试看。我 去 问问　我们　公司 的 人事部。
Wǒ shìshi kàn.　Wǒ qù wènwen wǒmen gōngsī de rénshìbù.
我们　公司 可能 要 人。
Wǒmen gōngsī kěnéng yào rén.

B: 谢谢 你的 帮助。
Xièxie nǐde　bāngzhù.

A: 不 客气。 我 一有 消息 就 给你打 电话。
   Bú kèqì.　　Wǒ yì yǒu xiāoxi jiù gěi nǐ dǎ diànhuà.

* 　　* 　　* 　　* 　　*

A: 小　 王， 我们　 学校　 在 找　 一位 中文　　 老师。
   Xiǎo Wáng, wǒmen xuéxiào zài zhǎo yí wèi Zhōngwén lǎoshī.
   你有 兴趣　 吗？
   Nǐ yǒu xìngqù ma?

B: 你们 要 全职　 老师 还是 半职 老师？
   Nǐmen yào quánzhí lǎoshī háishi bànzhí lǎoshī?

A: 我们　 要 全职　 老师。
   Wǒmen yào quánzhí lǎoshī.

B: 我 对 教书 很　 有 兴趣， 可是 我 只 能　　 做 半职
   Wǒ duì jiāoshū hěn yǒu xìngqù,　kěshì wǒ zhǐ néng zuò bànzhí
   工作。
   gōngzuò.

A: 你知道 不 知道 别人 有 没 有 兴趣 教 中文？
   Nǐ zhīdào bu zhīdào biérén yǒu méi yǒu xìngqù jiāo Zhōngwén?

B: 我 可以 问问　 我的 朋友们。　 你 能　 不 能　 告诉 我
   Wǒ kěyǐ wènwen wǒde péngyoumen. Nǐ néng bu néng gàosù wǒ
   你们 学校　 的 工资　 和 福利？
   nǐmen xuéxiào de gōngzī hé fúlì?

A: 工资　 要看 学历 和 经验。我们　 提供 医疗 保险　 和
   Gōngzī yàokàn xuélì hé jīngyàn. Wǒmen tígòng yīliáo bǎoxiǎn hé
   退休金。 每　 年 有 三十 天 的假。
   tuìxiūjīn.　　Měi nián yǒu sānshí tiān de jià.

B: 好， 我 一有 消息 就 给你打 电话。你 也 可以 在
   Hǎo, wǒ yì　yǒu xiāoxi jiù gěi nǐ dǎ diànhuà. Nǐ yě kěyǐ zài
   中文　　 报纸 上　 做 一个 广告，　 一定 会 有 很
   Zhōngwén bàozhǐ shang zuò yí ge guǎnggào, yídìng huì yǒu hěn
   多 人 来 申请。
   duō rén lái shēnqǐng.

A: 好 主意。
Hǎo zhǔyì.

*   *   *   *   *

A: 我 是 来 申请 贵 公司 电脑 工程师 的 工作 的。
Wǒ shì lái shēnqǐng guì gōngsī diànnǎo gōngchéngshī de gōngzuò de.

B: 你 是 怎么 知道 我们 要 电脑 工程师 的？
Nǐ shì zěnme zhīdào wǒmen yào diànnǎo gōngchéngshī de?

A: 我 是 在 报纸 上 看 到 你们的 广告 的。
Wǒ shì zài bàozhǐ shang kàn dào nǐmende guǎnggào de.

B: 谢谢 你 对 我们 公司 的 兴趣。 你 能 介绍 一下儿
Xièxie nǐ duì wǒmen gōngsī de xìngqù.   Nǐ néng jièshào yīxiàr
你自己 吗？
nǐ zìjǐ   ma?

A: 当然。 这 是 我的 学历。我 是 去年 从 大学 毕业 的。
Dāngrán. Zhè shì wǒde xuélì.   Wǒ shì qùnián cóng dàxué bìyè   de.
毕业后 在 美国 电话 公司 工作。
Bìyè hòu zài Měiguó Diànhuà Gōngsī gōngzuò.

B: 美国 电话 公司 是 个 大 公司，你 为什么 要 离开？
Měiguó Diànhuà Gōngsī shì ge dà gōngsī,   nǐ wèishénme yào líkāi?

A: 不错，美国 电话 公司 是 个 大 公司，但是 我 做 的
Bú cuò, Měiguó Diànhuà Gōngsī shì ge dà gōngsī,   dànshì wǒ zuò de
工作 和 电脑 没 有 关系。我 想 在 贵 公司 能
gōngzuò hé diànnǎo méi yǒu guānxì.   Wǒ xiǎng zài guì gōngsī néng
有 更 多 的 机会。
yǒu gèng duō de jīhuì.

B: 你 在 大学 学 的 是 什么 专业？
Nǐ zài dàxué xué de shì shénme zhuānyè?

A: 我 学 的是 电脑。我的 学历 上　写着 我 做 过 的
Wǒ xué de shì diànnǎo. Wǒde xuélì shang xiě zhe wǒ zuò guo de
工作。
gōngzuò.

B: 你 什么　时候 能　开始 工作?
Nǐ shénme shíhou néng kāishǐ gōngzuò?

A: 三 个星期 以后。
Sān ge xīngqī yǐhòu.

B: 好。我们　会 考虑 你的 申请，　在 一个星期 里 给你
Hǎo. Wǒmen huì kǎolǜ nǐde shēnqǐng, zài yí ge xīngqī lǐ gěi nǐ
答复的。
dáfù de.

A: 谢谢。
Xièxie.

B: 你有 没 有 问题 问 我?
Nǐ yǒu méi yǒu wèntí wèn wǒ?

A: 现在　没 有。
Xiànzài méi yǒu.

READING PASSAGE

中国的学校，特别是大学，每年要找很多外国英语老师
去教英语。他们要求外国老师有大学文凭，英语是第一
语言。外国老师的工资不太高，但是他们不用付房租。
大多数学校还提供飞机票。中国的东西很便宜，所以虽
然工资不高，但是生活没有问题。很多人去中国教英语
是想用这个机会学中文和了解中国文化。外国老师一般
每星期工作十五个小时。他们教的课有口语、阅读、
作文，等等。你有兴趣去中国教英语吗？

Zhōngguó de xuéxiào, tèbié shì dàxué, měi nián yào zhǎo hěn duō wàiguó
Yīngyǔ lǎoshī qù jiāo Yīngyǔ. Tāmen yāoqiú wàiguó lǎoshī yǒu dàxué
wénpíng, Yīngyǔ shì dìyī yǔyán. Wàiguó lǎoshī de gōngzī bú tài gāo,
dànshì tāmen bú yòng fù fángzū. Dàduōshù xuéxiào hái tígòng fēijīpiào.
Zhōngguó de dōngxi hěn piányi, suǒyǐ suīrán gōngzī bù gāo, dànshì
shēnghuó méi yǒu wèntí. Hěn duō rén qù Zhōngguó jiāo Yīngyǔ shì xiǎng
yòng zhè ge jīhuì xué Zhōngwén hé liǎojiě Zhōngguó wénhuà. Wàiguó
lǎoshī yìbān měi xīngqī gōngzuò shíwǔ ge xiǎoshí. Tāmen jiāo de kè yǒu
kǒuyǔ, yuèdú, zuòwén, děngděng. Nǐ yǒu xìngqù qù Zhōngguó jiāo
Yīngyǔ ma?

(*English translation, page 191*)

NEW WORDS AND EXPRESSIONS

被	bèi	*passive marker*
解雇	jiěgù	lay off
生意	shēngyì	business
什么样	shénmeyàng	what kind of
秘书	mìshū	secretary
人事部	rénshìbù	personnel department
一 ... 就 ...	yí ... jiù ...	as soon as
消息	xiāoxi	news; word
问	wèn	ask
兴趣	xìngqu	interest
全职	quánzhí	full time
半职	bànzhí	part time
工资	gōngzi	salary
福利	fúlì	benefits
学历	xuélì	academic credentials; resume
经验	jīngyàn	experience
提供	tígòng	provide
退休金	tuìxiūjīn	pension
广告	guǎnggào	advertisement; commercial
申请	shēnqǐng	apply; application
工程师	gōngchéngshī	engineer
自己	zìjǐ	oneself; one's own
离开	líkāi	leave (*v.*)
和 ... 有关系	hé ... yǒu guānxi	have to do with ...
更	gèng	even more
考虑	kǎolù	consider
答复	dáfù	reply (*n./v.*)
要求	yāoqiu	requirement; require

房租	fángzū	rent
生活	shēnghuo	livelihood; life
了解	liáojiě	gain understanding
文化	wénhuà	culture
文凭	wénpíng	diploma; degree
阅读	yuèdú	reading

SUPPLEMENTARY WORDS AND EXPRESSIONS

需要	xūyào	need
雇主	gùzhǔ	employer
雇员	gùyuán	employee
职员	zhíyuán	staff; clerk
失业	shīyè	lose one's job; be out of work
辞职	cízhí	resign; resignation (from a job)
老板	lǎobǎn	boss
空缺	kòngquē	vacancy
面试	miànshì	(job) interview
特长	tècháng	specialty; expertise
经济	jīngjì	economy; economic; economical
条件	tiáojiàn	terms; conditions
行业	hángyè	profession; trade
退休	tuìxiū	retire

LANGUAGE POINTS

我被解雇了 wǒ bèi jiěgù le

Chinese does not make a distinction between the active voice and the passive voice. A lot depends on the context. For example, if there is no object or prior reference, 鱼吃了 yú chī le can only mean *the fish was eaten*. If there is an object, 鱼 yú would be the agent such as 大鱼吃了小鱼 dà yú chī le xiǎo yú (*the big fish ate the small fish*). There are, however, a number of passive markers in Chinese that are used to make the agent explicit in a sentence when the recipient of an action is expressed as the subject. The most common of these passive markers is 被 bèi:

> 他被老师批评了。
> Tā bèi lǎoshī pīpíng le.
> He was criticized by the teacher.

The agent can often be omitted from the sentence, but 被 bèi must be retained:

> 他被批评了。
> Tā bèi pīpíng le.
> He was criticized.

> 汽车被偷了。
> Qìchē bèi tōu le.
> The car was stolen.

Verbs used with 被 bèi or the 被 bèi phrase tend to suggest an undesirable action, as shown in the above sentences.

帮我的忙 bāng wǒde máng

"帮 bāng" and "忙 máng" in "帮我的忙 bāng wǒde máng" (*do me a favor*) are part of the word 帮忙 bāngmáng (*help*). A disyllabic word, 帮忙 bāngmáng belongs to a class of verbs in Chinese that internally consist of a verb and an object. In this case, the verb is 帮 bāng and the object is 忙 máng (literally meaning *render assistance*). Since there is already a built-in object in the verb, 帮忙 bāngmáng can't take an object. For example, we can't say 帮忙我 bāngmáng wǒ. To express the idea of *help me* or *do me a favor* by using 帮忙 bāngmáng, we'll need to say 帮我的忙 bāng wǒde máng. The three words are in the following relationship:

帮	我的	忙
bāng	wǒde	máng
verb	*attribute*	*noun object*

There is another word in the lesson that also means *help*: 帮助 bāngzhù. It differs from 帮忙 bāngmáng in that: 1) 帮忙 bāngmáng is always a verb, whereas 帮助 bāngzhù can be a verb as well as a noun; 2) when both words are used as a verb, 帮助 bāngzhù can take on object, but 帮忙 bāngmáng can't for the reason explained above; and 3) 帮忙 bāngmáng refers more to a physical act or an action that involves physical effort, whereas 帮助 bāngzhù is not restricted to physical acts. So for example, when a person lends you money to tide you over in a time of financial difficulty, or if he helps you move (house), what he does is 帮忙 bāngmáng. But if a person helps you with your Chinese or gives you advice, what he does is 帮助 bāngzhù. Below are some of the commonly used sentence patterns involving these two words:

你 能 帮 我一个 忙　吗？
Nǐ néng bāng wó yí ge máng ma?
Can you do me a favor?

你帮 了我 一个大忙。
Nǐ bāng le wǒ yí ge dà máng.
You did me a big favor.

我 一点儿忙　也 没 帮。
Wǒ yìdiǎnr máng yě méi bāng.
I didn't help at all.

你 帮 我的忙，我 帮　你的忙。
Nǐ bāng wǒde máng, wǒ bāng nǐde máng.
You help me, and I will help you.

谢谢 你的帮助。
Xièxie nǐde bāngzhù.
Thank you for your help.

没 有 你的 帮助， 我 找 不 到 工作。
Méi yǒu nǐde bāngzhù, wǒ zhǎo bú dào gōngzuò.
Without your help, I can't find a job.

我的 美国 朋友 帮助 我 学 英语。
Wǒde Měiguó péngyou bāngzhù wǒ xué Yīngyǔ.
My American friend helps me with my English.

我们 互相 帮助 吧。
Wǒmen hùxiāng bāngzhù ba.
Let's help each other.

我一有消息就给你打电话 wǒ yì yǒu xiāoxi jiù gěi nǐ dǎ diànhuà

The pattern "一 … 就 yī … jiù" is used to indicate that one action (expressed by 就 jiù) closely follows another action (expressed by 一 yī).

你一来 我 就 走。
Nǐ yì lái wǒ jiù zǒu.
As soon as you come, I'll leave.

Note that **a)** the main clause (in this case, 我就走 wǒ jiù zǒu) always follows the subordinate clause; **b)** the subject of the main clause (in this case 我 wǒ) always precedes 就 jiù instead of following it; and **c)** if the verb in the main clause shares the subject with the verb in the subordinate clause, the subject in the main clause is always left out. The sentence cited from the text is a case in point.

我对教书很有兴趣 wǒ duì jiāoshū hěn yǒu xìngqù

Both 教 jiāo and 教书 jiāoshū mean *teach*, but there is an important difference. 教 jiāo is a transitive verb and must be followed by an object, whereas 教书 jiāoshū (a verb + object structure) is an intransitive verb and cannot be followed by an object. So for *he teaches at a middle school*, we can't say 他在中学教 tā zài zhōngxué jiāo; we can only say 他在中学教书 tā zài zhōngxué jiāoshū (*he teaches at a middle school*). If there is an object in the sentence, it would be fine to use 教 jiāo: 他在中学教数学 tā zài zhōngxué jiāo shùxué (*he teaches math at a middle school*).

The Chinese structure for *to be interested in* is 对 … 有兴趣 duì … yǒu xìngqù:

> 你 对 什么 有 兴趣？
> Nǐ duì shénme yǒu xìngqù?
> What are you interested in?

> 我 对 中医 有 很 大的 兴趣。
> Wǒ duì zhōngyī yǒu hěn dà de xìngqù.
> I'm very interested in Chinese medicine.

The negative form is 对 … 没有兴趣 duì … méi yǒu xìngqù:

> 我 对音乐 没 有 兴趣。
> Wǒ duì yīnyuè méi yǒu xìngqù.
> I'm not interested in music.

贵公司 guì gōngsi

This 贵 guì is the same 贵 guì as in 您贵姓 nín guì xìng (*what is your last name*). It is an honorific prefixed to a place name to show respect to your addressee. Other examples include 贵校 guì xiào (*your school*), 贵国 guì guó (*your country*), 贵店 guì diàn (*your store*).

你能介绍一下儿你自己吗 nǐ néng jièshào yīxiàr nǐ zìjǐ ma?

自己 zìjǐ is mainly used in the following two ways:

1. Used with a personal pronoun to mean *oneself* or *one's own*:

> 我自己 wǒ zìjǐ (*myself*)
> 你自己 nǐ zìjǐ (*yourself*)
> 他自己 tā zìjǐ (*himself*)
> 我自己的房子 wǒ zìjǐ de fángzi (*my own house*)

2. Used in the sense of *by oneself* or *alone*:

> 你自己去还是 和 别人 去？
> Nǐ zìjǐ qù háishi hé biérén qù?
> Are you going alone or with somebody else?

很多人去中国教英语是想用这个机会学中文和了解中国文化
hěn duō rén qù Zhōngguó jiāo Yīngyǔ shì xiǎng yòng zhè ge jīhuì
xué Zhōngwén hé liǎojiě Zhōngguó wénhuà

Used after a verb or a verb phrase, 是 shì indicates purpose or reason. The above sentence means *many people go to teach English in China because they would like to use the opportunity to learn Chinese and understand Chinese culture.* Other examples of this usage include:

我 来 是 工作   的，不 是 玩儿 的。
Wǒ lái shì gōngzuò de,   bú shì wánr   de.
I came to work, not to play.

他 给 你 打 电话 是 想   请 你去吃饭。
Tā gěi nǐ   dǎ diànhuà shì xiǎng qǐng nǐ qù chīfàn.
He called you to invite you to go (to his place) to eat.

EXERCISES

Answer key, pages 284-286

I. Answer the following questions:

1. 你 工作 吗？你喜欢 你现在 的工作 吗？
   Nǐ gōngzuò ma? Nǐ xǐhuān nǐ xiànzài de gōngzuò ma?

---

2. 你有没有 被解雇过？你被解雇后 是怎么 找 到
   Nǐ yǒu méiyou bèi jiěgù guò? Nǐ bèi jiěgù hòu shì zěnme zhǎo dào
   工作 的？
   gōngzuò de?

---

3. 你觉得找 什么样 的工作 容易，什么样 的
   Nǐ juéde zhǎo shénmeyàng de gōngzuò róngyì, shénmeyàng de
   工作 不容易？
   gōngzuò bù róngyì?

---

4. 你找 工作 的时候，有 没有 去面试？ 他们 问
   Nǐ zhǎo gōngzuò de shíhou, yǒu méiyou qù miànshì? Tāmen wèn
   了你什么 问题？
   le nǐ shénme wèntí?

---

5. 什么样 的人可以去中国 教 英语？
   Shénmyàng de rén kěyǐ qù Zhōngguó jiāo Yīngyǔ?

---

6. 你对什么样 的电影 有 兴趣？
   Nǐ duì shénmyàng de diànyǐng yǒu xìngqù?

---

7. 在 美国，面试 的时候，雇主 不能 问 什么 问题？
   Zài Měiguó, miànshì de shíhou, gùzhǔ bù néng wèn shénme wèntí?

8. 你 现在 的工作　和你在大学学 的专业　有 没 有
   Nǐ xiànzài de gōngzuò hé nǐ zài dàxué xué de zhuānyè yǒu méi yǒu
   关系？
   guānxì?

   _____

9. 你们 单位 的 福利怎么样？　你们 有 什么 福利？
   Nǐmen dānwèi de fúlì   zěnmeyàng? Nǐmen yǒu shénme fúlì?

   _____

10. 学历 和 经验，你觉得 哪一个更　重要？
   Xuélì hé jīngyàn, nǐ juéde nǎ yī gè gèng zhòngyào?

   _____

II. How do you say the following:

1. got laid off

   _____

2. look for a job

   _____

3. found a job

   _____

4. within three months

   _____

5. in a year

   _____

6. more opportunities

   _____

7. saw the news on TV

   _____

8. very interested in music

   _____

9. not interested in swimming

_____

10. He didn't do me the favor.

_____

11. I didn't ask him to do me the favor.

_____

12. Where does your wife teach? She teaches fine arts at a college.

_____

13. Salary is commensurate with experience.

_____

14. I came here to buy, not to sell.

_____

15. This matter has nothing to do with our company.

_____

III. Change the following active sentences to passive sentences:

1. 医生　治好了病人。
   Yīshēng zhì hǎo le bìngrén.

_____

_____

2. 学生们　　把书带回家了。
   Xuéshengmen bǎ shū dài huí jiā le.

_____

_____

3. 他喝了茶。
   Tā hē le chá.

_____

_____

4. 我 爸爸 卖了他的汽车。
   Wǒ bàba mài le tāde qìchē.

_____

_____

5. 我的 女朋友　关　掉 了她的手机。
Wǒde nǚpéngyou guān diào le tāde　shǒujī.

_____

_____

6. 老板　考虑 了你的申请。
Lǎobǎn kǎolǜ le nǐde　shēnqǐng.

_____

_____

IV. Change the following passive sentences to active sentences:

1. 鱼 被 猫　吃了。
Yú bèi māo chī le.

_____

_____

2. 桌子　被 老师 拿 进来了。
Zhuōzi bèi lǎoshī ná jìn lai le.

_____

_____

3. 词典 被 他 放 在 书架上　了。
Cídiǎn bèi tā fàng zài shūjià shang le.

_____

_____

4. 圣诞节　的礼物被 孩子们 看 到 了。
Shèngdànjié de lǐwù bèi háizimen kàn dào le.

_____

_____

5. 毛衣 被 妈妈 洗了。
Máoyī bèi māma xǐ le.

_____

_____

6. 这 个 问题 已经 被 很 多 人 问 过 了。
Zhè ge wèntí yǐjīng bèi hěn duō rén wèn guo le.

_____

_____

V. Fill in the blanks with either 帮助 bāngzhù, 帮忙 bāngmáng **or a variation of them:**

1. 你 _____ 了她一个大 _____。

    Nǐ _____ le tā yí ge dà _____.

2. 我_____ 你学中文，你 _____ 我学英语。

    Wǒ _____ nǐ xué Zhōngwén, nǐ _____ wǒ xué Yīngyǔ.

3. 我 刚 来美国 的时候 英语 不好，她给了我很大

    Wǒ gāng lái Měiguó de shíhou Yīngyǔ bù hǎo, tā gěi le wǒ hěn dà

    的 _____。

    de _____.

4. 老师 要 重新   布置 教室。我们 去 _____。

    Lǎoshī yào chóngxīn bùzhī jiàoshì.   Wǒmen qù _____.

    好 不好？

    Hǎo buhǎo?

5. 谢谢 你的_____。

    Xièxie nǐde _____.

6. 你不能 _____ 他这 个_____。

    Nǐ bù néng _____ tā zhè ge _____.

VI. Translate the following into Chinese:

1. Elementary and secondary schools in New York City need a lot of English teachers.

    _____

    _____

2. I'm not interested in jobs that do not provide medical insurance.

    _____

    _____

3. Please write your expertise on your resume.

    _____

    _____

4. To some employers, experience is more important than a diploma.

   _____

   _____

5. I only did you a small favor. You don't need to give me money.

   _____

   _____

6. He has changed jobs three times in the last two years.

   _____

   _____

7. What I'm doing now has a lot to do with what I studied at college.

   _____

   _____

8. I don't have a college degree. Do you think they would hire me?

   _____

   _____

9. When are you available to start to work and how long can you commit to working here?

   _____

   _____

10. She has been looking for a job for two months, but has not found one.

   _____

   _____

VII. Translate the following into English:

1. 现在 经济 越来越 差， 很 多 雇主 在 解雇 员工。
   Xiànzài jīngjì yuèláiyuè chà, hěn duō gùzhǔ zài jiěgù yuángōng.

   _____

   _____

2. 他的 工作 虽然 工资 不 高， 但是 福利 很 好。
   Tāde gōngzuò suīrán gōngzī bù gāo, dànshì fúlì   hěn hǎo.

   _____

   _____

3. 我们 一做 决定 就会 给你 答复。
Wǒmen yí zuò juédìng jiù huì gěi nǐ dáfù.

_____

_____

4. 三 年 前 电脑 工作 很 好 找，现在 不好 找。
Sān nián qián diànnǎo gōngzuò hěn hǎo zhǎo, xiànzài bù hǎo zhǎo.

_____

_____

5. 医生 要 你 在 家 休息 是 不 想 要 你 太 累。
Yīshēng yào nǐ zài jiā xiūxi shì bù xiǎng yào nǐ tài lèi.

_____

_____

6. 我 一个 月 后 才 能 开始 给 你们 工作。
Wǒ yí ge yuè hòu cái néng kāishǐ gěi nǐmen gōngzuò.

_____

_____

7. 你 没 有 大学 文凭， 英语 不 是 你的 第一 语言，
Nǐ méi yǒu dàxué wénpíng, Yīngyǔ bú shì nǐde dìyī yǔyán,
所以 我们 不 能 考虑 你的 申请。
suǒyǐ wǒmen bù néng kǎolǜ nǐde shēnqǐng.

_____

_____

8. 他 要 你 做 的 是 给 他的 秘书 写 信。
Tā yào nǐ zuò de shì gěi tāde mìshū xiě xìn.

_____

_____

9. 面试 时 请 把 你的 文凭 带来。
Miànshì shí qǐng bǎ nǐde wénpíng dài lai.

_____

_____

10. 全职　雇员 有 退休金，半职 雇员 没 有。
Quánzhí gùyuán yǒu tuìxiūjīn,　bànzhí gùyuán méi yǒu.

_____

_____

VIII. Topics for discussion/writing:

Describe your job.

Describe a job-hunting experience of yours.

ENGLISH TRANSLATION OF THE TEXT

Conversations (*pages 170-173*)

A: Why didn't you go to work today?
B: I was laid off last month. I don't have a job anymore.
A: You were laid off? How could this be possible?
B: Business at our company is not good, so it laid off a lot of people.
A: Have you found a new job?
B: I have been looking for a month, but I have not found one yet. Do you know a place where they need people?
A: What kind of work would you like to find?
B: I worked as a secretary. I would still like to look for a secretary's job. Can you help me?
A: Let me try. I'll check with the personnel department of our company. Our company may need people.
B: Thank you for your help.
A: You are welcome. I'll call you as soon as I hear from them.

*   *   *   *   *

A: Xiao Wang, our school is looking for a Chinese teacher. Are you interested?
B: Are you looking for a full-time teacher or part-time teacher?
A: We are looking for a full-time teacher.
B: I'm very interested in teaching, but I can only work part-time.
A: Do you know someone else who might be interested in teaching Chinese?
B: I can ask my friends. Can you let me know your salary and benefits?
A: Salary is commensurate with academic credentials and experience. We provide medical insurance and pension. There are 30 vacation days a year.
B: Good. I'll call you as soon as I find something. You can also put an ad in the Chinese newspapers. I'm sure there will be many people applying.
A: Good idea.

*   *   *   *   *

A: I'm here to apply for a computer engineer's position at your company.

B: How did you learn that we need a computer engineer?

A: I saw your ad in the newspaper.

B: Thank you for your interest in our company. Can you say a few things about yourself?

A: Sure. This is my resume. I graduated from college last year. Since then, I have been working for the American Telephone Company.

B: The American Telephone is a big company. Why do you want to leave?

A: Yes, American Telephone is a big company, but the work I do there is not related to computers. I think I'll have more opportunities at your company.

B: What was your major at college?

A: I studied computer science. The work I have done is described on my resume.

B: When can you start?

A: In three weeks.

B: Good. We'll consider your application and give you a reply in a week.

A: Thank you.

B: Do you have questions for me?

A: Not for the moment.

Reading Passage (*page 174*)

Schools in China, particularly universities, are looking for a lot of foreign English teachers to teach English there every year. They require that the foreign teachers have a college degree and English as their first language. Salary for foreign teachers is not very high, but they don't have to pay rent. Additionally, most schools also provide airfare. Besides, things are very inexpensive in China. Although the salary is not high, making a living is not a problem. Many people want to teach in China in order to use this opportunity to study Chinese and understand Chinese culture. Generally, foreign teachers work fifteen hours a week. The classes that they teach include conversation, reading, writing and so on. Are you interested in teaching in China?

LESSON 9

NEWSPAPERS & INTERNET

CONVERSATIONS

(*English translation, pages 216-217*)

A: 你每 天 都 看 报 吗？
Nǐ měi tiān dōu kàn bào ma?

B: 差不多 每 天 都 看。
Chàbuduō měi tiān dōu kàn.

A: 你一般看 什么 报？
Nǐ yìbān kàn shénme bào?

B: 我 一般看 "华尔街 时报"。报 上 的内容 跟
Wǒ yìbān kàn "Huá'ěrjiē Shíbào". Bào shang de nèiróng gēn
我的 工作 有 很 大 的关系。你呢？ 你看 不看
wǒde gōngzuò yǒu hěn dà de guānxi. Nǐ ne? Nǐ kàn bu kàn
"华尔街 时报"？
"Huá'ěrjiē Shíbào"?

A: 我 很 少 看。我 对金融 没 有 兴趣。我 一般看
Wǒ hěn shǎo kàn. Wǒ duì jīnróng méi yǒu xìngqù. Wǒ yìbān kàn
"纽约 时报"。你看 不看 "纽约 时报"？
"Niǔyuē Shíbào." Nǐ kàn bu kàn "Niǔyuē Shíbào"?

B: 我 有时 也看。
Wǒ yǒushí yě kàn.

A: 你有 没有 看 今天 的 "纽约 时报"？
Nǐ yǒu méiyou kàn jīntiān de "Niǔyuē Shíbào"?

B: 没有。 我 今天很 忙，连标题 都没 有 时间 看。
Méiyou. Wǒ jīntiān hěn máng, lián biāotí dōu méi yǒu shíjiān kàn.
今天 有 什么 重要 的新闻？
Jīntiān yǒu shénme zhòngyào de xīnwén?

A: 股票 跌得很 厉害。昨天 跌了差不多 两 百 点。
Gǔpiào diē de hěn lìhai. Zuótiān diē le chābuduō liǎng bǎi diǎn.

B: 你 担心 不 担心？
Nǐ dānxīn bù dānxīn?

A: 我 很 担心。我 有 很 多 股票。
Wǒ hěn dānxīn. Wǒ yǒu hěn duō gǔpiào.

＊　　＊　　＊　　＊　　＊

A: 你 喜欢 看 星期天 的 报纸 吗？
Nǐ xǐhuan kàn xīngqītiān de bàozhǐ ma?

B: 喜欢。其实我只 看 星期天 的 报纸。平常　 太 忙，
Xǐhuan. Qíshí wǒ zhǐ kàn xīngqītiān de bàozhǐ. Píngcháng tài máng,
没 有 时间 看 报。
méi yǒu shíjiān kàn bào.

A: 星期天 的 报纸 内容 太 多，你 都 看 吗？
Xīngqītiān de bàozhǐ nèiróng tài duō, nǐ dōu kàn ma?

B: 我 不都 看。除了 国际, 国内 新闻，我 大多 看 体育
Wǒ bù dōu kàn. Chúle guójì, guónèi xīnwén, wǒ dàduō kàn tǐyù
消息。你呢，你喜欢 看 星期天 的报纸 吗？
xiāoxi. Nǐ ne, nǐ xǐhuan kàn xīngqītiān de bàozhǐ ma?

A: 我 不太喜欢。我 只看 标题。我 觉得 里面 的
Wǒ bú tài xǐhuan. Wǒ zhǐ kàn biāotí. Wǒ juéde lǐmiàn de
广告　 太 多。
guǎnggào tài duō.

B: 是 这样。我 买 了星期天 的 报纸 后 做 的第一件
Shì zhèyàng. Wǒ mǎi le xīngqītiān de bàozhǐ hòu zuò de dì yī jiàn
事 就是把 广告　 扔　 掉。
shì jiù shì bǎ guǎnggào rēng diào.

＊　　＊　　＊　　＊　　＊

A: 我 想 去 中国 学 中文。 你 能 给 我 介绍 一
Wǒ xiǎng qù Zhōngguó xué Zhōngwén. Nǐ néng gěi wǒ jièshào yí
个学校 吗？
ge xuéxiào ma?

B: 中国 的很 多 大学 给外国 学生 开中文 课。
Zhōngguó de hěn duō dàxué gěi wàiguó xuésheng kāi Zhōngwén kè.
我 离开 中国 已经 很 多 年 了，对 它们 也不
Wǒ líkāi Zhōngguó yǐjīng hěn duō nián le, duì tāmen yě bù
很 熟悉。
hěn shúxī.

A: 我 怎么 能 找 到 这些 学校 的资料 呢？
Wǒ zěnme néng zhǎo dào zhèxiē xuéxiào de zīliào ne?

B: 你可以上 网 去查。每个大学 都 有 网站。
Nǐ kěyǐ shàng wǎng qù chá. Měi ge dàxué dōu yǒu wǎngzhàn.

A: 你 知道它们的 网站 地址吗？
Nǐ zhīdào tāmende wǎngzhàn dìzhǐ ma?

B: 我 知道 一些。我 回家查一下，发 电子信 告诉你，
Wǒ zhīdào yìxiē. Wǒ huí jiā chá yíxià, fā diànzǐxìn gàosù nǐ,
好 不 好？
hǎo bu hǎo?

A: 好，谢谢 你。
Hǎo, xièxie nǐ.

B: 对 了，你打算 什么 时候去中国 学 中文？
Duì le, nǐ dǎsuan shénme shíhou qù Zhōngguó xué Zhōngwén?

A: 我 打算 放 了假 就去。
Wǒ dǎsuan fàng le jià jiù qù.

*   *   *   *   *

A: 你 爸爸 妈妈 也 在 美国　吗？
Nǐ bàba māma yě zài Měiguó ma?

B: 不 在，他们 在 中国。
Bú zài,　tāmen zài Zhōngguó.

A: 你 常　给 他们 写 信 吗？
Nǐ cháng gěi tāmen xiě xìn ma?

B: 以前 常　写，我现在　一般 打 电话 或 写 电子信。
Yǐqián cháng xiě, wǒ xiànzài yìbān dǎ diànhuà huò xiě diànzǐxìn.

A: 你爸爸 妈妈 也会 写 电子信 吗？
Nǐ bàba māma yě huì xiě diànzǐxìn ma?

B: 会，就 连 我 爷爷，奶奶 也 会 写。
Huì,　jiù lián wǒ yéye,　nǎinai yě huì xiě.

A: 你给 他们 写 电子信 的 时候 用 中文　还是 英语？
Nǐ gěi tāmen xiě diànzǐxìn de shíhou yòng Zhōngwén háishi Yīngyǔ?

B: 他们 不 懂 英语，我 用 中文　给 他们 写，但是
Tāmen bù dǒng Yīngyǔ, wǒ yòng Zhōngwén gěi tāmen xiě,　dànshì
我 给 朋友　写 的时候，用　英语。
wǒ gěi péngyou xiě de shíhou, yòng Yīngyǔ.

A: 我 能　用 中文　给你写电子信 吗？
Wǒ néng yòng Zhōngwén gěi nǐ xiě diànzǐxìn ma?

B: 你 如果 用 中文　给我写电子信 就太 好 了！
Nǐ rúguǒ yòng Zhōngwén gěi wǒ xiě diànzǐxìn jiù tài háo le!

READING PASSAGE

互联网和电子信给我们带来了很大的方便，现在我们可
以在网上查资料，买东西，看报，聊天等等。以前我们
跟国外的朋友联系的时候要写信或打电话。信在路上要
走很多天，打电话又很贵。但是现在写电子信就可以了。
没有电脑的人可以去网吧。中国的每个城市都有网吧，
也很便宜，所以很方便。

Hùliánwǎng hé diànzǐxìn gěi wǒmen dài lai le hěn dà de fāngbiàn, xiànzài
wǒmen kěyǐ zài wǎng shang chá zīliào, mǎi dōngxī, kàn bào, liáotiān děngǐ
deng. Yǐqián wǒmen gēn guówài de péngyou liánxì de shíhou yào xiě xìn
huò dǎ diànhuà. Xìn zài lù shang yào zǒu hěn duō tiān, dǎ diànhuà yòu
hěn guì. Dànshì xiànzài xiě diànzǐxìn jiù kěyǐ le. Méi yǒu diànnǎo de rén
kěyǐ qù wǎngbā. Zhōngguó de měi ge chéngshì dōu yǒu wǎngbā, yě hěn
piányi, suǒyǐ hěn fāngbiàn.

(*English translation, page 217*)

NEW WORDS AND EXPRESSIONS

华尔街	Huá'ěrjiē	Wall Street
时报	Shíbào	(newspaper title) Times
内容	nèiróng	content
金融	jīnróng	finance
连	lián	even
标题	biāotí	headline
新闻	xīnwén	news
股票	gǔpiào	stockS
跌	diē	fall (*v.*)
厉害	lìhai	terrible; formidable
担心	dānxīn	worry
其实	qíshí	actually
平常	píngcháng	ordinarily; generally
国际	guójì	international
国内	guónèi	domestic; national
扔掉	rēng diào	throw away
开	kāi	offer; start (a class or a business)
熟悉	shúxi	familiar
查	chá	check; consult; look up
网站	wǎngzhàn	website
发	fā	send email, text message, etc.
电子信	diànzǐxìn	email
爷爷	yéye	(paternal) grandfather
奶奶	nǎinai	(paternal) grandmother
得	děi	have to
互联网	hùliánwǎng	the Internet
资料	zīliào	information; data; material
聊天	liáotiān	chat

| 国外 | guówài | overseas; abroad |
| 网吧 | wǎngbā | Internet café |

SUPPLEMENTARY WORDS AND EXPRESSIONS

订	dìng	subscribe to
日报	rìbào	(newspaper title) Daily
电子报	diànzǐbào	e-paper
报摊	bàotān	newspaper stand
记者	jìzhě	reporter
社论	shèlùn	editorial
商业	shāngyè	business; commerce
杂志	zázhì	magazine
文章	wénzhāng	article
报道	bàodǎo	report (*n.*)
篇	piān	*classifier* (for articles, reports)
无线	wúxiàn	wireless
上网	shàngwǎng	go on Internet; get online
网址	wǎngzhǐ	web address
搜索	sōusuǒ	search

LANGUAGE POINTS

连标题都没有时间看 lián biāotí dōu méi yǒu shíjiān kàn

连 lián in the sense of *even* is usually used in conjunction with 也 yě, 都 dōu, or 还 hái to form a special construction: 连 lián ... 也 yě/都 dōu/还 hái to give prominence to the item following 连 lián. This item can be the subject or the object of the sentence:

连 我 都 会 做饭。
Lián wǒ dōu huì zuòfàn.
Even I can cook.

我的 美国 朋友 连 上海话 都 会 说。
Wǒde Měiguó péngyou lián Shànghǎihuà dōu huì shuō.
My American friend can even speak Shanghai dialect.

连 lián can be intensified by another adverb, such as 就 jiù:

就 连 我 爷爷，奶奶 也 会 写 电子信。
Jiù lián wǒ yéye,   nǎinai yě huì xiě diànzǐxìn.
Even my grandfather and grandmother can write email.

The sentence cited at the beginning (连标题都没有时间看 lián biāotí dōu méi yǒu shíjiān kàn) is an example where the item highlighted is the object of the sentence. It means *(I) don't even have time to read the headlines.*

我不都看 wǒ bù dōu kàn

The position of the negative word in Chinese is very important. Negation extends to the section of the sentence that lies to the right of the negative word, but not the section that lies to the left of the negative word. 我不都看 wǒ bù dōu kàn means *I don't read all of them;* whereas 我都不看 wǒ dōu bù kàn would mean *I read none of them.* This explains why the following sentence for *my wife doesn't work in a school* is incorrect:

我 太太在 学校 不工作。
Wǒ tàitai zài xuéxiào bù gōngzuò.

What we should negate in the sentence is 在学校 zài xuéxiào, but since the phrase lies to the left of the negative word, it is not negated. What gets negated by mistake is the verb 工作 gōngzuò. If we force an interpretation, the sentence would mean *my wife is in school, but she doesn't work*—implying that she does something else. The correct sentence should therefore be:

我 太太不 在学校　工作。
Wǒ tàitai bú zài xuéxiào gōngzuò.

This explains why in the sentence that contains a complement of result, the negative word appears before the complement instead of the verb. For example:

他修 不好 你的 汽车。
Tā xiū bù hǎo nǐde qìchē.
He can't fix your car.

The logic is that he performed the action of repairing, but didn't produce the result.

Similarly, for the English sentence *I don't think he will come*, the Chinese is:

我 想　他不会 来。
Wǒ xiǎng tā bú huì lái.

Again, note the position of the negative word 不 bù. It is illogical to the Chinese to put *don't* before *think*. To do so would imply that the thinking didn't even take place. If you didn't even think, how could you know he was not coming?

In the sentence cited: 我不都看 wǒ bù dōu kàn (*I don't read all*), the object (*newspaper*) didn't appear because it appeared earlier. If it is to appear in the sentence, it cannot be placed after the verb 看 kàn. The general rule is that when 都 dōu refers to the object, the object must be placed at the beginning of the sentence:

In response to a question such as:

你喜欢 米饭 还是 面条?
Nǐ xǐhuan mǐfàn háishi miàntiáo?
Do you like rice or noodles?

The object is always left out:

我 都 喜欢。
Wǒ dōu xǐhuan.
I like both.

Or:

我 都 不 喜欢。
Wǒ dōu bù xǐhuan.
I like neither.

It is ungrammatical to say:

我 都 喜欢 米饭 和 面条。
Wǒ dōu xǐhuan mǐfàn hé miàntiáo.
I like both rice and noodles.

The only way to include the object in the sentence is to relocate it to the beginning of the sentence:

米饭 和 面条 我 都 喜欢。
Mǐfàn hé miàntiáo wǒ dōu xǐhuan.

However, when 都 dōu refers to the subject, the relocation of the object is not needed:

我 和我 太太 都 喜欢 面条。
Wǒ hé wǒ tàitai dōu xǐhuan miàntiáo.
Both my wife and I like noodles.

新闻 xīnwén and 消息 xiāoxi

These two words are often used interchangeably to mean *news* as transmitted by mass media, but there are three main differences between them. First, 新闻 xīnwén is more inclusive than 消息 xiāoxi. It can be long or short, but 消息 xiāoxi usually refers to brief news dispatches, flashes, or releases. Second, a news report (新闻报道 xīnwén bàodào) can not only take the forms of printed language or spoken language, but also of pictures, photos, videos, etc. 消息 xiāoxi, on the other hand, can only take the form of printed or spoken language. Third, 消息 xiāoxi can be used in the sense of *information* or *word* such as:

> 你 有 没 有 他的消息?
> Nǐ yǒu méi yǒu tāde   xiāoxi?
> Do you have any news about him?

新闻 xīnwén does not have this sense.

把广告扔掉 bǎ guǎnggào rēng diào

掉 diào is a verb often used as a complement after a verb to indicate the result, suggesting a clean break. It is very similar to *off* and *away* in the English expressions: *wash off the dirt*, *turn off the cell phone*, and *throw away the garbage*. Chinese examples include:

> 关 掉 手机
> guān diào shǒujī
> turn off the cell phone

> 扔 掉 垃圾
> rēng diào lājī
> throw away the garbage

> 客人 走 掉 了。
> Kèrén zǒu diào le.
> The guest has left.

发电子信 fā diànzǐxìn

Note that the verb for *send* varies depending on what is sent. If what is sent is a regular letter, the verb is 寄 jì. If what is sent is a fax, text message, or email, the verb is 发 fā.

爷爷 yéye, 奶奶 nǎinai

Chinese kinship terminology belongs to a system where each relative is called by a different term. It is much more complicated than that in English, where different types of kin are often called by the same term. Other than the terms for the nuclear family, which we have already learned, here are a few more terms for members of the extended family. The distinction between father's family and mother's family is an important one. The terms below are grouped under these two families:

On father's side:	On mother's side:
爷爷 yéye grandfather	外公 wàigōng grandfather
奶奶 nǎinai grandmother	外婆 wàipó grandmother
伯伯 bóbo uncle (*older than father*)	舅舅 jiùjiu uncle
叔叔 shūshu uncle (*younger than father*)	
婶婶 shěnshen aunt	姨姨 yíyi aunt

Hopefully, you have noticed at least two things from the above list. First, uncles on the father's side have to be distinguished in terminology by seniority in relation to one's father, whereas no such distinction is maintained for uncles on the mother's side. Second, no seniority distinction is made for aunts on either the father's side or the mother's side. What conclusion can we draw from this observation? This reveals that in Chinese culture, relatives on the father's side are considered more important than relatives on the mother's side and male relatives are more important than female relatives. This is a phenomenon we call "cultural emphasis," where there are more terms for things considered culturally important.

对了，你打算什么时候去中国学中文？
duì le, nǐ dǎsuan shénme shíhou qù Zhōngguó xué Zhōngwén?

对了 duì le is used at the beginning of a sentence in a conversation to introduce a new topic or an afterthought about a topic previously brought up.

我打算放了假就去 **wǒ dǎsuan fàng le jià jiù qù.**

了 le in the sentence indicates the completion of an action either in the past or in the future. The pattern of this sentence:

$$S + V_1 + 了\ le + (O) + (S) + (就\ jiù)\ V_2$$

This pattern suggests that V_2 will take place after V_1. If the connection is immediate, 就 jiù will be used. If both verbs share the same subject, it is always left either before V_1 or V_2. Other examples include:

今天 下 了班 我 要 去 同事 的家。
Jīntiān xià le bān wǒ yào qù tóngshì de jiā.
I'm going to my colleague's home after I get off work.

昨天 晚上 我看 了电影 就 回 家了。
Zuótiān wǎnshang wǒ kàn le diànyǐng jiù huí jiā le.
I went home right after I saw the movie last night.

This pattern is similar in meaning to the following we have learned, but it is used more frequently in colloquial speech:

$$S + V_1 + (O) + 以后\ yǐhòu, (S) + (就\ jiù)\ V_2$$

The sentence cited would be like this, using this pattern:

我 打算 放假 以后 就去。
Wǒ dǎsuan fàngjià yǐhòu jiù qù.
I'm planning to go right after vacation begins.

Note that in this pattern, 了 le is often not used after V_1 because the completion of the action is made explicit by the time word 以后 yǐhòu.

EXERCISES

Answer key, pages 286-289

I. Answer the following questions:

1. 你 每 天 看 报 吗? 你平常　　看 什么　报?
   Nǐ měi tiān kàn bào ma? Nǐ píngcháng kàn shénme bào?

   _____

2. 你 对报 上　的什么　内容　有 兴趣?
   Nǐ duì bào shang de shénme nèiróng yǒu xìngqù?

   _____

3. 你 今天 看 报了 吗? 今天 报 上　有 什么　重要
   Nǐ jīntiān kàn bào le ma? Jīntiān bào shang yǒu shénme Zhòngyào
   的 新闻?
   de xīnwén?

   _____

4. 你 订 杂志 吗? 你 一般 喜欢 看 什么　杂志?
   Nǐ dìng zázhì ma? Nǐ yìbān xǐhuan kàn shénme zázhì?

   _____

5. 你 每 天 都 收到　很 多 电子 广告　吗?
   Nǐ měi tiān dōu shōudào hěn duō diànzǐ guǎnggào ma?

6. 你 今天 看 电视 了吗? 今天 有 什么　新闻?
   Nǐ jīntiān kàn diànshì le ma? Jīntiān yǒu shénme xīnwén?

   _____

7. 你 每 天 都 写 电子信 吗? 给 谁 写?
   Nǐ měi tiān dōu xiě diànzixìn ma? Gěi shuí xiě?

   _____

8. 你 会 用 中文　　写 电子信 吗?
   Nǐ huì yòng Zhōngwén xiě diànzixìn ma?

   _____

9. 你在网 上 买 过 东西 吗? 买 过 什么 东西?
   Nǐ zài wǎng shang mǎi guo dōngxi ma?   Mǎi guo shénme dōngxi?
   你觉得 方便 不 方便?
   Nǐ juéde fāngbiàn bu fāngbiàn?

   _____

   _____

10. 在 网 上 学 外语 是 不 是 一个好 方法?
    Zài wǎng shang xué wàiyǔ shì bu shì yí ge hǎo fāngfǎ?

   _____

II. How do you say the following in Chinese?

1. local news; national news; international news; front-page news

   _____

   _____

2. know about three hundred characters

   _____

3. work out almost every day

   _____

4. seldom get on the Internet

   _____

5. very familiar with Beijing

   _____

6. movie about China; book about Japan

   _____

   _____

7. throw away the old newspaper

   _____

8. I actually have not heard of that place.

   _____

9. He is worried that he might be laid off.

   _____

10. The stocks rose (涨 zhǎng) dramatically yesterday.

___

III. Insert the negative word in the appropriate places according to translations given.

(*You may need to make necessary changes after inserting the negative word.*)

1. 我 在 家 吃 中饭。
   Wǒ zài jiā chī zhōngfàn.
   I don't eat lunch at home.

___

2. 他 中文　说 得 流利。
   Tā Zhōngwén shuō de liúlì.
   He doesn't speak fluent Chinese.

___

3. 医生　治 好 了 这 个 病。
   Yīshēng zhì hǎo le zhè ge bìng.
   The doctor can't cure this disease.

___

4. 书 在 桌子 上　放 着。
   Shū zài zhuōzi shang fàng zhe.
   The book is not lying on the table.

___

5. 老师　给 我 打 了 电话。
   Lǎoshī gěi wǒ dǎ le diànhuà.
   The teacher didn't call me.

___

6. 学生们　都 学习 英语。
   Xuéshengmen dōu xuéxí Yīngyǔ.
   Not all the students study English.

___

7. 大家 都 喜欢 这 个 餐馆。
Dàjià dōu xǐhuan zhè ge cānguǎn.
No one likes this restaurant.

---

8. 我 想　那儿有 医院。
Wǒ xiǎng nàr　yǒu yīyuàn.
I don't think there is a hospital there.

---

9. 我 觉得 今天 很 冷。
Wǒ juéde jīntiān hěn lěng.
I don't feel it is cold today.

---

10. 火车　开 得 快。
Huǒchē kāi de kuài.
The train does not travel fast.

IV. Translate the following into Chinese, using 都 dōu in each sentence and paying attention to its various uses:

1. I don't know all the foreign teachers at our school.

---

2. I don't know any of the foreign teachers at our school.

---

3. Our teacher gives us a quiz every day without fail.

---

4. The patient didn't eat anything today.

---

5. Both of my parents like Japanese food.

_____

_____

6. Does every company have a website?

_____

_____

**V. Translate the following into Chinese, using the 连 lián … 都 dōu/
也 yě structure:**

1. Even children know that.

_____

_____

2. I didn't even ask his name.

_____

_____

3. He can't even drive.

_____

_____

4. The doctors are so busy today that they don't even have time to eat
   lunch.

_____

_____

5. My American friend can even speak the Shanghai dialect.

_____

_____

VI. Rewrite the following senetences with the pattern:
   "S + V$_1$ + 了 le + (O) + (S) + (就 jiù) V$_2$"

1. 我 到 洛杉矶 以后 就给 你打电话。
   Wǒ dào Luòshānjī yǐhòu jiù gěi nǐ dǎ diànhuà.

_____

_____

2. 他们 结婚 以后 要 去 香港　度 蜜月。
   Tāmen jiéhūn yǐhòu yào qù Xiānggǎng dù mìyuè.

   _____

   _____

3. 你下课 以后来图书馆，好 吗?
   Nǐ xiàkè yǐhòu lǎi túshūguǎn, hǎo ma?

   _____

   _____

4. 飞机到 北京 以后 就 去上海。
   Fēijī dào Běijīng yǐhòu jiù qù Shànghǎi.

   _____

   _____

5. 我们 下班 以后 要 开会。
   Wǒmen xiàbān yǐhòu yào kāihuì.

   _____

   _____

VII. Translate the following into Chinese:

1. I only read the headlines because I'm too busy.

   _____

   _____

2. Is there any report in today's paper about their wedding?

   _____

   _____

3. Do you offer classes on Chinese history?

   _____

   _____

4. Nowadays, even young children can send email and use the Internet.

   _____

   _____

5. I'm not familiar with the city. Can you tell me something about it?

   _____

   _____

6. You may find information about the company on the Internet.

   _____

   _____

7. Many people are now doing their shopping on the Internet.

   _____

   _____

8. The email address you gave me last time is not correct.

   _____

   _____

9. My friend is now taking a Chinese class over the Internet.

   _____

   _____

10. There are more Internet cafés in China than in America.

    _____

    _____

VIII. Translate the following into English:

1. 互联网　给我们　带来了很　大的方便。　现在
   Hùliánwǎng gěi wǒmen dài lai le hěn dà de fāngbiàn. Xiànzài
   我们 在 网　上　可以看 到 中国　　的 报纸。
   wǒmen zài wǎng shang kěyǐ   kàn dào Zhōngguó de bàozhǐ.

   _____

   _____

2. 经济 好不 好 和 股票 市场 (*market*) 有　很　大的关系。
   Jīngjì hǎo bu hǎo hé gǔpiào shìchǎng   yǒu hěn dà de guānxì.

   _____

   _____

3. 我 学 中文　　已经学了两　个月 了，可是连"大"
   Wǒ xué Zhōngwén yǐjīng xué le liǎng ge yuè le,   kěshì lián "dà"
   字都 不会 写。
   zì dōu bú huì xiě.

   _____

   _____

4. 我 妈妈买 到 报纸 后 做 的第一件 事 就 是 看
Wǒ māma mǎi dào bàozhǐ hòu zuò de dì yī jiàn shì jiù shì kàn
广告。
guǎnggào.

_____

_____

5. 中国　　的很 多 网站　是 用　中文　写 的，不
Zhōngguó de hěn duō wǎngzhàn shì yòng Zhōngwén xiě de,　bù
懂　中文　的人看 不 懂。
dǒng Zhōngwén de rén kàn bù dǒng.

_____

_____

6. 她 每 天 收到 各种　电子信，但是 没有　时间
Tā měi tiān shōudào gè zhǒng diànzǐxìn,　dànshì méi yǒu shíjiān
全 看。
quán kàn.

_____

_____

7. 他 没有　收到　我 的 电子信。他给我 的 地址一定 错
Tā méiyou shōudào wǒde diànzǐxìn.　Tā gěi wǒ de dìzhǐ yídìng cuò
了。
le.

_____

_____

8. 很 多人工作　太忙，只能 在 坐 地铁上班　的
Hěn duō rén gōngzuò tài máng, zhǐ néng zài zuò dìtiě shàngbān de
时候看 报。
shíhu kàn bào.

_____

_____

9. 小 报 上　的本地 新闻 比大报 多。
Xiǎo bào shang de běndì xīnwén bǐ dà bào duō.

_____

_____

10. 我 对 股票 一点儿兴趣 也 没 有。体育新闻 更
Wǒ duì gǔpiào yìdiǎnr xìngqù yě méi yǒu. Tǐyù xīnwén gèng
有意思。
yǒuyìsī.

_____

_____

IX. Topics for discussion and writing:

1. Talk or write about a piece of news you read in today's paper or heard on TV.

2. Talk or write about your experience using the Internet.

ENGLISH TRANSLATION OF THE TEXT

Conversations (*pages 194-197*)

A: Do you read the newspaper every day?
B: Almost every day.
A: What paper do you usually read?
B: I usually read the Wall Street Journal. Its contents have a lot to do with my job.
    How about you? Do you read the Wall Street Journal?
A: I seldom read the Wall Street Journal. I'm not interested in finance and investment.
    I usually read the New York Times. Do you read the New York Times?
B: I sometimes do.
A: Did you read the New York Times today?
B: No. I'm so busy today that I don't even have time to read the headlines. Is there
    any important news there today?
A: The stocks have dropped sharply. It fell almost two hundred points yesterday.
B: Are you worried?
A: I'm very worried. I have a lot of stocks.

*   *   *   *   *

A: Do you like to read Sunday's paper?
B: Yes, I do. As a matter of fact, I only read Sunday's paper. I'm so busy during the
    week that I don't even have time to read the paper.
A: There is too much stuff in Sunday's paper. Do you read everything?
B: I don't read everything. Besides international and national news, I mostly read
    sports news. How about you? Do you like to read Sunday's paper?
A: I don't. I only read headlines. I think there are too many ads there.
B: That's true. The first thing that I do after I buy the Sunday paper is to throw away
    the ads.

*   *   *   *   *

A: I'd like to go to study Chinese in China. Can you introduce (recommend) a school
    to me?
B: Many universities in China offer Chinese classes for foreign students. I left China
    many years ago and am not familiar with the schools there.
A: How do I find information about these schools?
B: You can check on the Internet. Every university has a website.
A: Do you know their web addresses?
B: I know some. I'll check when I go home. I'll let you know by email. How does
    that sound?
A: Great, thank you.
B: By the way, when are you planning to go to study Chinese in China?

A: I'm planning to leave as soon as vacation starts.

*   *   *   *   *

A: Are your parents also in the U.S.?
B: No, they are in China.
A: Do you often write to them?
B: I often wrote them in the past, but now I usually call them or email them.
A: Do your parents also know how to write emails?
B: Yes, even my grandparents also know how to write emails.
A: Do you use Chinese or English when you write them?
B: They don't understand English, so I write them in Chinese, but when I write to my friends, I use English.
A: Can I write emails to you in Chinese?
B: If you write emails to me in Chinese, that would be excellent!

Reading Passage (*page 198*)

The Internet and email have brought us a lot of convenience. We can now check information, go shopping, read newspapers, chat and so on. When we wanted to get in touch with our friends abroad in the past, we would need to write letters and make phone calls. It took days for letters to arrive and making phone calls was also expensive. We can do this by email now. People who do not have a computer can go to the internet café. Every city in China has Internet cafés, which are quite inexpensive. For this reason, it is quite convenient.

Lesson 10

CHINA & AMERICA

CONVERSATIONS

(English translation, pages 244-245)

A: 麦克，好 久 没 见。你最近有 没 有 什么 新闻？
Màikè, hǎo jiǔ méi jiàn. Nǐ zuìjìn yǒu méi yǒu shénme xīnwén?

B: 有，我们 全 家去了中国。
Yǒu, wǒmen quán jiā qù le Zhōngguó.

A: 真的 吗？你们 玩儿 得 怎么样？
Zhēnde ma? Nǐmen wánr de zěnmeyàng?

B: 我们 玩儿得 非常 高兴。
Wǒmen wánr de fēicháng gāoxìng.

A: 这 是 你们 第一次去中国 吗？
Zhè shì nǐmen dìyī cì qù Zhōngguó ma?

B: 这 是 我 和 我太太第二次去中国， 但是 对 孩子们
Zhè shì wǒ hé wǒ tàitai dì'èr cì qù Zhōngguó, dànshì duì háizimen
来 说，这 是 第一次。
lái shuō, zhè shì dìyī cì.

A: 你和你太太上 次 是 什么 时候 去中国 的？
Nǐ hé nǐ tàitai shàng cì shì shénme shíhou qù Zhōngguó de?

B: 我们 是 十年 前 去的。
Wǒmen shì shí nián qián qù de.

A: 你觉得 中国 在 这 十 年 里有 没 有 变化？
Nǐ juéde Zhōngguó zài zhè shí nián lǐ yǒu méi yǒu biànhuà?

B: 变化 太大了。很 多 我以前 去过 的地方 变 得
Biànhuà tài dà le. Hěn duō wǒ yǐqián qù guo de dìfang biàn de
完全 不 一样 了。
wánquán bù yíyàng le.

A: 你们 这 次 去了中国　　 的什么　 地方？
Nǐmen zhè cì qù le Zhōngguó de shénme dìfāng?

B: 我们　去了香港，　　 西安, 北京, 上海。
Wǒmen qù le Xiānggǎng, Xī'ān, Běijīng, Shànghǎi.

A: 这些 地方，你最喜欢 哪儿？
Zhèxiē dìfang, nǐ zuì xǐhuan nǎr?

B: 我 都喜欢。每 一个地方 都 有 自己 的特点。
Wǒ dōu xǐ huan. Měi yí ge dìfang dōu yǒu zìjǐ　de tèdiǎn.

A: 你能 不 能 说说　　它们的 特点？
Nǐ néng bu néng shuōshuo tāmende tèdiǎn?

B: 当然。香港　　 跟 纽约 一样，是 一个 国际城市，
Dāngrán. Xiānggǎng gēn Niǔyuē yíyàng, shì yí ge guójì chéngshì,
你 能 看 到 各个 国家 的人。西安 有 很 久的历史，
nǐ néng kàn dào gè ge guójiā de rén.　Xī'ān yǒu hěn jiǔ de lìshǐ,
我 最喜欢 那儿的博物馆。
wǒ zuì xǐhuan nàr　de bówùguǎn.

A: 北京　给 你留下了什么　 印象？
Běijīng gěi nǐ　liú xià le shénme yìnxiàng?

B: 北京　给 我留下了很 深 的印象。这 是 一个伟大
Běijīng gěi wǒ liú xià le hěn shēn de yìnxiàng. Zhè shì yí ge wěidà
的城市。长城　　 是 个 奇迹，故宫 也是一个非常
de chéngshì. Chángchéng shì ge qíjī,　Gùgōng yě shì yí ge fēicháng
有意思 的地方。
yǒuyìsī de dìfang.

A: 你觉得上海　 怎么样？
Nǐ juéde Shànghǎi zěnmeyàng?

B: 在 我们 去过 的 城市　中，上海　是 我 最 喜欢
Zài wǒmen qù guo de chéngshì zhōng, Shànghǎi shì wǒ zuì xǐhuan
的城市。 我 觉得上海 比中国　 别的 城市　发展
de chéngshì. Wǒ juéde Shànghǎi bǐ Zhōngguó biéde chéngshì fāzhǎn
得都 快。
de dōu kuài.

A: 你 能 不 能 说说 上海 有 什么 变化？
Nǐ néng bù néng shuōshuo Shànghǎi yǒu shénme biànhuà?

B: 上海 在 过去几年 里建了很 多 高楼，建了十
Shànghǎi zài guòqù jǐ nián lǐ jiàn le hěn duō gāo lóu, jiàn le shí
条 地铁，三 座 大桥，一条 高速 公路，一个新 机场。
tiáo dìtiě, sān zuò dàqiáo, yì tiáo gāosù gōnglù, yí ge xīn jīcháng.
建 这么 多 的 东西 在美国 至少 也要二十年。
Jiàn zhème duō de dōngxi zài Měiguó zhìshǎo yě yào èrshí nián.

A: 你 知道 上海 的City Bird 是 什么 吗？
Nǐ zhīdào Shànghǎi de City Bird shì shénme ma?

B: 不 知道，是 什么？
Bù zhīdào, shì shénme?

A: 是 "crane"。
Shì "crane".

B: 我 怎么 没 听说 过？为什么 是 "crane"？
Wǒ zěnme méi tīngshuō guo? Wèishénme shì "crane"?

A: 这 个 crane 不是 鸟，是 起重机。你 知道 吗？几年
Zhè ge crane bú shì niǎo, shì qǐzhòngjī. Nǐ zhīdào ma? Jǐ nián
前，全 世界百分之 三十 的起重机 都 在上海。
qián, quán shìjiè bǎifēn zhī sānshí de qǐzhòngjī dōu zài Shànghǎi.

B: 真 有意思。我们 打算 明年 再 去一次上海。
Zhēn yǒuyìsī. Wǒmen dǎsuan míngnián zài qù yí cì Shànghǎi.

* * * * *

A: 老 李，你 来美国 多少 年 了？
Lǎo Lǐ, nǐ lái Měiguó duōshao nián le?

B: 我 来美国 已经 三十 多 年 了。
Wǒ lái Měiguó yǐjīng sānshí duō nián le.

A: 你 一直 住 在西海岸 吗?
Nǐ yìzhí zhù zài xī hǎi'àn ma?

B: 不，我 是 三 年 前 退休 时 从 东 海岸 搬 到 西
Bù, wǒ shì sān nián qián tuìxiū shí cóng dōng hǎi'àn bān dào xī
海岸 的。
hǎi'àn de.

A: 那你 一定 对 东 海岸 和西海岸 都 很 熟悉 了。
Nà nǐ yídìng duì dōng hǎi'àn hé xī hǎi'àn dōu hěn shúxi le.

B: 我 知道 一些，不能 说 很 熟悉。你有 问题 吗?
Wǒ zhīdào yìxiē, bù néng shuō hěn shúxi. Nǐ yǒu wèntí ma?

A: 对，你能 不能 给我 介绍 一下儿东 海岸 有
Duì, nǐ néng bu néng gěi wǒ jièshào yíxiàr dōng hǎi'àn yǒu
什么 著名 的 城市?
shénme zhùmíng de chéngshì?

B: 可以。东 海岸 著名 的 城市 有 华盛顿，
Kěyǐ. Dōng hǎi'àn zhùmíng de chéngshì yǒu Huáshèngdùn,
费城， 纽约，波士顿，等等。
Fèichéng, Niǔyuē, Bōshìdùn, děngdeng.

A: 这些 城市 我 都 听说 过，特别是华盛顿，
Zhèxiē chéngshì wǒ dōu tīngshuō guo, tèbié shì Huáshèngdùn,
美国 的 首都。
Měiguó de shǒudū.

B: 美国 和中国 有 一点儿不一样。中国 的首都
Měiguó hé Zhōngguó yǒu yìdiǎnr bù yíyàng. Zhōngguó de shǒudū
在 最大的 城市，而华盛顿 比纽约 和波士顿
zài zuì dà de chéngshì, ér Huáshèngdùn bǐ Niǔyuē hé Bōshìdùn
这样 的城市 小 得多。
zhèyàng de chéngshì xiǎo de duō.

A: 是的。西海岸 有 什么 著名 的 城市?
Shì de. Xī hǎi'àn yǒu shénme zhùmíng de chéngshì?

B: 西海岸 最 著名 的 城市 有 洛杉矶，旧金山 和
Xī hǎi'àn zuì zhùmíng de chéngshì yǒu Luòshānjī, Jiùjīnshān hé
西雅图。
Xīyǎtú.

A: 旧金山 大还是 洛杉矶 大？
Jiùjīnshān dà háishi Luòshānjī dà?

B: 旧金山 大，但是 洛杉矶 更 大。
Jiùjīnshān dà,   dànshì Luòshānjī gèng dà.

A: 人口 呢？
Rénkǒu ne?

B: 旧金山 的人口 也没有 洛杉矶 的人口 多。
Jiùjīnshān de rénkǒu yě méiyou Luòshānjī de rénkǒu duō.

A: 你是 不 是 更 喜欢 洛杉矶？
Nǐ shì bu shì gèng xǐhuan Luòshānjī?

B: 不 是, 我 更 喜欢 旧金山。旧金山 夏天 没有
Bú shì, wǒ gèng xǐhuan Jiùjīnshān. Jiùjīnshān xiàtiān méiyou
洛杉矶 那么热。
Luòshānjī nàme rè.

READING PASSAGE

我虽然在旧金山住了十年，但是没有去过那儿的中国城。
上个周末我跟我的中国朋友去了一次中国城，今天我们
又去了一次。我们先去参观了中国城的博物馆，然后去
了一家书店，那里有各种各样的中文书和词典。从书店
出来后，我们又去了一家百货公司，里面有很多中国产
品，非常便宜。买完东西以后，我们去一家餐馆里吃了
Dim Sum。我以前没有见过这种吃法。我觉得很有意思。
我要介绍我的朋友们都来中国城看一看。

Wǒ suīrán zài Jiùjīnshān zhù le shí nián, dànshì méiyou qù guo nàr de
Zhōngguóchéng. Shàng ge zhōumò wǒ gēn wǒde Zhōngguó péngyou qù
le yí cì Zhōngguóchéng, jīntiān wǒmen yòu qù le yí cì. Wǒmen xiān qù
cānguān le Zhōngguóchéng de bówùguǎn, ránhòu qù le yì jiā shūdiàn, nàlǐ
yǒu gèzhònggèyàng de Zhōngwén shū hé cídiǎn. Cóng shūdiàn chū lai
hòu, wǒmen yòu qù le yì jiā bǎihuògōngsī, lǐmiàn yǒu hěn duō Zhōngguó
chǎnpǐn, fēicháng piányi. Mǎi wán dōngxi yǐhòu, wǒmen qù yì jiā cānguǎn
lǐ chī le Dim Sum. Wǒ yǐqián méiyou jiàn guo zhè zhòng chīfǎ. Wǒ juéde
hěn yǒuyìsi. Wǒ yào jièshào wǒde péngyǒumen dōu lái Zhōngguóchéng
kàn yi kàn.

(*English translation, page 245*)

NEW WORDS AND EXPRESSIONS

久	jiǔ	long time
变化	biànhuà	change (v./n.)
变	biàn	change (v.)
完全	wánquán	completely; entirely
特点	tèdiǎn	characteristic; trait; feature
印象	yìnxiàng	impression
伟大	wěidà	great
深	shēn	deep
奇迹	qíjī	miracle
故宫	gùgōng	Palace Museum / Forbidden City
发展	fāzhǎn	develop; development
建	jiàn	build; construct; erect
座	zuò	*classifier* (for bridge, building, mountain, monument, etc.)
桥	qiáo	bridge
高速公路	gāosù gōnglù	highway; expressway
至少	zhìshǎo	at least
鸟	niǎo	bird
起重机	qǐzhòngjī	crane (construction machinery)
百分之	bǎifēn zhī	percent
一直	yìzhí	all along; straight; always
海岸	hǎi'àn	coast
搬	bān	move (house or an object)
著名	zhùmíng	famous; renowned
费城	Fèichéng	Philadelphia
波士顿	Bōshìdùn	Boston
首都	shǒudū	capital (of a country)
西雅图	Xīyǎtú	Seattle

更		gèng	even more
人口		rénkǒu	population
又		yòu	again
参观		cānguān	visit
先 … 然后	xiān … ránhòu	first … then
产品		chǎnpǐn	product

SUPPLEMENTARY WORDS AND EXPRESSIONS

省	shěng	province
市	shì	city
州	zhōu	(U.S.) state
区	qū	district; borough; region; zone
长	zhǎng	head; chief
都市	dūshì	metropolis; large city
总统	zǒngtǒng	president (of a country)
总理	zǒnglǐ	prime minister; premier
主席	zhǔxí	chairman
党	dǎng	(political) party
游	yóu	tour (*v.*)
建筑	jiànzhù	architecture
家乡	jiāxiāng	hometown
景色	jǐngsè	scenery
移民	yímín	immigrant

LANGUAGE POINTS

好久没见 hǎo jiǔ méi jiàn

This is the expression that the English *long time no see* is derived from. It can also be expressed as 好久不见 hǎo jiǔ bú jiàn. In the expression, 好 hǎo is not an adjective meaning *good*, rather it is an adverb meaning *quite a few*; *quite some*; *a good number of*. It is often used before words such as 几 jǐ, 些 xiē, and 多 duō:

好 几本 日语书
hǎo jǐ běn Rìyǔ shū
several Japanese books

好 些 年
hǎo xiē nián
many years

好 多 人
hǎo duō rén
many people

你最近有没有什么新闻 Nǐ zuìjìn yǒu méi yǒu shénme xīnwén?

Questions may arise as to what type of interrogative sentence this is. It looks like a yes/no question from the phrase 有没有 yǒu méi yǒu, but there is also the presence of the question word 什么 shénme. This 什么 shénme is actually not an interrogative word. It is a pronoun with the meaning of *some, something, any,* or *anything*. The cited sentence means *have you had any news (to share) recently*. Similar examples are:

他 在 吃 什么 东西。
Tā zài chī shénme dōngxi.
He is eating something.

我 最近没有 看 什么 电影。
Wǒ zuìjìn méiyou kàn shénme diànyǐng.
I haven't seen any movies recently.

Ways to indicate comparisons

The following patterns and structures are commonly used to indicate comparisons in Chinese:

1. A + 和 hé/跟 gēn B + 一样 yíyàng

This is equivalent to "A is the same as B" in English. Since 和 hé/跟 gēn B modifies 一样 yíyàng, it is placed before it:

我的 电话 号码 和 传真   号码 一样。
Wǒde diànhuà hàomǎ hé chuánzhēn hàomǎ yíyàng.
My telephone number and my fax number are the same.

In the negative sentence, 不 bù can be placed either before 和 hé/跟 gēn or before 一样 yíyàng:

我的 专业   跟 我 女朋友   的专业 不 一样。
Wǒde zhuānyè gēn wǒ nǚpéngyou de zhuānyè bù yíyàng.

我的 专业 不 跟 我 女朋友   的专业   一样。
Wǒde zhuānyè bù gēn wǒ nǚpéngyou de zhuānyè yíyàng.
My major is not the same as my girlfriend's major.

2. A + 和 hé/跟 gēn B + 一样 yíyàng + Adj.

This is equivalent to "A is as Adj. as B" in English.

和 hé/跟 gēn B and 一样 yíyàng both modify the adjective and both are therefore placed before it. Examples include:

香港   的东西 和 上海   的东西 一样 贵。
Xiānggǎng de dōngxi hé Shànghǎi de dōngxi yíyàng guì.
Things in Hong Kong are as expensive as things in Shanghai.

中国   菜 跟 韩国 菜 一样 好吃。
Zhōngguó cài gēn Hánguó cài yíyàng hǎochī.
Chinese food tastes as good as Korean food.

The negative form of the pattern is:
A + 没有 méiyou + B (+ 那么 nàme) + Adj.

This is equivalent to "A is not as/so Adj. as B" in English. Other examples include:

旧金山 的 人口 没有 洛杉矶 的人口 多。
Jiùjīnshān de rénkǒu méiyou Luòshānjī de rénkǒu duō.
The population of San Francisco is not as large as that of Los Angeles.

今天 没有 昨天 那么热。
Jīntiān méiyou zuótiān nàme rè.
It is not so hot today as it was yesterday.

3. A + 比 bǐ B + Adj.

This is equivalent to "A is Adj. (in comparative-degree form) than B" in English.

比 bǐ in the pattern is a preposition with the meaning of *in comparison with*. Since the prepositional phrase "比 bǐ" modifies the adjective, it is placed before it. Other examples include:

我 妈妈 的身体 比我 爸爸的身体 好。
Wǒ māma de shēntǐ bǐ wǒ bàba de shēntǐ hǎo.
My mother's health is better than my father's health.

对 她来 说，法语比西班牙语 难。
Duì tā lái shuō, Fǎyǔ bǐ Xībānyáyǔ nán.
As far as she is concerned, French is more difficult than Spanish.

Note that the adjective in Chinese does not need to be further modified by words like *more* or undergo an inflectional change by affixing *–er* as in the English examples of *more beautiful*; *prettier*. The comparative meaning is indicated by the structure itself.

The adjective in A + 比 bǐ B + Adj. cannot be modified by an intensifying adverb such as 很 hěn, 非常 fēicháng or 太 tài. For example, we can't say:

北京 的 冬天 比上海 的 冬天 很 冷。
Běijīng de dōngtiān bǐ Shànghǎi de dōngtiān hěn lěng.
Beijing's winter is much colder than Shanghai's winter.

我们的　学校　比他们的 学校　太大。
Wǒmende xuéxiào bǐ tāmende xuéxiào tài dà.
Our school is much larger than their school.

However the adjective can be modified (with additional implied meanings) by the following two adverbs: 更 gèng and 还 hái:

他比我 更　高。
Tā bǐ wǒ gèng gāo.
He is even taller than I am.
(*The implied meaning is that both people are tall.*)

这 个 国家 的 人口 比那个 国家的 人口　还 多。
Zhè ge guójiā de rénkǒu bǐ nà ge guójiā de rénkǒu hái duō.
This country's population is even larger than that country's population.
(*The implied meaning is that the population in both countries is large.*)

The implied meaning is absent if the adverb is not used.

In the negative form, 不 bù is to be placed before 比 bǐ rather than the adjective.

There are three variations of the pattern A + 比 bǐ B + Adj.:

a) A + 比 bǐ B + Adj. + 得多 de duō

While the adjective cannot be modified by an intensifying adverb as pointed above, it can be followed by a complement of degree 得多 de duō, as in this pattern. 得多 de duō in the pattern functions to emphasize the adjective with the meaning of *much more*:

飞机比火车　快　得多。
Fēijī bǐ huǒchē kuài de duo.
The plane is much faster than the train.

华盛顿　比 纽约 和 波士顿 这样　的 城市
Huáshèngdùn bǐ Niǔyuē hé Bōshìdùn zhèyàng de chéngshì
小 得多。
xiǎo de duō.
Washington is much smaller than cities such as New York and Boston.

b) A + V. + 得 de + 比 bǐ B + Adj.

In this case, the comparison between two things is about the verb complement, which is in the form of an adjective:

上海　发展得比中国　别的城市　都快。
Shànghǎi fāzhǎn de bǐ Zhōngguó biéde chéngshì dōu kuài.
Shanghai has developed faster than all the other cities in China.

Note the variation of the pattern when the verb is a transitive one. In this case, the verb needs to be repeated: A + V. + O. + V. + 得 de 比 bǐ B + Adj.:

他说中文　说得比我好。
Tā shuō Zhōngwén shuō de bǐ wǒ hǎo.
He speaks Chinese better than I do.

The negative form is A + V. (+ O. + V.) + 得 de + 没有 méiyou + B (+ 那么 nàme) + Adj.

我说中文　说得没有他那么好。
Wǒ shuō Zhōngwén shuō de méiyou tā nàme hǎo.
I don't speak Chinese as well as he does.

c) A + 比 bǐ B + Adj. + Quantifier

The quantifier specifies the difference between two items:

我比我太太大三岁。
Wǒ bǐ wǒ tàitai dà sān suì.
I'm three years older than my wife.

他们公司比我们公司多五百个人。
Tāmen gōngsī bǐ wǒmen gōngsī duō wǔ bǎi ge rén.
Their company has five hundred more people than our company does.

咖啡比茶贵两毛钱。
Kāfēi bǐ chá guì liǎng máo qián.
Coffee is twenty cents more expensive than tea.

4. A + Adj., B + 更 gèng + Adj.

更 gèng (*more*) is not necessary before the adjective in A + 比 bǐ B + Adj., but there is a difference when 更 gèng is used. In 洛杉矶比旧金山大 Luòshānjī bǐ Jiùjīnshān dà (*Los Angeles is larger than San Francisco*), there is no implication that Los Angeles is large. It simply says that in comparison with San Francisco, Los Angeles is large. Maybe both cities are small. In 洛杉矶比旧金山更大 Luòshānjī bǐ Jiùjīnshān gèng dà (*Los Angeles is even larger than San Francisco*), there is clearly the implication that both cities are large.

全世界百分之三十的起重机都在上海
quán shìjiè bǎifēnzhī sānshí de qǐzhòngjī dōu zài Shànghǎi

One of the cardinal principles, mentioned in *Beginner's Chinese,* that govern the word order in Chinese is that larger units precede smaller units and general precedes specific. This is also referred to as whole preceding part. There are two examples in this lesson.

To indicate a percentage, Chinese places percent (whole) before the specific number (part): 百分之十 bǎifēn zhī shí (*10%*), 百分之九十五 bǎifēn zhī jiǔshí wǔ (*95%*). 之 zhī in the expression is a remnant of classic Chinese with the same meaning as the possessive 的 de except that it is only used in set expressions or structures.

The way to express a fraction is similar to that for percentage:

十分 之 一	五分 之 四	三分 之 二
shífēn zhī yī	wǔfēn zhī sì	sānfēn zhī èr
one-tenth	four-fifths	two-thirds

The other example in the lesson that shows the whole-part sequence is:

这些 地方，你最喜欢 哪儿？
Zhèxiē dìfang, nǐ zuì xǐhuan nǎr?
Of these places, which one do you like the most?

This is the only order possible in Chinese.

中国的首都在最大的城市，而华盛顿比纽约和波士顿这样的
城市小得多
Zhōngguó de shǒudū zài zuì dà de chéngshì, ér Huáshèngdùn bǐ
Niǔyuē hé Bōshìdùn zhèyàng de chéngshì xiǎo de duō
而 ér is a conjunction used to indicate a contrast, similar to *whereas* in
English. The above sentence means *the capital of China is in the largest
city, whereas Washington is much smaller than cities such as New York
and Boston.*

我们明年要再去上海 wǒmen míngnián yào zài qù Shànghǎi
and 今天我们又去了一次 jīntiān wǒmen yòu qù le yí cì

Both 再 zài and 又 yòu are equivalent to *again* in English, but there is an
important difference. While 再 zài indicates the intention of repeating an
action in the future, 又 yòu indicates that the repletion of the action has
already taken place. The first cited sentence means *we'll go to Shanghai
again next year* (the intended repetition has not taken place) and the second cited sentence means *we went there again today* (the repeated action
has already taken place).

EXERCISES

Answer key, pages 289-292

I. Answer the following questions:

1. 你 有 没有 去过 中国?　你 是 什么　时候 去 的?
   Nǐ yǒu méiyou qù guo Zhōngguó? Nǐ shì shénme shíhou qù de?
   你去过 中国　 的 什么　地方?
   Nǐ qù guò Zhōngguó de shénme dìfang?

   _____

   _____

2. 你去过 欧洲　吗? 你去过 欧洲　 的 什么　地方?
   Nǐ qù guo Ōuzhōu ma? Nǐ qù guo Ōuzhōu de shénme dìfang?

   _____

   _____

3. 你的家乡　 在 哪儿? 那里最近 发展 得 怎么样?
   Nǐde jiāxiāng zài nǎr?　Nàlǐ zuìjìn fāzhǎn de zěnmeyàng?

   _____

   _____

4. 你去过 中国城　　吗? 你对 中国城　　的印象
   Nǐ qù guo Zhōngguóchéng ma? Nǐ duì Zhōngguóchéng de yìnxiàng
   怎么样?
   zěnmeyàng?

   _____

   _____

5. 你觉得你住 的 城市　这 十 年 里有 没 有 变化?
   Nǐ juéde nǐ zhù de chéngshì zhè shí nián lǐ yǒu méi yǒu biànhuà?
   有 什么　变化?
   Yǒu shénme biànhuà?

   _____

   _____

6. 华盛顿　　有 什么 特点?
   Huáshèngdùn yǒu shénme tèdiǎn?

   _____

   _____

7. 上海　　这 几年 有 什么　变化?
   Shànghǎi zhè jǐ nián yǒu shénme biànhuà?

   _____

   _____

8. 北京 的什么　有名?
   Běijīng de shénme yǒumíng?

   _____

   _____

9. 你 吃 过 dim sum 吗? 你 觉得 这 种　吃法 怎么样?
   Nǐ chī guo *dim sum* ma?　Nǐ juéde zhè zhòng chīfǎ zěnmeyàng?

   _____

   _____

10. 你最近 有 没 有 什么　新闻?
    Nǐ zuìjìn yǒu méi yǒu shénme xīnwén?

   _____

   _____

II. How do you say the following in Chinese:

1. characteristics of the old architecture

   _____

   _____

2. impression of the city

   _____

   _____

3. have been to this place many times

   _____

   _____

4. in the world

_____

_____

5. at least three days

_____

_____

6. completely changed

_____

_____

7. 50%, 75%, 100%, ¼, ⅗, ⅔

_____

_____

8. have not read this book

_____

_____

9. plan to go to China again next year

_____

_____

10. went to the bank again today

_____

_____

III. Comparative sentences

A. Fill in the blanks with the appropriate adjectives:

1. 咖啡比茶 _____ 。
   Kāfēi bǐ chá _____.

2. 飞机票 比汽车票 _____ 。
   Fēijīpiào bǐ qìchē piào _____.

3. 今年 的经济比去年 的经济 _____ 得 多。
   Jīnnián de jīngjì bǐ qùnián de jīngjì _____ de duō.

4. 法国 菜 比 英国　菜 _____。
   Fǎguó cài bǐ Yīngguó cài _____.

5. 你学 开车比我学 得 _____。
   Nǐ xué kāi chē bǐ wǒ xué de _____.

B. Rewrite the following sentences using comparative structures:

1. 哥哥十岁，弟弟八岁。
   Gēge shí suì,　dìdi　bā suì.

   _____
   _____

2. 这 条 高速 公路 长，　那条 高速 公路 短。
   Zhè tiáo gāosù gōnglù cháng, nà tiáo gāosù gōnglù duǎn.

   _____
   _____

3. 我们　班 有 三十 个学生，　他们班 有 二十五个
   Wǒmen bān yǒu sānshí ge xuésheng, tāmen bān yǒu èrshí wǔ ge
   学生。
   xuésheng.

   _____
   _____

4. 这 个汉字 难，那个汉字 不 难。
   Zhè ge hànzì nán,　nà ge hànzì bù nán.

   _____
   _____

5. 他 走 得 快，我 走 得慢。
   Tā zǒu de kuài,　wǒ zǒu de màn.

   _____
   _____

6. 姐姐 写字写得好看，妹妹　写 字写 得不 好看。
   Jiějie xiě zì xiě de hǎokàn, mèimei xiě zì　xiě de bù hǎokàn.

   _____
   _____

7. 中国　的产品　便宜，日本 的 产品　贵。
Zhōngguó de chǎnpǐn piányi,　Rìběn de chǎnpǐn guì.

_____

_____

8. 我 妈妈 做 菜 做 得 好，我 爸爸 做 菜 做 得 不好。
Wǒ māma zuò cài zuò de hǎo, wǒ bàba zuò cài zuò de bù hǎo.

_____

_____

9. 今天 股票 跌得 厉害，昨天 股票 跌 得不 厉害。
Jīntiān gǔpiào diē de lìhài,　zuótiān gǔpiào diē de bú lìhài.

_____

_____

10. 我 家 有 五 口 人，他家也 有 五 口 人。
Wǒ jiā yǒu wǔ kǒu rén,　tā jiā yě yǒu wǔ kǒu rén.

_____

_____

IV. Fill in the blanks with 又 yòu or 再 zài as appropriate:

1. 你的话 我 不懂，请 你 _____ 说 一遍。
Nǐde huà wǒ bù dǒng, qǐng nǐ _____ shuō yí biàn.

2. 我 姐姐 昨天 打来一个电话，今天 _____ 打来一个
Wǒ jiějie zuótiān dǎ lái yí ge diànhuà, jīntiān _____ dǎ lái yí ge
电话。
diànhuà.

3. 他们 今年 去过 亚洲，明年 要 _____ 去一次。
Tāmen jīnnián qù guo Yàzhōu, míngnián yào _____ qù yí cì.

4. 这 本 书 我很 多 年 前 看 过，但 都 忘 了。
Zhè běn shū wǒ hěn duō nián qián kàn guo, dàn dōu wàng le.
我 最近 _____看 了一遍。
Wǒ zuìjìn _____ kàn le yī biàn.

5. 我的病 已经 好 了，不用 _____ 去看 医生 了。
Wǒde bìng yǐjing hǎo le, búyòng _____ qù kàn yīshēng le.

V. Translate the following into Chinese:

1. We had a good time in Europe.

    _____

    _____

2. As far as I am concerned, Xi'an is the most interesting place in China.

    _____

    _____

3. Great changes have taken place in China in the past twenty years.

    _____

    _____

4. Of all the places we have been to, my wife likes Paris (巴黎 Bālí) the most.

    _____

    _____

5. I didn't like the restaurant we went to last night.

    _____

    _____

6. It takes at least fifteen hours to go to Hong Kong from Shanghai by train.

    _____

    _____

7. One-fourth of the people in the world are Chinese.

    _____

    _____

8. My wife and I moved to Florida (佛罗里达 Fúluólǐdá) five years ago when I retired.

    _____

    _____

9. He has lived in Japan all his life and is very familiar with the country.

    _____

    _____

10. Some people don't like changes. They don't think new things are as good as old things.

_____

_____

VI. Translate the following into English:

1. 中文　　的特点 是 语法 简单，但是 发音难。
   Zhōngwén de tèdiǎn shì yǔfǎ jiǎndān, dànshì fāyīn nán.

   _____

   _____

2. 北京　现在 有 五 条 环城 (beltway) 高速 公路。
   Běijīng xiànzài yǒu wǔ tiáo huánchéng   gāosù gōnglù.

   _____

   _____

3. 三十 年　前，上海　　的 浦东　是 农村 (countryside)，但
   Sānshí nián qián, Shànghǎi de Pǔdōng shì nóngcūn,   dàn
   现在 那儿有 很 多 高 楼，是 一 个 全 新 的 地方。
   xiànzài nàr   yǒu hěn duō gāo lóu,   shì yí ge quán xīn de dìfang.

   _____

   _____

4. 如果 要看 中文　　报纸，至少　要 认识 两 千 个
   Rúguǒ yàokàn Zhōngwén bàozhǐ,   zhìshǎo yào rènshì liǎng qiān gè
   中国　字。
   Zhōngguó zì.

   _____

   _____

5. 很 多 西方 人(Westerner) 喜欢 dim sum，因为 他们
   Hěn duō Xīfāng rén   xǐhuan *dim sum*, yīnwéi tāmen
   虽然 不 知道 菜 的 名字，但是 可以选 自己喜欢 的菜。
   suīrán bù zhīdào cài de míngzì, dànshì kěyǐ xuǎn zìjǐ xǐhuan de cài.

   _____

   _____

6. 我 很 喜欢 纽约。在纽约 你 能 见 到 从 各个
   Wǒ hěn xǐhuan Niǔyuē. Zài Niǔyuē nǐ néng jiàn dào cóng gè ge
   国家 来 的 人。你 能 听 到 各种 语言。
   guójiā lái de rén.　Nǐ néng tīng dào gè zhòng yǔyán.

   _____

   _____

7. 这 个 学校 百分 之 二十的 学生 是 外国 学生。
   Zhè ge xuéxiào bǎifēn zhī èrshí de xuésheng shì wàiguó xuésheng.

   _____

   _____

8. 我 先生 对金融 没 有 兴趣，很少 看 "华尔街
   Wǒ xiānsheng duì jīnróng méi yǒu xìngqù,　hěnshǎo kàn "Huá'ěrjiē
   日报"。
   Rìbào".

   _____

   _____

9. 我 有 十年 没有 见 到 他了。他 变 得 跟 以前
   Wǒ yǒu shí nián méiyou jiàn dào tā le.　　Tā biàn de gēn yǐqián
   完全 不 一样 了。
   wánquán bù yíyàng le.

   _____

   _____

10. 他们 结婚 后 一直 住 在 波士顿。
    Tāmen jiéhūn hòu yìzhí zhù zài Bōshìdùn.

    _____

    _____

VII. Topics for discussion and writing:

1. 在 你 去 过 的 国家 和 城市 中， 哪一个 给 你 留下 了
   Zài nǐ qù guo de guójiā hé chéngshì zhōng, nǎ yí ge gěi nǐ liú xià le
   最 深 的 印象？
   zuì shēn de yìnxiàng?

2. 你去 过 中国城 吗？ 请 谈谈 你 对 中国城
   Nǐ qù guo Zhōngguóchéng ma? Qǐng tántan nǐ duì Zhōngguóchéng
   的 印象。
   de yìnxiàng.

ENGLISH TRANSLATION OF THE TEXT

Conversations (*pages 220-224*)

A: Mike, long time no see. Any news recently?
B: Sure. Our whole family went to China.
A: Really? Did you have a good time?
B: We had a wonderful time.
A: Was this your first visit to China?
B: This was the second time for me and my wife to visit China, but it was the first time for the children.
A: When did you and your wife go to China last time?
B: We went there ten years ago.
A: Did you notice any changes in China during these ten years?
B: The changes are tremendous. Many places I had been to before have completely changed.
A: Where in China did you go this time?
B: We went to Hong Kong, Xi'an, Beijing and Shanghai.
A: Which of these places do you like the most?
B: I like them all. Each place has its own characteristics.
A: Can you say something about their characteristics?
B: Of course. Hong Kong, like New York, is a cosmopolitan city, where you can see people from various countries. Xi'an has a very long history. I like the museums there the most.
A: What impression did Beijing leave you with?
B: Beijing left a deep impression on me. It is a great city. The Great Wall is a miracle and the Forbidden City is also an amazing work of architecture.
A: How did you like Shanghai?
B: Of the cities we went to, I like Shanghai the most. I find that Shanghai has developed faster than any other city in China.
A: Can you talk about the changes in Shanghai?
B: In the last few years, Shanghai built many high-rise buildings, ten subway lines, three bridges, a highway, and a new airport. It would take at least twenty years in the U.S. to build so many things.
A: Do you know what the city bird is for Shanghai?
B: No, I don't. What is it?
A: It is the crane.
B: How come I have never heard of it? Why is it the crane?
A: This crane is not a bird. It is the mechanical crane. Do you know 30% of the cranes in the world were in Shanghai a few years ago?
B: That is so interesting! We are planning to go to Shanghai again next year.

*   *   *   *   *

A: Lao Li, how long have you been in the U.S.?
B: I have been in the U.S. for more than thirty years.
A: Have you always lived on the West Coast?
B: No, it was only three years ago when I retired that I moved from the East Coast to the West Coast.
A: You must be familiar with both the East Coast and the West Coast.
B: I know a few things, but I can't say I'm very familiar with them. Do you have any questions?
A: Yes. Can you tell me something about the famous cities on the East Coast?
B: Sure. Famous cities on the East Coast include Washington, Philadelphia, New York, Boston and so on.
A: I have heard of all these cities, particularly Washington, capital of the United States.
B: There is a little difference between the United States and China. China's capital is in the largest city, but Washington is much smaller than cities like New York and Boston.
A: That's true. What are the famous cities on the West Coast?
B: The most famous cities on the West Coast are Los Angeles, San Francisco and Seattle.
A: Which is larger, San Francisco or Los Angeles?
B: San Francisco is large, but Los Angeles is larger.
A: How about the population?
B: The population in San Francisco is not as large as that in Los Angeles.
A: Is it true that you like Los Angeles better?
B: No, I actually like San Francisco better. It is not as hot as Los Angeles during the summer.

Reading Passage (*page 225*)

Although I have lived in San Francisco for ten years, I had never been to its Chinatown. I went with my Chinese friend last weekend and we went there again today. First we went to visit the museum in Chinatown and then we went to a bookstore, where there are all kinds of Chinese books and dictionaries. After we came out of the bookstore, we went to a department store. There are many Chinese products there, which are very cheap. After we were done with shopping, we ate Dim Sum in a restaurant. I had not seen such a way of eating. I found it very interesting. I'll let all of my friends know and ask them to come for a visit to Chinatown.

GLOSSARY

For easy reference, this is a combined glossary of the new words and expressions learned in *Beginners Chinese* and *Intermediate Chinese*.

SC=simplified characters; TC=traditional characters; L=lesson number; BC=*Beginners Chinese*; IC=*Intermediate Chinese*.

SC	TC	Pinyin	English	L
A				
安全		ānquán	safe	IC3
澳门	澳門	Aòmén	Macao	IC1
B				
吧		ba	*sentence-final particle*	IC1
八		bā	eight	BC4
把		bǎ	*preposition*	IC4
把 ... 作为	把 ... 作為	bǎ ... zuòwéi	treat ... as	IC6
爸爸		bàba	father	BC1
白酒		báijiǔ	liquor	BC8
摆	擺	bǎi	place (*v.*); put; arrange	IC7
百分之		bǎifēnzhī	percent	IC10
百货公司	百貨公司	bǎihuògōngsī	department store	BC7
班		bān	class	IC2
搬		bān	move (houses)	IC10
半		bàn	half	BC5
办法	辦法	bànfǎ	way; means; method	IC2
半职	半職	bànzhí	part time	IC8
帮助	幫助	bāngzhù	help; assist	IC2
包		bāo	bag	IC7
北京		Běijīng	Beijing	BC3

SC	TC	Pinyin	English	L
被		bèi	*passive marker*	IC8
本		běn	*classifier*	BC4
比		bǐ	than	BC10
弊		bì	drawback; disadvantage	IC3
必须	必須	bìxū	must	IC5
毕业	畢業	bìyè	graduate (*v.*)	IC5
毕业生	畢業生	bìyèshēng	graduate (*n.*)	IC5
变	變	biàn	change (*v.*)	IC10
变化	變化	biànhuà	change (*v./n.*)	IC10
标题	標題	biāotí	headline	IC9
别人		biérén	other people	IC3
病		bìng	become sick; sickness	IC6
波士顿	波士頓	Bōshìdùn	Boston	IC10
博士		bóshì	Ph.D.; doctoral degree (holder)	IC5
不是 … 而是		bù shī … ér shī	not ... but rather	IC6
不要紧		bú yàojǐn	doesn't matter; not important	IC7
不		bù	not	BC1
部		bù	*classifier*	IC3
部		bù	part; section	IC4
不一定		bù yīdìng	not necessarily	BC7
不同		bùtóng	difference; different	IC7
布置		bùzhì	arrange (furniture); decorate	IC4

C

猜		cāi	guess	IC7
才		cái	as late as; not until	IC2
菜		cài	dishes	BC8
菜单	菜單	càidān	menu	BC8
参观	參觀	cānguān	visit	IC10
餐馆	餐館	cānguǎn	restaurant	BC3
参加	參加	cānjiā	participate (in); join; take part (in)	IC1

SC	TC	Pinyin	English	L
厕所	廁所	cèsuǒ	restroom	BC3
叉子		chāzi	fork	IC4
查		chá	check; consult; look up	IC9
差		chà	not good; poor	IC2
差不多		chàbùduō	approximately; more or less	IC9
产品	產品	chǎnpǐn	product	IC10
常		cháng	often	BC9
长	長	cháng	long	BC7
常常		chángcháng	often	BC10
长城	長城	Chángchéng	Great Wall	IC4
长江	長江	Chángjiāng	Yangtze River	IC4
炒饭	炒飯	chǎofàn	fried rice	IC3
车	車	chē	vehicle	BC9
城		chéng	town; city	BC3
成绩	成績	chéngjī	grade; result; achievement	IC5
城市		chéngshì	city	IC2
吃		chī	eat	BC8
重新		chóngxīn	again; anew	IC4
出		chū	go out	BC10
初		chū	primary; beginning (of a time period)	IC5
出		chū	go out; exit	IC5
除夕		chúxī	eve	IC7
窗子		chuāngzi	window	IC4
春天		chūntiān	spring	BC10
词典		cídiǎn	dictionary	IC4
次		cì	time (occurrence)	BC8
从	從	cóng	from	BC6
从 … 到 …	從 … 到 …	cóng … dào …	from … to …	BC9
错	錯	cuò	wrong; bad	BC1

D

答复		dáfù	reply (*n./v.*)	IC8
打		dǎ	make (a phone call); hit	IC3

SC	TC	Pinyin	English	L
打算		dǎsuan	plan (v./n.)	IC1
大		dà	big	BC10
大多数	大多數	dàduōshù	majority; most of	IC5
大概		dàgài	probably	BC9
大家		dàjiā	everyone; people	IC7
大人		dàren	adult; grown-up	IC7
大学	大學	dàxué	university	BC3
大学生	大學生	dàxuéshēng	college student	BC4
大衣		dàyī	coat	BC7
带		dài	bring; take; carry	BC10
单位	單位	dānwèi	workplace	BC3
担心	擔心	dānxīn	worry	IC9
但是		dànshì	but	BC6
当然	當然	dāngrán	of course	BC7
当时	當時	dāngshí	at that time	IC7
刀		dāo	knife	IC4
到		dào	arrive; reach	IC2
到时	到時	dàoshí	at that (future) time	IC1
的		de	*possessive marker*	BC2
得		de	*verb complement marker*	IC2
得到		dédào	receive; obtain; acquire	IC7
得		děi	have to	IC9
等		děng	wait	BC7
等等		děngděng	so on	IC3
第		dì	*ordinal number indicator*	BC7
地方		dìfāng	place	BC9
地铁	地鐵	dìtiě	subway	BC9
地图	地圖	dìtú	map	IC4
地址		dìzhǐ	address	IC3
点	點	diǎn	o'clock	BC5
电话	電話	diànhuà	telephone	BC3
电脑	電腦	diànnǎo	computer	IC4
电子信	電子信	diànzǐxìn	email	IC9
跌		diē	fall (v.)	IC9

SC	TC	Pinyin	English	L
冬天		dōngtiān	winter	BC10
东西	東西	dōngxi	things; stuff	BC7
懂		dǒng	understand	BC6
都		dōu	both; all	BC8
豆腐		dòufu	tofu	IC3
读	讀	dú	study; read aloud	IC5
度		dù	degree	BC10
短期		duǎnqī	short-term	IC2
锻炼	鍛煉	duànliàn	physical exercise; workout	IC6
对	對	duì	right; correct	BC8
对	對	duì	to; for; regarding	IC3
对 ... 来说	對 ... 來說	duì ... lái shuō	as far as ... is concerned; for	IC7
对不起	對不起	duìbùqǐ	sorry	BC5
度假		dùjià	go on vacation	BC10
多		duō	many; much	BC7
多少		duōshao	*question word about numbers*	BC4

E

SC	TC	Pinyin	English	L
俄国	俄國	Éguó	Russia	IC4
儿子	兒子	érzi	son	BC4
二		èr	two	BC4

F

SC	TC	Pinyin	English	L
发	發	fā	send email, text message, etc.	IC9
发烧	發燒	fāshāo	have a fever	IC6
发展	發展	fāzhǎn	develop; development	IC10
发音	發音	fāyīn	pronounce; pronunciation	IC2
法国	法國	Fǎguó	France	BC6
法语	法語	Fǎyǔ	French language	BC6
饭店	飯店	fàndiàn	hotel	BC7
方便		fāngbiàn	convenient; convenience	IC3
方式		fāngshì	method; form; way	IC6
房租		fángzū	rent	IC8

SC	TC	Pinyin	English	L
放		fàng	put; lay	IC9
放假		fàngjià	have a vacation; have a day off	IC7
飞机	飛機	fēijī	airplane	BC9
费城		Fèichéng	Philadelphia	IC10
分		fēn	minute	BC5
分		fēn	monetary unit	BC7
分		fēn	divide; separate; distinguish	IC5
分钟	分鐘	fēnzhōng	minute	BC9
风	風	fēng	wind	BC10
风景	風景	fēngjǐng	scenery	IC1
福利		fúlì	benefits	IC8
服装店		fúzhuāngdiàn	clothing store	BC7
付		fù	pay (*v.*)	IC8

G

感觉	感覺	gǎnjué	feeling	IC6
感冒		gǎnmào	cold; have a cold	IC6
高		gāo	high; tall	IC5
高速公路		gāosùgōnglù	highway; expressway	IC10
高兴	高興	gāoxìng	happy	BC1
告诉	告訴	gàosu	tell	BC7
哥哥		gēge	older brother	BC4
跟		gēn	with; and	IC2
个	個	gè	*classifier*	BC4
各种各样	各種各樣	gèzhǒng gèyàng	various; all kinds of	IC6
给	給	gěi	give	BC8
给	給	gěi	to; give	IC3
更		gèng	even more	IC8
工程师	工程師	gōngchéngshī	engineer	IC8
公里		gōnglǐ	kilometer	IC4
工人		gōngrén	factory worker	BC2
公司		gōngsī	company	BC2
工资	工資	gōngzī	salary	IC8

SC	TC	Pinyin	English	L
工作		gōngzuò	work	BC3
够		gòu	enough	IC2
挂	掛	guà	hang	IC4
关掉	關掉	guān diào	turn off (a device)	IC3
广东	廣東	Guǎngdōng	Canton (the province); Guangdong	BC6
广告	廣告	guǎnggào	advertisement; commercial	IC8
广州	廣州	Guǎngzhōu	Canton (the city); Guangzhou	BC6
故宫		gùgōng	Palace Museum/ Forbidden City	IC10
股票	股票	gǔpiào	stocks	IC9
贵	貴	guì	distinguished	BC2
贵	貴	guì	expensive	BC7
过	過	guo	*aspect marker*	BC8
国	國	guó	country	BC6
国际	國際	guójì	international	IC9
国家	國家	guójiā	country	IC4
国内	國內	guónèi	domestic; national	IC9
国庆节	國慶節	guóqìngjié	National Day; Independence Day	IC7
国外	國外	guówài	overseas; abroad	IC9
国语	國語	Guóyǔ	Mandarin	BC6
过敏	過敏	guòmǐn	allergic	IC6

H

还	還	hái	also; additionally	IC1
还	還	hái	fairly; passably; still	IC2
海岸		hǎi'an	coast	IC10
海滩	海灘	hǎitān	beach	BC10
海鲜	海鮮	hǎixiān	seafood	BC8
韩国	韓國	Hánguó	(South) Korea	IC4
汉字	漢字	hànzì	Chinese characters	IC2
杭州		Hángzhōu	Hangzhou	BC9
好		hǎo	good	BC1
好		hǎo	become well; recover	IC6

SC	TC	Pinyin	English	L
好象		hǎoxiàng	seem	BC8
号	號	hào	number	BC5
号码	號碼	hàomǎ	(telephone) number	IC3
喝		hē	drink	BC8
和		hé	and	BC4
和…有关系	和…有關係	hé … yǒu guānxì	have to do with	IC8
很		hěn	very	BC1
很少		hěn shǎo	seldom; rarely	IC5
红酒	紅酒	hóngjiǔ	wine	BC8
后边	後邊	hòubian	behind; at the back of	IC4
互联网	互聯網	hùliánwǎng	Internet	IC9
花		huā	spend (time or money)	IC7
华尔街	華爾街	Huá'ěrjiē	Wall Street	IC9
华盛顿	華盛頓	Huáshèngdùn	Washington	BC9
滑雪		huáxuě	ski	BC10
话	話	huà	speech; dialect	BC6
欢迎	歡迎	huānyíng	welcome	BC8
换		huàn	change; exchange	BC7
回		huí	return (to a place); reply	IC1
会	會	huì	know how to	BC6
会	會	huì	will (*modal verb*)	IC1
婚礼	婚禮	hūnlǐ	wedding	IC1
或		huò	or	IC5

J

SC	TC	Pinyin	English	L
机会	機會	jīhuì	opportunity	IC2
极了	極了	jíle	extremely	BC8
几	幾	jǐ	*question word about numbers*	BC4
季节	季節	jìjié	season	BC10
家		jiā	home; family	BC3
加州		Jiāzhōu	California	BC9
检查	檢查	jiǎnchá	exam; examination	IC6
件		jiàn	*classifier*	BC7

SC	TC	Pinyin	English	L
建		jiàn	build; construct; erect	IC10
交换		jiāohuàn	exchange (*v./n.*)	IC7
交谈	交談	jiāotán	converse; chat	IC2
交通工具		jiāotōng gōngjù	means of transportation	IC6
饺子	餃子	jiǎozi	dumpings	IC7
叫		jiào	call	BC2
教		jiāo	teach	IC1
教室		jiàoshì	classroom	IC4
接		jiē	pick up; answer (a phone call)	IC3
结婚	結婚	jiéhūn	get married	IC1
节日	節日	jiérì	holiday; festival	IC7
解雇	解僱	jiěgù	lay off	IC8
介绍	介紹	jièshào	introduce; introduction	IC7
介意		jièyì	mind (*v.*)	IC1
金融		jīnróng	finance	IC9
今天		jīntiān	today	BC5
进	進	jìn	enter; come in	IC4
进步	進步	jìnbù	progress (*n./v.*)	IC2
经理	經理	jīnglǐ	manager	BC2
经验	經驗	jīngyàn	experience	IC8
景点	景點	jǐngdiǎn	scenic spot; tourist attraction	IC4
九		jiǔ	nine	BC4
久		jiǔ	long time	IC10
就		jiù	right away	IC1
就		jiù	as early as; already; then	IC2
觉得	覺得	juéde	feel; think	BC7
举行	舉行	jǔxíng	hold (an event)	IC1

K

SC	TC	Pinyin	English	L
开	開	kāi	operate; drive	BC9
开	開	kāi	offer; start (a class or a business)	IC9
开会	開會	kāihuì	attend a meeting	IC3

SC	TC	Pinyin	English	L
开药	開藥	kāiyào	prescribe medicine	IC6
看书	看書	kàn shū	read	BC5
考虑	考慮	kǎolǜ	consider	IC8
考试	考試	kǎoshì	exam (*v.*); examination	IC5
烤鸭	烤鴨	kǎoyā	roast duck	BC8
咳嗽		késou	cough (*n./v.*)	IC6
课	課	kè	class; lesson	BC5
客气	客氣	kèqi	be polite; be formal	BC2
可能		kěnéng	maybe; possible	BC9
可以		kěyǐ	may	BC7
可以		kěyǐ	pretty good; not bad	IC2
口		kǒu	*classifier*	BC4
口语		kǒuyǔ	spoken language	IC2
块	塊	kuài	monetary unit	BC7
快 ... 了		kuài ... le	about to	IC1
裤子	褲子	kùzi	pants	BC7

L

辣		là	spicy	BC8
老年人		lǎoniánrén	old people	IC6
老师	老師	lǎoshī	teacher	BC3
冷		lěng	cold	BC10
离	離	lí	away from	BC9
利		lì	benefit; advantage	IC3
连	連	lián	even	IC9
联系	聯繫	liánxì	contact (*v./n.*)	IC3
脸色	臉色	liǎnsè	look (*n.*); complexion	IC6
练	練	liàn	practice (*v.*)	IC2
练习	練習	liànxí	practice (*n./v.*)	IC2
聊		liáo	chat	IC3
聊天		liáotiān	chat	IC9
了解		liǎojiě	gain understanding	IC8
离开	離開	líkāi	leave	IC8
里边	裡邊	lǐbian	in; inside	IC4

SC	TC	Pinyin	English	L
礼物	禮物	lǐwù	gift; present	IC7
厉害	厲害	lìhai	terrible; formidable	IC9
历史	歷史	lìshǐ	history	BC4
零		líng	zero	BC4
溜冰		liūbīng	ice skate	BC10
流利		liúlì	fluent	IC2
留		liú	leave (a message)	IC3
六		liù	six	BC4
楼	樓	lóu	floor; building	BC6
路		lù	road; route	BC9
旅馆	旅館	lǚguǎn	hotel	BC9

M

SC	TC	Pinyin	English	L
吗	嗎	ma	*particle*	BC1
妈妈	媽媽	māma	mother	BC1
马马虎虎	馬馬虎虎	mǎmahūhū	so-so	BC1
买	買	mǎi	buy	BC7
卖	賣	mài	sell	BC7
慢		màn	slowly	BC6
慢跑		màn pǎo	jogging; jog	IC6
曼哈顿	曼哈頓	Mànhādùn	Manhattan	BC3
毛		máo	*monetary unit*	BC7
毛衣		máoyī	sweater	BC7
没		méi	not	BC2
没关系	沒關係	méi guānxi	That's all right.	BC5
每		měi	every; each	BC5
美		měi	pretty; beautiful	IC1
美国	美國	Měiguó	United States	BC2
美术	美術	měishù	fine art	IC5
美元		měiyuán	U.S. dollars	BC7
们	們	men	*plural suffix*	BC2
门	門	mén	door; gate	IC4
蒙古		Měnggǔ	Mongolia	IC4
面包		miànbāo	bread	BC8
面条	面條	miàntiáo	noodle	BC8

SC	TC	Pinyin	English	L
米饭	米飯	mǐfàn	cooked rice	BC8
秘书	秘書	mìshū	secretary	IC8
蜜月		mìyuè	honeymoon	IC1
明年		míngnián	next year	BC5
明天		míngtiān	tomorrow	BC5
名字		míngzi	name	BC2
N				
拿		ná	take; hold	IC4
哪		nǎ	which	BC4
哪里	哪裡	nǎli	*polite response to a compliment*	IC2
那		nà	that	BC7
那么	那麼	nàme	so; to such degree	IC5
奶奶		nǎinai	(paternal) grandmother	IC9
难	難	nán	hard; difficult	IC2
男孩		nánhái	boy	BC4
哪儿	哪兒	nǎr	what place	BC3
那儿	那兒	nàr	there	BC3
呢		ne	*particle*	BC1
内容		nèiróng	content	IC9
能		néng	can	BC7
你		nǐ	you	BC1
年		nián	year	BC9
年级	年級	niánjí	(of school) grade	IC5
鸟	鳥	niǎo	bird	IC10
您		nín	you (*polite form*)	BC2
牛肉		niúròu	beef	BC8
纽约	紐約	Niǔyuē	New York	BC3
女		nǚ	female	BC2
女儿	女兒	nǚ'ér	daughter	BC2
女孩		nǚhái	girl	BC4
P				
盘子		pánzi	plate	IC4
旁边	旁邊	pángbiān	beside; next to	IC4

SC	TC	Pinyin	English	L
朋友		péngyou	friend	BC2
啤酒		píjiǔ	beer	BC8
便宜		piányi	cheap	BC7
票		piào	ticket	BC9
瓶		píng	bottle	BC8
平常		píngcháng	ordinarily; generally	IC9
普通		pǔtōng	common; ordinary	IC3
普通话	普通話	Pǔtōnghuà	Mandarin	BC6

Q

七		qī	seven	BC4
骑	騎	qí	ride	BC9
奇迹	奇蹟	qíjī	miracle	IC10
其实	其實	qíshí	actually	IC9
起重机	起重機	qǐzhòngjī	crane (construction machinery)	IC10
钱	錢	qián	money	BC7
前边	前邊	qiánbian	in front of; ahead of	IC4
墙	牆	qiáng	wall	IC4
桥	橋	qiáo	bridge	IC10
青岛	青島	Qīngdǎo	Qingdao	BC8
晴		qíng	sunny	BC10
请帖	請帖	qǐngtiě	invitation card/letter	IC1
请问	請問	qǐngwèn	May I ask ...	BC3
秋天		qiūtiān	fall; autumn	BC10
全		quán	completely; entirely	IC6
全职	全職	quánzhí	full time	IC8

R

让	讓	ràng	ask (sb. to do sth.); let	IC3
热	熱	rè	hot	BC10
人口		rénkǒu	population	IC10
人们	人們	rénmen	people	IC6
人民币	人民幣	rénmínbì	*Renminbi*	BC7
人事部		rénshìbù	personnel department	IC8

SC	TC	Pinyin	English	L
认识	認識	rènshi	know	BC1
扔掉		rēng diào	throw away	IC9
日本		Rìběn	Japan	BC3
容易		róngyì	easy	IC5
肉		ròu	meat	BC8
如果		rúguǒ	if	IC2
S				
三		sān	three	BC4
伞	傘	sǎn	umbrella	BC10
散步		sànbù	take a walk	IC6
沙发	沙發	shāfā	sofa	IC4
上		shàng	up	BC9
上班		shàngbān	go to work	BC5
上边	上邊	shàngbian	on; over; above	IC4
上海		Shànghǎi	Shanghai	BC6
上网	上網	shàngwǎng	get on the Internet	IC3
上午		shàngwǔ	morning	BC5
上学	上學	shàngxué	go to school	BC9
深		shēn	deep	IC10
申请	申請	shēnqǐng	apply; application	IC8
身体	身體	shēntǐ	health; body	IC6
什么	什麼	shénme	what	BC2
什么样	什麼樣	shénmeyàng	what kind of	IC8
生		shēng	give birth to; be born; produce	IC7
生活		shēnghuó	livelihood; life	IC8
生日		shēngrì	birthday	BC5
生意		shēngyì	business	IC8
圣诞节	圣誕節	Shèngdànjié	Christmas	BC9
十		shí	ten	BC4
时报	時報	shíbào	(newspaper title) Times	IC9
时候	時候	shíhou	time	BC5
时间	時間	shíjiān	time	BC5
是		shì	be	BC1

SC	TC	Pinyin	English	L
试	試	shì	try	BC7
事		shì	matter; thing (to do)	IC1
世界		shìjiè	world	IC4
收		shōu	accept	BC7
收到		shōu dào	receive	IC1
手表		shǒubiǎo	watch	BC5
首都		shǒudū	capital (of a country)	IC10
手机	手機	shǒujī	cell phone	IC3
售票员	售票員	shòupiàoyuán	sales clerk	BC7
书包	書包	shūbāo	book bag	IC4
书架	書架	shūjià	bookshelf	IC4
舒服		shūfu	feeling well; comfortable	IC6
熟悉		shúxī	familiar	IC9
属	屬	shǔ	born in the Chinese zodiac year of	IC7
树	樹	shù	tree	IC7
数学	數學	shùxué	mathematics	IC5
谁	誰	shuí	who	BC4
说	說	shuō	speak; say	BC6
硕士	硕士	shuòshì	master's degree (holder)	IC5
私		sī	private	IC1
四		sì	four	BC4
四川		Sìchuān	Sichuan	BC6
送		sòng	deliver; take sb. or sth. to	IC3
苏州	蘇州	Sūzhōu	Suzhou	BC9
酸		suān	sour	BC8
素菜		sùcài	vegetable dish	BC8
所以		suǒyǐ	therefore	IC5

T

他		tā	he	BC1
她		tā	she	BC1
太		tài	too	BC3
太极拳	太極拳	tàijíquán	taiji (taichi)	IC6

SC	TC	Pinyin	English	L
太平洋		Tàipíngyáng	the Pacific Ocean	IC4
汤	湯	tāng	soup	BC8
特别		tèbié	especially; particularly	IC6
特点	特點	tèdiǎn	characteristic; trait; feature	IC10
疼		téng	hurt; pain (v.)	IC6
天		tiān	day; weather	BC5
天气	天氣	tiānqì	weather	BC10
天堂		tiāntáng	paradise	BC9
提供		tígòng	provide	IC8
条	條	tiáo	classifier	BC7
听说	聽說	tīngshuō	it is said	BC7
体育	體育	tǐyù	physical education	IC5
通过	通過	tōngguò	pass	IC5
头	頭	tóu	head	IC6
团聚	團聚	tuánjù	get together	IC7
退休金		tuìxiūjīn	pension	IC8
W				
外语		wàiyǔ	foreign language	IC5
玩		wán	play	BC9
完		wán	finish (v.)	IC6
完全		wánquán	completely; entirely	IC10
晚上		wǎnshang	evening	BC5
网吧	網吧	wǎngbā	Internet café	IC9
网站	網站	wǎngzhàn	website	IC9
伟大	偉大	wěidà	great	IC10
位		wèi	classifier	BC8
喂	餵	wèi	hello	IC9
味道		wèidao	taste	BC8
为了	為了	wèile	for; for the sake of; in order to	IC6
为什么	為什麼	wèishénme	why	BC10
文化		wénhuà	culture	IC8
文凭	文憑	wénpíng	diploma; degree	IC8

SC	TC	Pinyin	English	L
问	問	wèn	ask	IC8
问题	問題	wèntí	question	BC7
我		wǒ	I	BC1
五		wǔ	five	BC4

X

SC	TC	Pinyin	English	L
西班牙语	西班牙語	Xībānyáyǔ	Spanish language	BC6
西雅图	西雅圖	Xīyǎtú	Seattle	IC10
西医	西醫	xīyī	Western medicine	IC6
习惯	習慣	xíguàn	habit; custom	IC7
喜欢	喜歡	xǐhuan	like	
下		xià	down; fall	BC9
下班		xiàbān	get off work	BC5
下边	下邊	xiàbian	under; below; underneath	IC4
夏天		xiàtiān	summer	BC10
下午		xiàwǔ	afternoon	BC5
先		xiān	first	IC4
先 … 再		xiān … zài	first … then	IC5
先 … 然后	先 … 然後	xiān … ránhòu	first … then	IC10
先生		xiānsheng	Mr.; husband	BC1
现在	現在	xiànzài	now	BC5
香港		Xiānggǎng	Hong Kong	BC6
想		xiǎng	would like; think	BC9
消息		xiāoxi	news; word	IC8
小		xiǎo	small	BC10
小费		xiǎofèi	tip	BC8
小姐		xiǎojie	Miss	BC1
小时	小時	xiǎoshí	hour	BC9
小学生	小學生	xiǎoxuéshēng	elementary school student	BC4
谢谢	謝謝	xièxie	thank (you)	BC2
辛苦		xīnkǔ	hard (*adj.*); toilsome	IC5
新郎		xīnláng	bridegroom	IC1
新娘		xīnniáng	bride	IC1
新闻	新聞	xīnwén	news	IC9
星期		xīngqī	week	BC5

SC	TC	Pinyin	English	L
姓		xìng	family name	BC2
兴趣	興趣	xìngqù	interest	IC8
休息		xiūxi	rest; relax	IC6
选	選	xuǎn	select; choose	IC5
学	學	xué	study	BC3
学历	學歷	xuélì	academic credential; resumé	IC8
学期	學期	xuéqī	semester	IC4
学生	學生	xuésheng	student	BC1
学习	學習	xuéxí	study	BC4
雪		xuě	snow	BC10

Y

SC	TC	Pinyin	English	L
严格	嚴格	yángé	rigorous; strict; tough	IC5
研究生		yánjiūshēng	graduate student	IC5
颜色		yánsè	color	BC7
要求		yāoqiú	requirement; require	IC8
要		yào	want; take (time, etc)	BC7
要看		yào kàn	It depends	BC7
爷爷	爺爺	yéye	(paternal) grandfather	IC9
也		yě	also	BC1
一 ... 就 ...		yī ... jiù ...	as soon as	IC8
一		yī	one	BC4
一流		yīliú	first-rate; first-class	IC5
医生		yīshēng	(medical) doctor	IC6
衣服		yīfu	clothes	BC7
一遍		yíbiàn	once	BC6
一定		yídìng	certainly; definitely	BC8
一共		yígòng	altogether	BC7
一样	一樣	yíyàng	the same	IC7
以后	以後	yǐhòu	after; later; in the future	IC1
已经	已經	yǐjīng	already	IC2
以前	以前	yǐqián	before; previously; in the past; ago	IC1
椅子		yǐzi	chair	IC4

SC	TC	Pinyin	English	L
一会儿	一會兒	yīhuìr	a little while	IC3
一些		yìxiē	somewhat; a little	IC2
一直		yìzhí	all along; straight; always	IC10
意思		yìsi	meaning	BC6
阴	陰	yīn	cloudy	BC10
印象		yìnxiàng	impression	IC10
因为	因為	yīnwèi	because	IC7
应该	應該	yīnggāi	should; ought to	IC2
英国	英國	Yīngguó	United Kingdom	BC6
英语	英語	Yīngyǔ	English language	BC6
银行	銀行	yínháng	bank	BC3
用		yòng	use	BC6
游	遊	yóu	tour (v.)	IC10
有		yǒu	have; there is/are	BC2
有的 ... 有的	有的	yǒude ... yǒude	some…, others …	BC7
有点儿	有點兒	yǒudiǎnér	a little; somewhat	BC8
有名		yǒumíng	famous	BC8
有时 ... 有时	有時 ... 有時	yǒushí ... yǒushí	sometimes …, sometimes …	BC5
有意思		yǒuyìsi	interesting	IC1
又		yòu	further	IC5
又		yòu	again	IC10
雨		yǔ	rain	BC10
语法	語法	yǔfǎ	grammar	IC2
语言	語言	yǔyán	language	BC6
圆	圓	yuán	round; circular	IC7
元旦		yuándàn	(Western) New Year	IC7
月		yuè	month	BC5
月饼	月餅	yuèbǐng	moon cake	IC7
阅读	閱讀	yuèdú	reading	IC8
越来越		yuèláiyuè	more and more; increasingly	IC3
月亮		yuèliang	moon	IC7

SC	TC	Pinyin	English	L
Z				
在		zài	in; at	BC3
在		zài	*progressive aspect marker*	IC2
再		zài	again	BC6
再见	再見	zàijiàn	good-bye	BC2
怎么	怎麼	zěnme	how	BC6
怎么样	怎麼樣	zěnmeyàng	how is ...?	BC1
张	張	zhāng	*classifier*	BC7
帐单	帳單	zhàngdān	check; bill	BC8
找		zhǎo	look for; find	BC9
着	著	zhe	*aspect marker*	IC7
这	這	zhè	this	BC1
这样	這樣	zhèyàng	so; like this	IC1
真		zhēn	really; truly	IC2
这儿	這兒	zhèr	here	BC3
知道		zhīdao	know	BC2
只		zhǐ	only	BC6
只是		zhǐshì	merely; only; just	IC3
治		zhì	treat (a disease)	IC6
至少		zhìshǎo	at least	IC10
中国	中國	Zhōngguó	China	BC2
中秋节	中秋節	zhōngqiūjié	Mid-Autumn Festival	IC7
中文		Zhōngwén	Chinese language	BC3
中学生	中學生	zhōngxuéshēng	secondary school student	BC4
中医	中醫	zhōngyī	Chinese medicine	IC6
种	種	zhǒng	kind; variety	BC6
重要		zhòngyào	important	IC7
周围	周圍	zhōuwéi	area around; surroundings	IC4
住		zhù	live	BC3
装		zhuāng	hold; load; install	IC7
装饰品	裝飾品	zhuāngshìpǐn	decorative objects; decorations	IC7
主意		zhǔyi	idea	IC2
祝贺	祝賀	zhùhè	congratulate; congratulations	IC1

SC	TC	Pinyin	English	L
著名		zhùmíng	famous; renowned	IC10
桌子		zhuōzi	table; desk	IC4
资料	資料	zīliào	information; material; data	IC9
自己		zìjǐ	oneself; one's own	IC8
自然科学	自然科學	zìrán kēxué	natural sciences	IC5
自行车	自行車	zìxíngchē	bicycle	BC9
走		zǒu	walk	BC9
最		zuì	the most	BC7
最好		zuìhǎo	best; had better	BC10
最近		zuìjìn	recently; shortly; these days	IC1
尊重		zūnzhòng	respect	IC3
昨天		zuótiān	yesterday	BC5
做		zuò	do	BC4
坐		zuò	sit; take (the bus, etc)	BC8
座		zuò	*classifier*	IC10

KEY TO THE EXERCISES

LESSON 1 (*Exercises on pages 18-23*)

II.
1. 结婚三十年了　jiéhūn sānshí nián le
2. 离婚五年了　líhūn wǔ nián le
3. 参加朋友的婚礼　cānjiā péngyou de hūnlǐ
4. 去夏威夷度假　qù Xiàwēiyí dù jià
5. 我们去吧　wǒmen qù ba
6. 新娘和新郎　xīnniáng hé xīnláng
7. 十年前　shí nián qián; 十年后　shí nián hòu
8. 上班前　shàngbān qián; 下班后　xiàbān hòu
9. 他们结婚的时候　tāmen jiéhūn de shíhou
10. 从美国回来　cóng Měiguó huí lái

III.
1. 以后　yǐhòu
2. 是 … 的　shì … de
3. 最近　zuìjìn
4. 的时候　de shíhou
5. 以前　yǐqián
6. 要　yào
7. 以前　yǐqián
8. 以后　yǐhòu
9. 的时候　de shíhou
10. 是 … 的　shì … de

IV.
1. 老师们每天七点上班。Lǎoshīmen měi tiān qī diǎn shàngbān.
2. 老师们每天工作七个小时。Lǎoshīmen měi tiān gōngzuò qī ge xiǎoshí.

3. 我的美国朋友在广州住了三年。 Wǒde Měiguó péngyou zài Guǎngzhōu zhù le sān nián.
4. 大卫和玛丽下个月结婚。 Dàwèi hé Mǎlì xià ge yuè jiéhūn.
5. 你在澳门玩儿了几天? Nǐ zài Àomén wánr le jǐ tiān?

V.
1. 好吃　hǎochī
2. 好听　hǎotīng
3. 好喝　hǎohē
4. 好看　hǎokàn
5. 好玩儿　hǎowánr

VI.

新 _____ 汽车	好吃 <u>的</u> 菜	短 _____ 大衣
xīn _____ qīchē	hǎochī <u>de</u> cài	duǎn _____ dàyī

不老 <u>的</u> 人	高兴 <u>的</u> 事	热 _____ 茶
bù lǎo <u>de</u> rén	gāoxìng <u>de</u> shì	rè _____ chá

VII.
1. 我今天没有去银行。 Wǒ jīntiān méiyou qù yínháng.
2. 她来美国以前是老师。她来美国后是学生。
   Tā lái Měiguó yǐqián shì lǎoshī. Tā lái Měiguó hòu shì xuésheng.
3. 听说苏州是个很有意思的地方。 Tīngshuō Sūzhōu shì ge hěn yǒuyìsi de dìfang.
4. 你今天是几点吃的中饭? Nǐ jīntiān shì jǐ diǎn chī de zhōngfàn?
5. 他们为这个公司工作了二十年。 Tāmen wèi zhè ge gōngsī gōngzuò le èrshí nián.
6. 你今天晚上打算做什么? Nǐ jīntiān wǎnshang dǎsuan zuò shénme?
7. 我妹妹快结婚了。 Wǒ mèimei kuài jiéhūn le.
8. 除了法国，我们还去了英国和德国。 Chúle Fǎguó, wǒmen hái qù le Yīngguó hé Déguó.
9. 孩子们看电影的时候喜欢问很多问题。 Háizimen kàn diànyǐng de shíhòu xǐhuān wèn hěn duō wèntí.
10. 她说她以后告诉我。 Tā shuō tā yǐhòu gàosù wǒ.

VIII.

1. My older sister lived in California before she got married.
2. There was no university in this place in the past.
3. Nowadays many people are not planning to get married.
4. It's about to rain.
5. She came back from China three weeks ago.
6. Besides English, my teacher can speak French and Spanish.
7. I have been busy recently and don't have time to study Chinese, but I will do it in the future.
8. They went to Washington by plane.
9. I'll be attending my friend's wedding this weekend.
10. It has snowed for two days.

LESSON 2 *(Exercises on pages 42-48)*

II.

1. 他正在看书。Tā zhèng zài kàn shū.
2. 他们在看电视。Tāmen zài kàn diànshì.
3. 她在打电话呢。Tā zài dǎ diànhuà ne.
4. 她正做饭呢。Tā zhèng zuò fàn ne.
5. 他在开车。Tā zài kāi chē.
6. 老师在上课。Lǎoshī zài shàng kè.

III.

1. 很流利   hěn liúlì
2. 太快   tài kuài
3. 很晚   hěn wǎn
4. 怎么样   zěnmeyàng
5. 大不大   dà bu dà

IV.

1. 老师来得不早。Lǎoshī lái de bù zǎo.
2. 我妈妈做饭做得不很好。Wǒ māma zuò fàn zuò de bù hěn hǎo.
3. 他开车开得不快。Tā kāi chē kāi de bú kuài.
4. 那个老人走得不慢。Nà ge lǎo rén zǒu de bú màn.

5. 他们在北京玩儿得不很高兴。Tāmen zài Běijīng wánr de bù hěn gāoxìng.

V.

1. 五天多 wǔ tiān duō; 二十多个人 èrshí duō ge rén
2. 够长 gòu cháng; 不够高 bú gòu gāo
3. 有的地方容易，有的地方难 yǒude dìfang róngyì, yǒude dìfang nán
4. 学习外语的最好的办法 xuéxí wàiyǔ de zuì hǎo de bànfǎ
5. 练习口语的机会 liànxí kǒuyǔ de jīhuì
6. 结婚十年了 jiéhūn shí nián le
7. 跟中国朋友学习中文 gēn Zhōngguó péngyǒu xuéxí Zhōngwén
8. 认识一些汉字 rènshí yìxiē hànzì
9. 很快的进步 hěn kuài de jìnbù
10. 用英语和外国朋友交谈 yòng Yīngyǔ hé wàiguó péngyou jiāotán

VI.

1. 就 jiù
2. 才 cài
3. 就 jiù
4. 才 cài
5. 才 cài
6. 就 jiù

VII.

1. 我们吃了两个小时。Wǒmen chī le liǎng ge xiǎoshí.
2. 他开车开了五个多小时。Tā kāi chē kāi le wǔ ge duō xiǎoshí.
3. 学生们正在上课。Xuéshēngmen zhèng zài shàng kè.
4. 你昨天回家的时候你妈妈在做什么？Nǐ zuótiān huí jiā de shíhòu nǐ māma zài zuò shénme?
5. 美国老师给美国打了三十分钟的电话。Měiguó lǎoshī gěi Měiguó dǎ le sānshí fēnzhōng de diànhuà.
6. 你昨天晚上睡得好吗？Nǐ zuótiān wǎnshang shuì de hǎo ma?
7. 我现在工作太忙，没有机会去旅行。Wǒ xiànzài gōngzuò tài máng, méi yǒu jīhuì qù lǚxíng.

8. 我学英语学了十年多了，可是我的英语还不够好。
   Wǒ xué Yīngyǔ xué le shí nián duō le, kěshì wǒde Yīngyǔ hái bú gòu hǎo.
9. 雪下得很大。 Xuě xià de hěn dà.
10. 她睡得晚，起得早。 Tā shuì de wǎn, qǐ de zǎo.

VIII.
1. You can only keep (read) the book for three days.
2. My wife worked in a middle school for 20 years.
3. He drove more than 30 hours before he got to California.
4. It takes me an hour by bus to get to work every day.
5. The students wrote the characters for 30 minutes.
6. The teacher speaks slowly.
7. The American friends had a good time in Beijing.
8. The children watched TV for two hours.
9. No one practices Chinese with me.
10. It only took us an hour to go from Shanghai to Suzhou by train.

LESSON 3 (*Exercises on pages 64–69*)

II.
1. 打电话 dǎ diànhuà; 接电话 jiē diànhuà; 回电话 huí diànhuà
2. 她对我很好。 Tā duì wǒ hěn hǎo.
3. 他对你说了什么？ Tā duì nǐ shuō le shénme?
4. 七点对我不好。 Qī diǎn duì wǒ bù hǎo.
5. 我能不能给她留个话？ Wǒ néng bu néng gěi tā liú ge huà?
6. 我今天下午送人去机场。 Wǒ jīntiān xiàwǔ sòng rén qù jīchǎng.
7. 昨天晚上我们全家都在家。 Zuótiān wǎnshang wǒmen quán jiā dōu zài jiā.
8. 我们的经理在开会。 Wǒmende jīnglǐ zài kāi huì.
9. 你如果有问题，请来我这儿。 Nǐ rúguǒ yǒu wèntí, qǐng lái wǒ zhèr.
10. 越来越多的人学中文。 Yuèláiyuè duō de rén xué Zhōngwén.

III.

1. 一会儿 yíhuìr
2. 一下儿 yíxiàr
3. 一点儿 yìdiǎnr
4. 一点儿 yìdiǎnr
5. 一会儿 yíhuìr
6. 一下儿 yíxiàr

IV.

1. 你在什么商店都能买电话卡。Nǐ zài shénme shāngdiàn dōu néng mǎi diànhuà kǎ.
2. 我今年什么电影也没有看。Wǒ jīnnián shénme diànyǐng yě méiyou kàn.
3. 她昨天什么东西也没有吃，今天她什么东西也不想吃。Tā zuótiān shénme dōngxi yě méiyou chī, jīntiān tā shénme dōngxi yě bù xiǎng chī.
4. 我什么时候给她打电话，她的电话都忙。Wǒ shénme shíhòu gěi tā dǎ diànhuà, tāde diànhuà dōu máng.
5. 这个孩子的爸爸怎么跟她说，她都不听。Zhè ge háizi de bàba zěnme gēn tā shuō, tā dōu bù tīng.

V.

1. 一边开车，一边打电话不安全。Yìbiān kāi chē, yìbiān dǎ diànhuà bù ānquán.
2. 对不起，我们的经理还没有来。你要不要给他留个话？Duìbuqǐ, wǒmende jīnglǐ hái méiyou lái. Nǐ yào bu yào gěi tā liú ge huà?
3. 如果你明天不能来学校，请给我打个电话。Rúguǒ nǐ míngtiān bù néng lái xuéxiào, qǐng gěi wǒ dǎ ge diànhuà.
4. 今天下午有人从北京大学给你打电话。她留了一个话，要你给她回话。Jīntiān xiàwǔ yǒu rén cóng Běijīng Dàxué gěi nǐ dǎ diànhuà. Tā liú le yí ge huà, yào nǐ gěi tā huí huà.
5. 如果你要告诉我什么事，请打我的手机。Rúguǒ yǒu yào gàosù wǒ shénme shì, qǐng dǎ wǒde shǒujī.
6. 老师让我告诉你明天没有课。Lǎoshī ràng wǒ gàosù nǐ míngtiān méi yǒu kè.
7. 我请老师看看我的作业。Wǒ qǐng lǎoshī kàn kan wǒde zuòyè.

8. 一边看电视一边学习不好。Yìbiān kàn diànshì yìbiān xuéxí bù hǎo.
9. 请问，你能告诉我哪儿有公用电话吗？Qǐngwèn, nǐ néng gàosù wǒ nǎr yǒu gōngyòng diànhuà ma?
10. 你能过一会儿给我打电话吗？Nǐ néng guò yīhuìr gěi wǒ dǎ diànhuà ma?

VI.

1. She asked me to call her, but forgot to tell me her phone number.
2. I hate people who call me when I'm having dinner.
3. He said that he had texted me, but I didn't receive it.
4. In the past, college students only studied, but didn't work. Now more and more college students work while they study.
5. Twnety years ago, most Chinese didn't have a phone at home, which was quite inconvenient. People couldn't set up a time when they wanted to visit a friend. Sometimes they walked a long distance to see a friend only to find that he was not home. Now most Chinese have a cell phone, which is quite convenient.

LESSON 4 *(Exercises on pages 89-95)*

II.

1. 东亚 dōngyà	2. 南亚 nányà	3. 南美 nánměi
4. 北美 běiměi	5. 北非 běifēi	6. 南非 nánfēi
7. 中非 zhōngfēi	8. 中亚 zhōngyà	9. 西欧 xī'ōu
10. 东欧 dōng'ōu	11. 北欧 běi'ōu	12. 南欧 nán'ōu

III.

1. 在 zài	6. 在 zài
2. 有 yǒu	7. 有 yǒu
3. 是 shì	8. 是 shì
4. 在 zài	9. 在 zài
5. 是 shì	10. 有 yǒu

IV.

1. behind the car   car in the back
2. in front of the school   the school in the front
3. on the book   the book on top
4. east of the store   the store in the east
5. across from the bank   the bank across

V.

1. 英国在法国的北边 Yīngguó zài Fǎguó de běibian
2. 印度在中国的西南 Yìndù zài Zhōngguó de xīnán
3. 墨西哥在美国的南边 Mòxīgē zài Měiguó de nánbian
4. 日本在韩国的东北 Rìběn zài Hánguó de dōngběi
5. 波兰在俄国的西边 Bōlán zà Éguó de xībian
6. 埃及在苏丹的北边 Āijí zài Sūdān de běibian

VI.
A.

1. 他把他的汽车卖了。Tā bǎ tāde qìchē mài le.
2. 我把我的手机关掉了。Wǒ bǎ wǒde shǒujī guān diào le.
3. 他们把茶喝了。Tāmen bǎ chá hē le.
4. 妈妈把那件毛衣洗了。Māma bǎ nà jiàn máoyī xǐ le.
5. 公司把我的工作换了。Gōngsī bǎ wǒde gōngzuò huàn le.

B.

1. 把书放在书包里 bǎ shū fàng zài shūbāo lǐ
2. 把钱包忘在家里 bǎ qiánbāo wàng zài jiā lǐ
3. 把饭送到学校 bǎ fàn sòng dào xuéxiào
4. 把朋友带回家 bǎ péngyou dài huí jiā
5. 把你的名字写在纸上 bǎ nǐde míngzì xiě zài shǐ shang

VII.

1. 猫在床的下面。Māo zài chuáng de xiàmiàn.
2. 大西洋在美国的东边。Dàxīyáng zài Měiguó de dōngbian.
3. 我们的学校在医院和银行的中间。Wǒmende xuéxiào zài yīyuàn hé yínháng de zhōngjiān.
4. 地图在门的后面。Dìtú zài mén de hòumiàn.
5. 我家在一家商店的旁边。Wǒ jiā zài yì jiā shāngdiàn de pángbiān.

6. 教室里有三个书架。Jiàoshì lǐ yǒu sān ge shūjià.
7. 孩子们在楼的外面玩。Háizimen zài lóu de wàimiàn wán.
8. 酒店在餐馆的对面。Jiǔdiàn zài cānguǎn de duìmiàn.
9. 中国的北边有两个国家。Zhōngguó de běibian yǒu liǎng ge guójiā.
10. 加州在美国的西部。Jiāzhōu zài Měiguó de xībù.

VIII.

The United States is in North America. It is the fourth largest country in the world (the largest being Canada, followed by Russia and China). North of the United States is Canada and south of it is Mexico. There are no countries to its east and west. To its east is the Atlantic Ocean and to its west is the Pacific Ocean.

LESSON 5 *(Exercises on pages 112-118)*

II.

1. 我们现在是老师了。Wǒmen xiànzài shì lǎoshī le.
2. 天冷了。Tiān lěng le.
3. 她现在会开车了。Tā xiànzài huì kā chē le.
4. 我爸爸不工作了。Wǒ bàba bù gōngzuò le.
5. 这个班的学生们现在有电脑了。Zhè ge bān de xuésheng men xiànzài yǒu diànnǎo le.

III.

1. 我们老师说的 wǒmén lǎoshī shuō de
2. 我们看的 wǒmén kàn de
3. 公司做的 gōngsī zuò de
4. 你要的 nǐ yào de
5. 他们不能做的 tāmen bù néng zuò de

IV.

1. 看到 kàn dào
2. 买到 mǎi dào
3. 吃到 chī dào
4. 找到 zhǎo dào
5. 买到 mǎi dào

V.
1. 还是 háishi
2. 或（者） huò (zhě)
3. 或（者） huò (zhě)
4. 还是 háishi
5. 还是 háishi

VI.
1. 这五本书都是我的。Zhè wǔ běn shū dōu shì wǒde.
2. 我想星期六或星期天去看电影。Wǒ xiǎng xīngqīliù huò xīngqītiān qù kàn diànyǐng.
3. 今年夏天很多人去中国旅行，我买不到飞机票。Jīnnián xiàtiān hěn duō rén qù Zhōngguó lǚxíng, wǒ mǎi bú dào fēijīpiào.
4. 如果不能去英国，我们就去法国。Rúguǒ bù néng qù Yīngguó, wǒmen jiù qù Fǎguó.
5. 我爸爸妈妈结婚40年了。Wǒ bàba māma jiéhūn sìshí nián le.
6. 汽车在房子的前面。Qìchē zài qiánmiàn de fángzi.
7. 老师对我们很好。Lǎoshī duì wǒmen hěn hǎo.
8. 你的美国朋友说中文说得很好。Nǐde Měiguó péngyou shuō Zhōngwén shuō de hěn hǎo.
9. 你昨天是怎么来学校的？Nǐ zuótiān shì zěnme lái xuéxiào de?
10. 他学中文学了两年多了。Tā xué Zhōngwén xué le liǎng nián duō le.

VII.
1. 我高中毕业以后没有上大学。Wǒ gāozhōng bìyè yǐhòu méiyou shàng dàxué.
2. 我儿子的班上有28个学生。Wǒ érzi de bān shang yǒu 28 ge xuésheng.
3. 学生们很高兴，因为老师说没有作业。Xuéshengmen hěn gāoxìng, yīnwèi lǎoshī shuō méi yǒu zuòyè.
4. 对不起我今天晚上不能跟你去看电影。明天有一个考试，我要学习。Duìbuqǐ wǒ jīntiān wǎnshang bù néng gēn nǐ qù kàn diànyǐng. Míngtiān yǒu yí ge kǎoshì, wǒ yào xuéxí.
5. 很多家长要他们的孩子毕业后当律师或医生。Hěn duō jiāzhǎng yào tāmende háizi bìyè hòu dāng lǜshī huò yīshēng.

6. 我们的暑假七月初开始。Wǒmende shǔjià qī yuè chū kāishǐ.
7. 老师让学生们下星期一交作业。Lǎoshī ràng xuéshengmen xià xīngqíyī jiāo zuòyè.
8. 学生们必须通过这些考试才能进大学。Xuéshengmen bìxū tōngguò zhèxiē kǎoshì cái néng jìn dàxué.
9. 很多大学生不想上研究生院。Hěn duō dàxuésheng bù xiǎng shàng yánjiūshēngyuàn.
10. 你有没有找到工作？Nǐ yǒu méiyou zhǎo dào gōngzuò?

VIII.
1. There are 12 grades at this school from elementary to high school.
2. Graduate students need to learn two foreign languages.
3. High school graduates must pass the foreign languge exam before they can go to college.
4. More and more secondary schools in America are now offering Chinese classes.
5. He can find a job, but he didn't look for one.
6. The English major is further divided into the English language and the English literature.
7. In China, students must first earn a master's degree before they can study for a Ph.D., but in America, students do not need to study for a masters first before they can study for a Ph.D.
8. Many college graudates go on to graduate school when they can't find a job.
9. I believe that in America, neither getting into college or getting out of college is easy.
10. Most foreign students must pass an English exam first before they are admitted into a college or graduate school in the U.S.

LESSON 6 (*Exercises pages 136-143*)

II.
1. 在上海工作的医生 zài Shànghǎi gōngzuò de yīshēng
2. 我们工作的地方 wǒmen gōngzuò de dìfang
3. 他们开始上课的时间 tāmen kāishǐ shàng kè de shíjiān
4. 教我们英语的老师 jiāo wǒmen Yīngyǔ de lǎoshī

5. 今天要做的事 jīntiān yào zuò de shì
6. 开门 kāi mén
7. 开电视 kāi diànshì
8. 开车 kāi chē
9. 开药 kāi yào
10. 开会 kāi huì

III.

1. 完 wán
2. 完 wán
3. 好 hǎo, 好 hǎo
4. 完 wán
5. 完 wán

IV.

1. 我家是我爸爸做饭。 Wǒ jiā shì wǒ bàba zuò fàn.
   你家是不是你爸爸做饭? Nǐ jiā shì bu shì nǐ bàba zuò fàn?
2. 他是在北京大学学习。 Tā shì zài Běijīng Dàxué xuéxí.
   他是不是在北京大学学习? Tā shì bu shì zài Běijīng Dàxué xuéxí?
3. 我太太是不喜欢看电影。 Wǒ tàitai shì bù xǐhuan kàn diànyǐng.
   你太太是不是喜欢看电影? Nǐ tàitai shì bu shì xǐhuan kàn diànyǐng?
4. 大多数中国人是起得很早。 Dàduōshù Zhōngguórén shì qǐ de hěn zǎo.
   大多数中国人是不是起得很早? Dàduōshù Zhōngguórén shì bu shì qǐ de hěn zǎo?
5. 打太极拳是对身体有帮助。 Dǎ tàijíquán shì duì shēntǐ yǒu bāngzhù.
   打太极拳是不是对身体有帮助? Dǎ tàijíquán shì bu shì duì shēntǐ yǒu bāngzhù?

V.

1. 我昨天肚子疼。 Wǒ zuótiān dùzi téng.
2. 我先生牙疼。 Wǒ xiānshēng yá téng.
3. 他嗓子疼。 Tā sǎngzi téng.
4. 那位先生背疼。 Nà wèi xiānshēng bèi téng.

5. 病人腿疼。Bìngrén tuǐ téng.

VI.

1, 3, 5, 7 and 9 are topic-comment sentences; 2, 4, 6, 8 and 10 are not.

VII.

1. then (*result*)
2. just (*for emphasis*)
3. soon (*for emphasis*)
4. then (*one action immediately follows the other*)
5. only (*referring to the previous action: earlier or better than expected*)

VIII.

1. 中国是不是在东亚？Zhōngguó shì bu shì zài Dōngyà?
2. 我是住在纽约。Wǒ shì zhù zài Niǔyuē.
3. 请把报纸放在桌子上。Qǐng bǎ bàozhǐ fàng zài zhuōzi shang.
4. 今天是星期天。你怎么还上班？Jīntiān shì xīngqí tiān. Nǐ zěnme hái shàngbān?
5. 你是什么时候开始发烧的？Nǐ shì shénme shíhòu kāishǐ fāshāo de?
6. 很多人信中医，因为他们觉得中医能治好西医治不好的一些病。Hěn duō rén xìn zhōngyī, yīnwèi tāmen juédé zhōngyī néng zhì hǎo xīyī zhì bù hǎo de yìxiē bìng.
7. 医生说你要吃一个月的药。Yīshēng shuō nǐ yào chī yí ge yuè de yào.
8. 你不会说中文没有关系。Nǐ bú huì shuō Zhōngwén méi yǒu guānxì.
9. 你对海鲜过敏吗？Nǐ duì hǎixiān guòmǐn ma?
10. 我看过很多医生，但是他们谁都治不好我的病。Wǒ kàn guo hěn duō yīshēng, dànshì tāmen shuí dōu zhì bù hǎo wǒde bìng.

IX.

1. There are no private doctors in China. When people are sick, they go to the hospital to see a doctor.
2. Without examining me, the doctor said that I didn't have any problem.

3. My mother is very good at cooking, especially at cooking Chinese food.
4. Although he came to work today, he was not completely recovered.
5. You don't just look unwell. You looked very unwell.
6. Many people only go to see a Chinese doctor when a Western doctor can't cure their disease.
7. Fever is the symptom of many diseases.
8. Most people who do taiji are middle-aged and old people.
9. Daily jogging is a very good way to exercise.
10. I study Chinese not to speak to the Chinese people, but rather to read books.

LESSON 7 (*Exercises on pages 159-165*)

II.
1. 黑板上写着五个字。Hēibǎn shang xiě zhe wǔ ge zì.
2. 桌上摆着晚饭。Zhuō shang bǎi zhe wǎnfàn.
3. 包里放着十本书。Bāo lǐ fàng zhe shí běn shū.
4. 墙上挂着世界地图。Qiáng shang guà zhe shìjiè dìtú.
5. 汽车里装着很多杯子和盘子。Qìchē lǐ zhuāng zhe hěn duō bēizi hé pánzi.
6. 请问他是不是学生。Qǐngwèn tā shì bu shì xuésheng.
7. 你能告诉我这儿有医院吗？Nǐ néng gàosù wǒ zhèr yǒu yīyuàn ma?
8. 你知道不知道我们如果不去他会不会不高兴？Nǐ zhī bù zhīdào wǒmen rúguǒ bú qù tā huì bú huì bù gāoxìng?
9. 圣诞节如果在星期天，我们星期一也放假。Shèngdànjié rúguǒ zài xīngqītiān, wǒmen xīngqī yī yě fàngjià.
10. 我想知道能不能在饭店换钱。Wǒ xiǎng zhīdào néng bu néng zài fàndiàn huàn qián.

III.
1. 十二月 shíèr yuè
2. 十月 shí yuè
3. 七月 qī yuè
4. 一月 yī yuè

5. 二月　èr yuè
6. 一月或二月　yī yuè huò èr yuè
7. 十一月　shíyī yuè
8. 五月　wǔ yuè
9. 五月　wǔ yuè
10. 九月或十月　jiǔ yuè huò shí yuè

V.

1. 对大多数美国人来说，圣诞节是最重要的节日。Duì dàduōshù Měiguórén lái shuō, Shèngdànjié shì zuì zhòngyào de jiérì.
2. 我最喜欢的节日是感恩节，因为我们全家会团聚。Wǒ zuì yǐhuan de jiérì shì Gǎnēnjié, yīnwèi wǒmen quán jiā huì tuánjù.
3. 我先来介绍一下我们的公司。Wǒ xiān lái jièshào yíxià wǒmende gōngsī.
4. 你能猜一猜我有多大吗？Nǐ néng cāi yi cāi wǒ yǒu duó dà ma?
5. 你能介绍一下你们国家的节日吗？Nǐ néng jièshào yíxià nǐ men guójiā de jiérì ma?
6. 美国餐馆里的中国菜和中国餐馆里的中国菜不一样。Měiguó cānguǎn lǐ de Zhōngguó cài hé Zhōngguó cānguǎn lǐ de Zhōngguó cài bù yíyàng.
7. 我没有喝酒的习惯。Wǒ méi yǒu hē jiǔ de xíguàn.
8. 中国新年也叫春节。Zhōngguó Xīnnián yě jiào Chūnjié.
9. 圣诞节虽然不是中国的节日，但是现在很多中国人也过。Shèngdànjié suīrán bú shì Zhōngguó de jiérì, dànshì xiànzài hěn duō Zhōngguórén yě guò.
10. 在中国，孩子们最喜欢新年，因为他们那天能得到很多红包。Zài Zhōngguó, háizimen zuì xǐhuan Xīnnián, yīnwèi tāmen nà tiān néng dédào hěn duō hóngbāo.

VI.

1. My younger brother is 12 years younger than I am. We were both born in the year of the sheep.
2. Chinese people are not in the habit of exchanging gifts on Chinese New Year.

3. In the past, people would say "Gōngxǐ fācái" on New Year's Day, but now people often say "Xīn Nián hǎo". They mean the same.
4. The Labor Day in China is May 1, whereas in America, the Labor Day is the first Monday in September.
5. In China, people don't get a day off on the Mid-Autumn Festival.
6. American people celebrate all kinds of holidays and festivals.
7. I like September the most, when there are most festivals.
8. During holidays, people in China like to go to the cities, but people in American like to get out of the city.
9. Many countries in Asia also celebrate the Chinese New Year.
10. I've used up my vacation days for this year.

LESSON 8 (*Exercises on pages 182-189*)

II.
1. 被解雇了 bèi jiěgù le
2. 找工作 zhǎo gōngzuò
3. 找到了工作 zhǎo dào le gōngzuò
4. 三个月里 sān ge yuè lǐ
5. 一年后 yì nián hòu
6. 更多的机会 gèng duō de jīhuì
7. 看了电视里的新闻 kàn le diànshì lǐ de xīnwén
8. 对音乐很有兴趣 duì yīnyuè hěn yǒu xìngqù
9. 对游泳没有兴趣 duì yóuyǒng méi yǒu xìngqù
10. 他没有帮我这个忙。 Tā méiyou bāng wǒ zhè ge máng.
11. 我没有请他帮我这个忙。 Wǒ méiyou qǐng tā bāng wǒ zhè ge máng.
12. 你太太在哪儿教书？她在大学教美术。 Nǐ tàitai zài nǎr jiāoshū? Tā zài dàxué jiāo měishù.
13. 工资多少要看经验。 Gōngzī duōshao yào kàn jīngyàn.
14. 我来这儿是买东西，不是卖东西的。 Wǒ lái zhèr shì mǎi dōngxi, bú shì mài dōngxi de.
15. 这件事和我们公司没有关系。 Zhè jiàn shì hé wǒmen gōngsī méi yǒu guānxì.

III.
1. 病人被医生治好了。Bìngrén bèi yīshēng zhì hǎo le.
2. 书被学生们带回家了。Shū bèi xuéshengmen dài huí jiā le.
3. 茶被他喝了。Chá bèi tā hē le.
4. 我爸爸的汽车被他卖了。Wǒ bàba de qìchē bèi tā mài le.
5. 我女朋友的手机被她关掉了。Wǒ nǚpéngyou de shǒujī bèi tā guān diào le.
6. 你的申请被老板考虑了。Nǐde shēnqǐng bèi lǎobǎn kǎolǜ le.

IV.
1. 猫吃了鱼。Māo chī le yú.
2. 老师把桌子拿进来了。Lǎoshī bǎ zhuōzi ná jìn lai le.
3. 他把字典放在书架上了。Tā bǎ zìdiǎn fàng zài shūjià shang le.
4. 孩子们看到了圣诞节的礼物。Háizimen kàn dào le Shèngdànjié de lǐwù.
5. 妈妈洗了毛衣。Māma xǐ le máoyī.
6. 很多人已经问过这个问题了。Hěn duō rén yǐjīng wèn guò zhè ge wèntí le.

V.
1. 帮 bāng _____ 忙 máng
2. 帮助 bāngzhù, 帮助 bāngzhù
3. 帮助 bāngzhù
4. 帮忙 bāngmáng
6. 帮助 bāngzhù
6. 帮 _____ 忙 bāngmáng

VI.
1. 纽约的中小学需要很多英语老师。Niǔyuē de zhōng xiǎoxué xūyào hěn duō de Yīngyǔ lǎoshī.
2. 我对不提供医疗保险的工作没有兴趣。Wǒ duì bù tígòng yīliáo bǎoxiǎn de gōngzuò méi yǒu xìngqù.
3. 请把你的特长写在你的简历上。Qǐng bǎ nǐde tècháng xiě zài nǐde jiǎnlì shang.
4. 对有的雇主来说，经验比学位更重要。Duì yǒude gùzhǔ lái shuō, jīngyàn bǐ xuéwèi gèng zhòngyào.

5. 我只帮了你一个小忙。你不用给我钱。Wǒ zhǐ bāng le nǐ yí ge xiǎo máng. Nǐ búyòng gěi wǒ qián.

6. 在过去两年里，他换了三次工作。Zài guòqù de liǎngnián lǐ, tā huàn le sān cì gōngzuò.

7. 我现在做的和我在大学学的有很大的关系。Wǒ xiànzài zuò de hé wǒ zài dàxué xué de yǒu hěn dà de guānxì.

8. 我没有大学文凭。你想他们会雇我吗？Wǒ méi yǒu dàxué wénpíng. Nǐ xiǎng tāmen huì gù wǒ ma?

9. 你什么时候能开始工作？你能工作多久？Nǐ shénme shíhòu néng kāishǐ gōngzuò? Nǐ néng gōngzuò duō jiǔ?

10. 她找工作找了两个月，但是还没有找到。Tā zhǎo gōngzuò zhǎo le liǎngge yuè, dànshì hái méiyou zhǎo dào.

VII.

1. As the economy is getting worse, many employers are laying off employees.

2. Although the pay is not good, his job provides good benefits.

3. We'll let you know as soon as we make the decision.

4. Computer jobs were easy to find three years ago, but not now.

5. The doctor wanted you to rest at home because he didn't want you to be too tired.

6. I can't start working for you until after a month.

7. Since you don't have a college degree and English is not your first language, we can't consider your application.

8. What he wants you to do is to write to his secretary.

9. Please bring your diploma when you come to the interview.

10. Full-time employees have pension, but part-time employees don't.

LESSON 9 (*Exercises on pages 207-215*)

II.

1. 地方新闻 dìfang xīnwén; 国内新闻 guónèi xīnwén; 国际新闻 guójì xīnwén; 头版新闻 tóubǎn xīnwén

2. 大概认识300个字 dàgài rènshi 300 ge zì

3. 差不多每天都锻炼 chàbùduō měi tiān dōu duànliàn

4. 很少上网 hěn shǎo shàng wǎng

5. 对北京很熟悉 duì Běijīng hěn shúxi
6. 关于中国的电影 guānyú Zhōngguó de diànyǐng;
   关于日本的书 guānyú Rìběn de shū
7. 把旧报纸扔掉 bǎ jiù bàozhǐ rēng diào
8. 我其实没有听说过那个地方。Wǒ qíshí méiyou tīngshuō guo nà ge dìfang.
9. 他很担心他会被解雇。Tā hěn dānxīn tā huì bèi jiěgù.
10. 股票昨天涨得很厉害。Gǔpiào zuótiān zhàng de hěn lìhài.

III.

1. 我不在家吃中饭。Wǒ bú zài jiā chī zhōngfàn.
2. 他中文说得不流利。Tā Zhōngwén shuō de bù liúlì.
3. 医生治不好这个病。Yīshēng zhì bù hǎo zhè ge bìng.
4. 书没有在桌子上放着。Shū méiyou zài zhuōzi shang fàng zhe.
5. 老师没有给我打电话。Lǎoshī méiyou gěi wǒ dǎ diànhuà.
6. 学生们不都学习英语。Xuéshengmen bù dōu xuéxí Yīngyǔ.
7. 大家都不喜欢这个餐馆。Dàjiā dōu bù xǐhuan zhè ge cānguǎn.
8. 我想那儿没有医院。Wǒ xiǎng nàr méi yǒu yīyuàn.
9. 我觉得今天不冷。Wǒ juéde jīntiān bù lěng.
10. 火车开得不快。Huǒchē kāi de bú kuài.

IV.

1. 我们学校的外国老师我不都认识。Wǒmen xuéxiào de wàiguó lǎoshī wǒ bù dōu rènshi.
2. 我们学校的外国老师我都不认识。Wǒmen xuéxiào de wàiguó lǎoshī wǒ dōu bú rènshi.
3. 我们的老师每天都给我们测验。Wǒmende lǎoshī měi tiān dōu gěi wǒmén cèyàn.
4. 病人今天什么都没有吃。Bìngrén jīntiān shénme dōu méiyou chī.
5. 我爸爸妈妈都喜欢日本菜。Wǒ bàba māma dōu xǐhuan Rìběn cài.
6. 每个公司都有网站吗？Měi ge gōngsī dōu yǒu wángzhàn ma?

V.

1. 连孩子都知道。Lián háizi dōu zhīdào.
2. 我连他的名字也没有问。Wǒ lián tāde míngzì yě méiyou wèn.

3. 他连开车都不会。Tā lián kāi chē dōu bú huì.
4. 医生们今天忙得连吃饭的时间也没有。Yīshéngmen jīntiān máng de lián chīfàn de shíjiān yě méi yǒu.
5. 我的美国朋友连上海话都会说。Wǒde Měiguó péngyǒu lián Shànghǎihuà dōu huì shuō.

VI.

1. 我到了洛杉矶就给你打电话。Wǒ dào le Luòshānjī jiù gěi nǐ dǎ diànhuà.
2. 他们结了婚就要去香港度蜜月。Tāmen jié le hūn jiù yào qù Xiānggǎng dù mìyuè.
3. 你下了课就来图书馆,好吗?Nǐ xià le kè jiù lái túshūguǎn, hǎo ma?
4. 飞机到了北京就去上海。Fēijī dào le Běijīng jiù qù Shànghǎi.
5. 我们下了班要开会。Wǒmen xià le bān yào kāihuì.

VII.

1. 我太忙,没有时间,所以我只读标题。Wǒ tài máng, méi yǒu shíjiān, suǒyǐ wǒ zhǐ dú biāotí.
2. 今天的报上有关于他们婚礼的报道吗?Jīntiānde bào shang yǒu guānyú tāmen hūnlǐde bàodào ma?
3. 你们有关于中国历史的课吗?Nǐmen yǒu guānyú Zhōngguó lìshǐ de kè ma?
4. 现在连小孩子都能发电子信,用互联网。Xiànzài lián xiǎoháizi dōu néng fā diànzǐxìn, yòng hùliánwǎng.
5. 我对这个城市不熟悉。你能给我介绍一下儿吗?Wǒ duì zhè ge chéngshì bù shúxi. Nǐ néng gěi wǒ jièshào yīxiàr ma?
6. 你可以在网上找到关于这个公司的资料。Nǐ kěyǐ zài wǎng shang zhǎo dào guānyú zhè ge gōngsī de zīliào.
7. 现在很多人在网上买东西。Xiànzài hěn duō rén zài wǎng shang mǎi dōngxī.
8. 你上次给我的电子信地址不对。Nǐ shàng cì gěi wǒ de diànzǐxìn dìzhǐ bú duì.
9. 我的朋友在网上上中文课。Wǒde péngyou zài wǎng shang shàng Zhōngwénkè.
10. 中国的网吧比美国的多。Zhōngguó de wǎngbā bǐ Měiguóde duō.

VIII.
1. The Internet brought us a lot of convenience. We can now read newspapers in China on the Internet.
2. The status of the economy has a lot to do with the stock market.
3. I have been learning Chinese for two months, but I can't even write the character for "big."
4. The first thing that my mother does after she buys the newspaper is to read the ads.
5. Many websites in China are written in Chinese. Those who don't read Chinese don't understand them.
6. She receives all kinds of emails everyday, but she does not have time to read them all.
7. The address he gave me must have been wrong. The emails that I sent him were all returned.
8. Many people are so busy that they can only read newspapers when they are on their way to work in the subway.
9. There is more local news in the tabloid than in big papers.
10. I have no interest in stocks at all. Sports news is more interesting.

LESSON 10 (*Exercises on pages 235-243*)

II.
1. 旧建筑的特点 jiù jiànzhù de tèdiǎn
2. 对这个城市的印象 duì zhè ge chéngshì de yìnxiàng
3. 到过这个地方很多次 dào guo zhè ge dìfang hěn duō cì
4. 世界上 shìjiè shang
5. 至少三天 zhìshǎo sān tiān
6. 完全变了 wánquán biàn le
7. 百分之五十 bǎifēnzhī wǔshí
    百分之七十五 bǎifēnzhī qīshí wǔ
    百分之百 bǎifēnzhī bǎi
    四分之一 sìfēnzhī yī
    五分之三 wǔfēnzhī sān
    三分之二 sānfēnzhī èr
8. 从来没有读过这本书 cónglái méiyou dú guo zhè běn shū
9. 打算明年再去中国。 dǎsuan míngnián zài qù Zhōngguó
10. 今天又去了银行 jīntiān yòu qù le yínháng

III.
A.
1. 好喝 hǎo hē
2. 贵 guì
3. 好 hǎo
4. 好吃 hǎo chī
5. 快 kuài

B.
1. 哥哥比弟弟大两岁。Gēge bǐ dìdi dà liǎng suì.
2. 这条公路比那条公路长。Zhè tiáo gōnglù bǐ nà tiáo gōnglù cháng.
3. 我们班比他们班多五个学生。Wǒmen bān bǐ tāmen bān duō wǔ ge xuésheng.
4. 这个汉字比那个汉字难。Zhè ge hànzì bǐ nà ge hànzì nán.
5. 他走得比我快。Tā zǒu de bǐ wǒ kuài.
6. 姐姐写字写得比妹妹写得好看。Jiějie xiě zì xiěde bǐ mèimei xiě de hǎokàn.
7. 中国的产品比日本的产品便宜。Zhōngguó de chǎnpǐn bǐ Rìběn de chǎnpǐn piányi.
8. 我妈妈做菜比我爸爸做得好。Wǒ māma zuò cài bǐ wǒ bàba zuò de hǎo.
9. 今天的股票跌得比昨天的股票跌得厉害。Jīntiān de gǔpiào diē dé bǐ zuótiānde gǔpiào diē dé lìhài.
10. 我家的人和他家的人一样多。Wǒ jiāde rén hé tājiā de rén yíyàng duō.

IV.
1. 再 zài
2. 又 yòu
3. 再 zài
4. 又 yòu
5. 再 zài

V.
1. 我们在欧洲玩儿得很高兴。Wǒmen zài Ōuzhōu wánr dé hěn gāoxìng.

2. 对我来说，西安是中国最有意思的地方。Duì wǒ lái shuō, Xī'ān shì Zhōngguó zuì yǒuyìsī de dìfang.

3. 在最近20年里，中国变化很大。Zài zuìjìn 20 nián lǐ, Zhōngguó biànhuà hěn dà.

4. 在我们去的地方中，我太太最喜欢巴黎。Zài wǒmen qù de dìfang zhōng, wǒ tàitai zuì xǐhuan Bālí.

5. 我不喜欢我们昨天晚上去的餐馆。Wǒ bù xǐhuan wǒmen zuótiān wánshang qù de cānguǎn.

6. 从上海坐火车去香港至少要15个小时。Cóng Shànghǎi zuò huǒchē qù Xiānggǎng zhìshǎo yào 15 ge xiǎoshí.

7. 世界上四分之一的人是中国人。Shìjiè shang sìfēnzhī yī de rén shì Zhōngguórén.

8. 我和我太太是五年前在我退休的时候搬到弗罗里达的。Wǒ hé wǒ tàitai shì wǔ nián qián zài wǒ tuìxiū de shíhou bān dào Fóluólǐdá de.

9. 他一直住在日本，对这个国家很熟悉。Tā yìzhí zhù zài Rìběn, duì zhè ge guójiā hěn shúxi.

10. 有的人不喜欢变化。他们觉得新的东西没有老的东西好。Yǒude rén bù xǐhuan biànhuà. Tāmen juédé xīn de dōngxi méiyou lǎo de dōngxi hǎo.

VI.

1. The characteristic of Chinese is that its grammar is simple, but its pronunciation is difficult.

2. There are five beltways in Beijing.

3. Thirty years ago in Shanghai, Pudong was the countryside, but now there are many high-rises there and it is a completely new place.

4. In order to read Chinese newspapers, you need to know at least 2,000 characters.

5. Many people in the West like Dim Sum because although they don't know the names of the food, they can choose what they like.

6. I like New York, where you can meet people from various countries and hear various languages.

7. 20% of the students in this school are foreign students.

8. My husband has no interest in finance. He never reads *Wall Street Journal*.

9. I haven't seen him for ten years. He has changed so much that he looks completely differently from before.
10. They have always lived in Boston after they got married.

Internet Resources for Students of Chinese

Guides & Portals

Chinese Home Page
http://www.uni.edu/becker/chinese.html
A complete reference to China/Chinese-related websites.

Chinese Language Webs
http://bubl.ac.uk/link/c/chineselanguage.htm
A catalog of Internet resources.

Chinese Language & Linguistics
http://chinalinks.osu.edu/c-links3.htm
Annotated links compiled by Marjorie Chan to more than two hundred China and Chinese language- and linguistics-related websites.

Confucius Institute Online
http://english.chinese.cn/
You can find almost anything and everything about Chinese culture and language as well as tons of resources.

Chinese Characters

2500 Chinese Characters
http://www.shuifeng.net/pinyin.asp
Click on any of the 2,500 characters alphabetically arranged according to pinyin to see its stroke order, radical, and number of strokes and to hear its pronunciation.

Animated Chinese Characters
http://lost-theory.org/ocrat/chargif/
Click on any Chinese character to see how to write it.

Character Flashcards
http://www.mandarintools.com/flashcard.html
Database contains 1,000 most frequently used characters.

Chinese Character Annotator
http://lost-theory.org/ocrat/reaf/
Copy and paste Chinese text into the box and hit Search. The Chinese text will be marked up with pinyin and link to sound clips of the pronunciation.

Chinese Course
http://www.chinese-course.com/
An audio flashcard system with multiple-choice tests.

Clavis Sinica
http://www.clavisinica.com/
Mobile apps to help you learn to read and write Chinese characters on the go.

eStroke
http://www.eon.com.hk/estroke/
In addition to showing the stroke order of any Chinese character through animation, eStroke also creates stroke sequence that can be pasted into your documents. eStroke can also create worksheets, export to animated gif and flash video.

Hanlexon
http://www.hanlexon.org
A great language learning tool to create and save character worksheets out of any Chinese text.

Learn to Read and Write Chinese Characters
http://www.csulb.edu/~txie/character.htm
A wealth of resources.

List of Character Radicals
http://www.yellowbridge.com/chinese/radicals.php
See the list of 214 radicals in Chinese and their names in English.

Online Chinese Flashcards
http://www.yellowbridge.com/chinese/flashcards.php
The characters in Beginners Chinese and Intermediate Chinese are ready made on this site.

Semanda Mandarin Chinese Flashcards
http://www.semanda.com
It provides basic Mandarin Chinese flashcards and vocabulary exercises for children and beginners. The wordlists cover a wide range of basic concepts, such as colors, animals, fruits, vegetables, vehicles, furniture etc.

Ting Flashcard Reader
http://hua.umf.maine.edu/Chinese/FlashCardReader/TingflashcardNetEnglish.html
Free download and you can study off-line.

TrainChinese
http://www.trainchinese.com
Get access to more than 50,000 Chinese flashcards with original audio recordings. You can learn in your browser or with free apps for your PC, Mac, Android phone or iPhone/iPad.

Write Characters Using the Mouse
http://www.nciku.com/
Find this and other Chinese learning features on the site.

Chinese etymology
http://www.chineseetymology.org/
Result of Richard Sears's 20 years of efforts to make Chinese character etymology information available online.

Chinese Grammar

Basic Chinese Grammar
http://www.rci.rutgers.edu/~rsimmon/chingram/
A slide show that reviews the basics of spoken standard Chinese grammar.

Learn Chinese Grammar
http://www.csulb.edu/~txie/grammar.htm
A list of links to various sites about Chinese grammar.

Chinese Podcasts

ChinesePod
http://chinesepod.com
Online service that provides daily podcasts, with an accompanying text expansion exercises and other extensive tutoring aid.

Popup Chinese
http://www.popupchinese.com
Large archive of free Chinese lessons and resources. You can listen to podcasts and view the online transcripts. You can also mouseover any words you don't recognize.

iMandarinPod
http://imandarinpod.com/hoola
Designed to teach Chinese by introducing topics about Chinese culture or what is happening in China today.

Pronunciation and Listening Comprehension

BBC Chinese
http://www.bbc.co.uk/languages/chinese/games/
Online drilling games for Chinese learners. One game is for practicing the four tones and the other for learning how to write Chinese characters.

Beginning Chinese Listening Comprehension
http://www.wellesley.edu/Chinese/Listening/contents.html
An interactive website with 18 audio lessons followed by listening comprehension questions.

Pinyin Info
http://pinyin.info/
This site presents rules for using pinyin as well as tools for writing pinyin with tone marks.

Pinyin Trainer
Free app designed for both iPhone and iPad available in the Apple Store.

Dictionaries

Chinese-English Dictionary
http://www.mandarintools.com/worddict.html
This dictionary provides a searchable interface. Searches can be conducted by characters, pinyin, or English. Results will show the Chinese word, the pinyin representation of the word, and the English definition. You can also click on the pinyin to hear how it is pronounced.

Chinese-English Talking Dictionary
http://www.yellowbridge.com/chinese/chinese-dictionary.php
Integrated word and character dictionary on the web lets you search by word, pinyin, or English. Unique features include: handwriting recognition, fuzzy pinyin that matches words even when you are unsure of the exact pronunciation, word and character decomposition, character etymology, and stroke order.

DianHua Dictionary
Chinese English dictionary for iPhone and iPod touch. Search support for English, Mandarin Pinyin (with or without tones), Traditional Characters, Simplified Characters, and mixed searches consisting of any combination of the above.

Pleco
http://www.pleco.com
One of the most popular dictionary apps for mobile devices. It has a free version and a paid-version. The paid-version allows you to look up a character

by handwriting it on the screen or simply hold your phone over the Chinese text to scan it and get the definitions.

Inputting Chinese characters on your computer

The easiest and most powerful way to type in Chinese is to download the google pinyin input at http://tools.google.com/pinyin/. It takes just a couple of minutes to install it in your computer. You don't need any extra software. Depending on the setting of your computer, you may need to install the East Asian Language Support. See how you can install it at: http://www.unclp.org/writing/install_lang_pack.html.

Online Tutorials, Courses & Programs

ActiveChinese
http://activechinese.com
Its interactive lessons use multimedia to engage students of all ages, which can be taught from CD-ROMs, mobile downloads, or through online access.

BBC Chinese
http://www.bbc.co.uk/languages/chinese/real_chinese/
A lively introduction to Mandarin Chinese in 10 short parts. Each topic contains: a slideshow with the key language, tips on pronunciation and grammar, cultural notes, a challenge, video clips from Real Chinese (broadband, UK only) and a shorter video clip from Real Chinese for narrowband or non-UK users.

Chinese Online
http://www.hanyu.com.cn/en/
Free e-class, webcast, e-magazine, culture and entertainment.

Learn Mandarin Chinese
http://www.chinese-tools.com/learn/chinese
40 free online lessons with audio, including reading, speaking, writing, vocabulary, grammar, calligraphy, examples and exercices. All texts and dialogs are in mp3 format for download.

Serge Melnyk
http://www.melnyks.com
100+ audio lessons in a daily theme-based and progressive manner together with PDF transcripts and worksheets in both traditional and simplified Chinese characters, along with pinyin and English translations.

Steps of Chinese
http://www.stepsofchinese.com/
Free course that introduces Chinese language and culture in a friendly and

interesting way. Three steps of lessons will take a complete beginner to the elementary level.

YoyoChinese
http://www.yoyochinese.com
Bite-size lively audio and video lessons.

Zhongwen Learner
http://www.zhongwenlearner.com
In addition to lessons, you can also watch live Chinese TV, use the Forums and a variety of tools for learning Chinese.

Software and Platforms

ChinesePlus
http://www.biderworld.com/chineseplus.asp
A comprehensive Chinese text input software. It allows for the two-way conversion of traditional to simplified Chinese text. The software converts character to pinyin with tone marks, and pinyin back to character. The software also features an interactive stroke-by-stroke demonstration of Chinese character writing.

GoChinese
http://eu.gochinese.net/goChinese/
Chinese language learning platform that allows users to doubleclick and highlight text to listen to the spoken Mandarin as well as view definitions and Pinyin phonetics of learning materials from publishers, instructors or text submitted by learners themselves.

NJStar
http://www.njstar.com
Word processing software which reads, writes, edits and prints Chinese text in English Windows environment. It includes English-Chinese /Chinese-English dictionary and has the function of converting a block of Chinese text to pinyin with tone.

Wenlin Software for Learning Chinese
http://wenlin.com/
A CD-ROM software, Wenlin tackles the most frustrating obstacles for students of Chinese with its versatile and easy-to-use interface. Wenlin combines a high-speed expandable Chinese dictionary, a full-featured text editor, and unique "flashcard" system all in one intuitive environment.

Also by YONG HO:

BEGINNER'S CHINESE WITH 2 AUDIO CDS
SECOND EDITION

Currently the #1 Mandarin Chinese self-study course available on the market, **Beginner's Chinese with 2 Audio CDs** has been revised and updated to make learning to speak, read, and write the language easier than ever!

This edition includes ten practical lessons with dialogues, vocabulary, and exercises; new audio CDs featuring professional actors from Beijing; updated cultural and language notes; an attractive, easy-to-read presentation of the Chinese characters; additional exercises for teaching stroke order and writing skills; and new sections on how to read and write Chinese characters on a computer.

Upon completion of the course, the student will be able to use 90 basic sentence patterns, 300 written characters, and numerous communicative skills.

326 pages · ISBN 978-0-7818-1257-3 · 5½ x 8½ · $32.00 pb

CHINESE-ENGLISH/ENGLISH-CHINESE
PRACTICAL DICTIONARY

This book includes: simplified Chinese characters, internationally standard pinyin Romanization for all entries, a pronunciation key, and an index of characters sorted by stroke count, to aid in identifying unfamiliar characters.

15,000 entries · ISBN 978-0-7818-1236-8 · 4½ x 7 · $19.95 pb

CONCISE CHINESE USAGE DICTIONARY

Previously published as the *Chinese-English Frequency Dictionary: A Study Guide to Mandarin Chinese's 500 Most Frequently Used Words* (2002), this edition incorporates new terms and usage changes which have occurred in the language within the last ten years. It is designed to make understanding simple by showing how characters are most often used in building words.

256 pages · ISBN 978-0-7818-1293-1 · 5½ x 8½ · $19.95 pb

CHINESE-ENGLISH/ENGLISH-CHINESE DICTIONARY & PHRASEBOOK (MANDARIN)

Containing a bilingual dictionary and a practical phrasebook, this is an essential book for students, travelers and businesspeople.

4,000 entries · ISBN 978-0-7818-1135-4 · 3¾ x 7½ · $13.95 pb

Prices subject to change without prior notice. **To purchase Hippocrene books**, contact your local bookstore, visit www.hippocrenebooks.com, call (212) 685-4373, or write to: HIPPOCRENE BOOKS, 171 Madison Ave, New York, NY 10016.

他 在 医院 住 了 一 个 星期